ENGLISH
PAST
AND PRESENT

ENGLISH
PAST
AND PRESENT

A Selection of Essays by Knud Sørensen
presented to him on his sixtieth birthday

Edited by Marianne Powell
and Bent Preisler

Acta Jutlandica LXIV:1
Humanities Series 62

AARHUS UNIVERSITY PRESS

Copyright: Aarhus University Press, 1988
Printed in Denmark by Special-Trykkeriet Viborg a-s
ISBN 87 7288 168 2
ISSN 0065 1354 (Acta Jutlandica)
ISSN 0106 0556 (Humanities Series)

CONTENTS

EDITORS' PREFACE

This collection of articles by Professor Knud Sørensen marks the occasion of his sixtieth birthday and semi-retirement. Spanning 30 years of impressive scholarship in the field of English philology, it is presented to him by former and present colleagues and students, inside and outside the Department, who wish to pay tribute to his work.

When Knud Sørensen was appointed Professor of English at the University of Aarhus in September, 1967, it meant a return to his place of birth. He was born in Aarhus on the 2nd February, 1928, but not long afterwards his family moved to Copenhagen, where he grew up. He completed his secondary education at Efterslægtsselskabets Gymnasium in 1946 and commenced his studies at the University of Copenhagen with English as his major and Latin as his minor subject.

In choosing an academic career Knud Sørensen, whose father was a market gardener, was making a new departure, which meant that he was thrown on his own resources to a considerable extent. To solve the problem of financing his studies, he succeeded in obtaining a post as stenographer in the Danish Parliament, a post which he held from 1948 to 1955.

Having completed his studies for the degree of *cand.mag.* in 1953 he was appointed lecturer at the Copenhagen School of Economics and Business Administration in August, 1955. In 1960 he received a doctorate from the University of Copenhagen for a dissertation on Thomas Lodge's translation of Seneca's *De Beneficiis,* and in 1962 he became acting professor of English at the Royal Danish School of Educational Studies. In 1964 he obtained the post of full professor, and three years later he was appointed Professor of English at the University of Aarhus.

Professor Sørensen's life-long contribution to the study and teaching of the English language has been characterized both by his keen interest in the relationship between English and Danish, and by his constant endeavour to combine theoretical with practical points of view. It is no coincidence, therefore, that his work has benefited the teaching of English at such a wide range of Danish institutions of higher education as those just mentioned.

The many-sidedness of Professor Sørensen's scholarly pursuits is reflected in his publications: his doctoral thesis pertains to the history of the English language, and his many articles on English grammar in general, as well as on the language of particular literary writers, often have a diachronic perspective. His best known work, however, written in collaboration with Professor Poul Steller of the Royal Danish School of Educational Studies, is a modern English grammar for Danish university students, which – not least because of its pedagogical approach – has been used in all Danish institutions of higher education where English is taught. Research carried out in cooperation with the Danish Language Committee (Dansk Sprognævn), furthermore, has resulted in a book on the influence of the English language on modern Danish. Among his contributions to the study of English language and stylistics both his description of modern English prose style and his treatment of Charles Dickens as linguistic innovator have attracted wide attention.

Professor Sørensen's versatility manifests itself in other ways: he has maintained his association with the Copenhagen School of Economics, where he is a highly esteemed external examiner of long standing. Since 1970 he has been the Danish editor of the distinguished international learned journal *English Studies*. He has been called upon to serve on numerous evaluation and selection committees (doctoral theses, professorships), in Denmark as well as in the rest of Scandinavia.

Professor Sørensen is a member of the International Association of University Professors of English, Det Lærde Selskab i Aarhus, Vetenskapssocieteten and Videnskabernes Selskab.

To his colleagues Knud Sørensen has been something of an enigma. His attitude to his subject has been characterized by a certain conservatism, but at the same time informed by thoroughly up-to-date knowledge of current trends. The phenomenal breadth of Knud Sørensen's reading has frequently been commented on, and he has followed developments in so many areas within English studies that he has continued to contribute constructively to the most diverse debates, not only linguistic, but also literary and historical. He has avoided over-specialization and has always been prepared to take on supervising students' work or evaluating theses, whether or not the area concerned has been involved in his own research. Extremely knowledgeable and versatile in his interests Knud Sørensen stands out as a true philologist in the original sense of the word: a lover of learning and scholarship.

In recent years Professor Sørensen has travelled a good deal in Europe ("before World War III breaks out", he comments with characteristically wry humour). In 1982 he and his wife spent the autumn term at Binghamton, New York, where Knud Sørensen was guest professor as part of the exchange programme between the English Department at Aarhus University and the State University of New York.

When not travelling the world, Professor Sørensen uses a characteristically modest means of transport, his bicycle. He has never acquired such a newfangled thing as a driving licence, but he has proved that punctuality can be achieved at all times on two wheels.

In addition to his scholarly pursuits Knud Sørensen has found time to cultivate his interest in classical music. As an amateur violinist he has devoted himself particularly to chamber music, and regrets that since moving to Aarhus he has lacked the time for active performance. As a means of relaxation he reads thrillers, and he enjoys sitting in his lovely garden though he does not enjoy cultivating it.

Although Professor Sørensen can be regarded as representing the classical tradition of professorship, he does not conform to the popular image. Knud Sørensen is not absent-minded, the books he reads are not dusty, and his scholarship bears the mark of precision and relevance. Conscientious in the extreme in both academic work and occupational responsibilities he has been exemplary in his helpfulness as colleague and teacher. Although Knud Sørensen has chosen to allow more of his time to be at his own disposition, we are happy that his unique combination of academic thoroughness, modesty, and steadfast individualism will continue to be an invaluable asset to the Department.

Department of English,   *Dr. Marianne Powell,*
University of Aarhus   Senior Lecturer

                                                                    Dr. Bent Preisler,
                                                                      Senior Lecturer

ACKNOWLEDGEMENTS

We wish to thank the publishers who have kindly permitted us to reprint the articles in the present collection. The original pagination of each article is given in parentheses. The articles concerned have been marked with (*) in the chronological bibliography of Knud Sørensen's works at the back of the book.

We are grateful to the *Aarhus University Research Foundation* and the *Learned Society in Aarhus* for their financial support.

I
GRAMMAR AND
STYLE

SUBSTANTIVE WITH TWO EPITHETS

In Present-Day English such a phrase as *twelve good men and true,* with the last adjective placed after its substantive, must be characterized as a rudiment of an on the whole outdated construction. Still it is possible, even in twentieth-century literature, to find the construction in quotations such as the following:

a small movement and unobtrusive. E. Raymond, *We, the Accused,* 310.
a better and a deeper man, and a more tried. J. Cary, *Herself Surprised,* 211.
with a sure heart and true. H. Waddell, *The Wandering Scholars,* 220.

In most cases today, however, either the *one*-construction is resorted to or both adjectives are placed before the substantive (Jespersen, MEG II 10.96: *a good man and a true one; a good and true man*). In what follows I shall attempt to analyse the use and meaning of the old construction, viewed in the light of its history.

In OE. the rule was for the second epithet to be placed after its substantive:

þā swētestan stefne ond þā fægrestan. Bede.
þone heardestan hungor and þone rēðestan. Apollonius.
þrȳ gelǣrede weras ond æþelborene.

although the modern construction occurs as well:

ongemang ōðrum mislīcum ond monigfaldum bisgum. Cura Pastoralis.

and in the combination pronominal word (*ān, eall, ōðer,* etc.) + adjective pre-position is the rule:

on āne dīgle stōwe. Orosius.
þæt is ealra ferscra wætera mǣst. Orosius.

Now the OE. regular construction adjective + substantive + adjective has a certain stylistic similarity with other OE. constructions. As Bøgholm points out,[1] the rule is for parallel words to be kept apart; thus, if a subject consists of several parts, these are often separated from each other:

Hēr Cynewulf benam Sigebryht his rīces ond Westseaxna wiotan. Chronicle.
þā ridon hīe þider ond his alderman Osrīc ond Wīferþ his þegn ond þā men þe hē beæftan him lǣfde ǣr.[2] Chronicle.

Similarly, the several units constituting an object may be separated:

ond (hīe) þone æþeling ofslōgon ond þā men þe mid him wǣrun alle. Chronicle.

---

[1] *English Speech From an Historical Point of View,* 1939, 134.
[2] Cf. a modern example: marshes . . where swans nested and rarer birds. S. Gibbons, *Nightingale Wood,* 14.

Further, two predicatives may be separated by the verb:

Ðēah þū stille sȳ ond unrōt. Apollonius.

In all these cases the impression one receives is that apparently the writer did not care (or perhaps, was unable) to think matters over before he wrote them down — hence the many additions which may often be interpreted as afterthoughts. It is tempting to term such a style slipshod and loose, and it is natural to mention in this connexion the many instances of anacoluthon found in the early stages of the language. In Bøgholm's[3] and C. A. Smith s[4] terminologies constructions like the above are the manifestations of short span or short circuit tendencies innate in English. Perhaps immaturity is too harsh a characterization of a language which in other respects was highly developed. Anyhow it is tempting to assume that the widespread use of the construction adjective + substantive + adjective in OE. was supported by, if not a direct outcome of, this general tendency towards looseness in construction.

In all the examples adduced so far the substantive and the last adjective were connected by *and*. There exists also a rarer construction without *and*. I have only a single OE. example: *of twispunnenum twine linenum* (Cura Pastoralis). In Mod. English it is not infrequently met with, especially in poetry. Milton has *human face divine*, Gray *purest ray serene*. This construction has been ascribed to Greek[5] and to Italian[6] influence.

As we approach Modern English, the old construction becomes rarer (it may to some extent have been supported by the many phrases adopted from French in which the adjective was placed after the noun), and already in Mandeville the modern construction is the one generally used. In the fifteenth century it is frequent in the conclusion of letters, where it has apparently become a mere formula, witness such examples as *God grante yow right goode lyf and longe, our Lord send yow lang lyff and gud,* etc. It is very frequent in More. Curiously enough, it seems to have been extinct in the eighteenth century[7]; Swift, for instance, uses the modern one-construction: *a short life and a merry one.*

It has been maintained that where the old phrase occurs today, it bears the stamp of conscious archaism[8]. This is true in most instances, as when we find

a soft little wind and gay. H. Waddell, *The Wandering Scholars*, 121,

---

[3] *op. cit.*

[4] *Studies in English Syntax*, 1906.

[5] V. K. Gokak, *The Poetic Approach to Language*, 1952, 146.

[6] G. Highet, *The Classical Tradition*, 1949, 611: 'It should be noticed that one of the most striking of Milton's stylistic devices, the adjective-noun-adjective phrase, as in

The Eternal King Omnipresent (6.227)

is neither Latin nor Greek, but Italian: caro figlio adorato.

[7] Jespersen, MEG II 10.962.

[8] Jespersen, l.c.; Mats Redin, *Word-Order in English Verse*, 1925, 147.

14

in a paraphrase of lyrics; and Dickens's

You must stand by me, Venus, like a good man and true. *Our Mutual Friend*, 618,

is obviously reminiscent of the old phrase. At the same time it seems to have preserved the connotation of *afterthought* — sometimes this is corroborated by the presence of a comma —, and it need not always be archaic:

Wegg was a knotty man, and a close-grained. Dickens, *op. cit.*, 43.
keeping a journal is the veriest pastime in the world, and the pleasantest. Mark Twain, *The Innocents Abroad*, 24.

The last quotation is not felt as archaic, since it is quite common to leave out *one* after a superlative. When the second adjective stands as a predicative and takes the indefinite article, the construction is usually felt as archaic:

It was a rare thing and a joyful. Mark Twain, *op. cit.*, 49,

whereas that need not be the case if the indefinite article is left out, since then the adjective may be interpreted as a predicative in its own right, as it were, not very closely connected with the preceding substantive:

he was a fair man and kindly. A. P. Herbert, *Holy Deadlock*, 175.
a small movement and unobtrusive. E. Raymond, *op. cit.*, 310.

When Maugham writes:

It was a pleasant sight and grateful to the sensibility jarred by those sordid ruins and perplexed. *The Gentleman in the Parlour*, 135-6,

the first occurrence of the construction is caused by the need for *linking up* the second adjective with what follows (while the last instance impresses the reader as being affected).

In all the above quotations the qualities expressed by the adjectives refer to one primary. There exists a notionally different construction of the type *black spirits and grey*, in which *grey* conveys, not the addition of another quality to *spirits*, but another category of *spirits*. This type is quite current and is often used to express *contrast*; the separation of the two epithets throws them in relief, and the phrasal end-position of the second adjective gives it particular weight. As the addition may take the form of an alternative possibility, it also occurs with *or*:

black spirits and grey, red spirits and white. Dickens, *op. cit.*, 202.
whether the fates had promised good fortune or ill you could tell from not one of those impressive faces. Maugham, *op. cit.*, 140.

When we find in a book catalogue:

WE BUY BOOKS in large lots and small,

it must in that context be considered a stylistic trick to catch the reader's attention.

The above remarks are offered as a tentative interpretation of the adjective-substantive-adjective construction. I have only hinted at the fact that the whole problem is bound up with the rules for the use of *one* as a prop-word — some of the quotations are instances of the incomplete regularization of this use. It may well be that the material is too scant, and that other shades of meaning may be brought to light.

ENGLISH AND ROMANCE:
SOME ASPECTS OF STYLE

Loanwords are generally adopted for one of two main reasons. It may be for their *informative function:* a real need may be felt in the adopting language for a foreign term that appears to have no counterpart in the vernacular (I deliberately use a subjective terminology to suggest that it is often a psychological want that is felt, since with a bit of ingenuity a vernacular term might perhaps have been made to do duty). Or it may be for their *stylistic function:* loanwords may be adopted for the sake of the cultural and social prestige that attaches to them (including their typographical and phonetic effectiveness), while they do not really fill a semantic gap. Thirdly, there may be cases of more or less unconscious borrowing, the users of the vernacular being so impregnated with a foreign language that they come to employ foreign words mechanically and automatically; but probably such cases are not very numerous.

If we throw a rapid glance at the history of English, bearing in mind the first two functions mentioned above, the informative and the stylistic, we shall find that in different periods their relative importance has been varying. In Old English literature loans were mainly adopted for their sheer informative value. This was also generally true of the Romance loans adopted in Middle English, though by then the stylistic function undoubtedly played a part as well; in many of the pairings of Romance and native words that occur in Middle English there is an obvious striving for rhetorical effect. Mainly informative are such well-known examples from *Ancrene Riwle* as *cherité þet is luve, pacience þet is þolemodnesse,* while Caxton's doublets *the volume intituled and named . . . composed and drawen out of dyuerce bookes . . . Which sayd translacion and werke . . . ended and fynysshid,*[1] etc. are mainly stylistic. The Renaissance saw an increase in the relative importance of the stylistic function. In the wake of the growing patriotism there followed a strongly developed linguistic consciousness which was behind the conflict between inkhornists and Euphuists on the one hand and purists on the other. Though many of the inkhorn terms were shortlived, foreign influence on English was so marked that a 'language bar'[2] arose, witness Shakespeare's use of Malapropism. In the later seventeenth century the stylistic function suffered a temporary setback as a consequence of the striving towards simplicity (the Royal Society), but it came to the fore again in the eighteenth century with its predilection for abstract poetic diction. And this brief survey takes us almost up to modern times.

In considering the contemporary use of Romance loans it may be helpful to apply the two criteria already mentioned: the informative function and the stylistic function, though they cannot always be rigidly distinguished. It is the stylistic uses of the loanwords that will be our main concern, and we shall especially deal with some cases in which the contrast between what is felt as native (familiar) and foreign (exotic) is exploited.

---

[1] *Prologues and Epilogues,* E. E. T. S. Orig. Ser. No. 176 (1956), p. 2.
[2] Cf. Victor Grove, *The Language Bar* (London 1959).

The well-read writer of English has at his command a vast store of Romance loanwords, often terms that are related both in form and in meaning. In employing such terms the competent stylist has an opportunity of conveying precise shades of meaning, as in the following quotations[3]:

On such matters, and on Swift's final disappointment, Ehrenpreis is *sensible* and *sensitive*. (NP)

At the same time, until he had made his name by his work, he can rarely have spoken to a single *literary* (or even *literate*) man of his own immediate date. (NP)

If Mr Storey has sacrificed the *authenticity* and *authority* of his earlier books ... it is for the sake of a much more ambitious theme. (NP)

... it is evident that he was never merely the *confluence* of his *influences*. (NP)

... it is obvious that Aubrey cannot be considered as an historian, for his genius was for *collection* rather than *selection* (*Aubrey's Brief Lives*, Peregrine 1962, p. 103).

In examples of this type the writer's use of the italicized words may be said to be primarily informative, though the fact that the pairs are phonetically similar gives the reader the impression that these are at the same time cases of mild punning. No doubt the writer of the following passage was also thinking mainly of his message while simultaneously hoping to achieve some rhetorical effect by means of homoeoteleūton:

There are scores of organizations in these days who will help soften the blow when situations arise which not long ago would have meant *destitution, prostitution* or an *institution*. (NP)

A slightly different use is seen below, where the writer is trying to capitalize the supposed fact that two phonetically similar words are at the same time etymologically related (that is, unless he is writing with his tongue in his cheek):

The author insists again and again that drugs make one *impregnable,* so it is inconsistent then to claim that his characters' words and thoughts are *pregnant*. (NP)

The quotations adduced so far contain concepts that are semantically distinct, though related. When a writer feels the need for stylistic variation of a single concept, he may frequently utilize Romance synonyms of native English words, especially Romance adjectives corresponding to nouns that are of native origin (or at least no longer felt to be foreign): *mind — mental, mouth — oral,* etc. Thus, in C. P. Snow's *The Affair* (Penguin pp. 60-61) a discussion turns on *Electing Masters and so on,* for which we later find the variant *magisterial elections.* A useful distinction may be drawn between *assistant editors* and *editorial assistants* (to be paralleled with *a flower garden* vs. *a garden flower).* In many such cases the emphasis is clearly on the informative function, and there need be no important stylistic difference. But very often there *is* a marked difference in tone between the foreign and the native terms, the former being felt as prestige-words, the latter as the plain terms. There is a good deal of snobbishness involved in the higher rating of the foreign words, which are esteemed by some partly on account of their 'elegance', partly because they are less direct and transparent and may therefore sometimes function as euphemisms. Here are some instances; first a snatch of dialogue from Waugh's *The Loved One:*

---

[3] NP = recent newspaper quotation.

'... Were you thinking of interment or incineration?'
'Pardon me?'
'Buried or burned?' (Penguin p. 19)

A similar contrast is seen in Katherine Mansfield's *The Garden Party*:

— .. 'it was dropsy that carried him off at the larst. Many's the time they drawn one and a half pints from 'im at the 'ospital ... It seemed like a judgmint.'
Alice burned to know exactly what it was that was drawn from him. She ventured, 'I suppose it was water.'
But Mrs Stubbs fixed Alice with her eyes and replied meaningly, 'It was *liquid*, my dear.'
(Penguin p. 44)

It is natural that business men should endeavour to enhance their reputation; here are some instances of occupational terms of prestige:

Smog and cold have made this a busy spring for Britain's 4,400 undertakers, or *funeral directors*, as they prefer to call themselves. (NP)
Although more than 50 per cent of bodies are now embalmed, most people fear the word and embalmers themselves would prefer the phrase *'temporary preservation'*. (NP)
George scorned the new phrase *'prison officer'*, which he classified with *'rodent operative'*.
(NP)

In other cases the contrast between English and Romance may be one of plainness vs. exoticism:

The coast [of England] was incredibly green, but with a *bright cosy greenness* quite unlike the *luxuriant, vehement verdure* of Eastern jungles. (S. Maugham, *The Door of Opportunity*, Modern English Short Stories, First Series, p. 114).

It is understandable that writers, especially journalists, should occasionally be tempted to play with their medium. Thus the highbrow will sometimes resort to the Latinization of a name, as an elegant variation or a mild joke:

Henry James excommunicated the dramatic critics of England for their failure to bring her playgoers to drink at the slightly opaque and brackish waters of *Henrico-Jacobean* drama. (C. E. Montague, *A Writer's Notes on his Trade*, Penguin p. 127).
For evocation, subtlety of mood, atmosphere — all the qualities the *Lupians* praise — the sensitive Mrs Woolf can be shamed by an old toughy like Simenon. (NP)

From here it is but a step to the deliberate exploitation of Romance words of the more exotic type for the purpose of achieving a humorous effect. This effect is caused by stylistic incongruity. The reader normally expects to find bookish and learned words in decidedly technical contexts. Thus the characteristic environment of a term like *piscine* would be in a passage like

The piscine modification of the vertebrate skeleton (OED q 1899),

and *piscatorial* would fit in well in the following passage:

the grandest specimen of piscatorial topography ever exhibited, in the official fishery map of the United States (OED q 1883).

But when Ellery Queen starts by introducing us to a *fish-faced man* and refers to him later as *the piscatorial flunkey* and *the piscine butler* (*Half-Way House*, London

1937, pp. 109, 112, 270), we are given a slight shock because these words are employed outside their normal context; we may or may not laugh — probably not much in this case, which is rather laboured; but the device can be quite effective. Its origin is perhaps to be sought in Johnsonese and in the less felicitous instances of eighteenth-century poetic diction, though this was not usually *meant* to be humorous. There are numerous instances of it in Dickens's facetious passages; generally they are not very successful, conveying the impression of forced gaiety, as in this typical example:

... they performed private dances of ecstasy among themselves, and stood on one leg apiece, and hopped, and indulged in other *salutory* tokens of gladness. (*Dombey and Son*, Ch. 58)

The point is of course that this stylistic trick should not be overworked, for the moment it degenerates into a mannerism, it loses much of its effect. — One of the contemporary writers who employ this substitution-technique with great virtuosity is P. G. Wodehouse. Here are some characteristic specimens:

Bredin was a pig. He looked like a pig; he ate like a pig; he grunted like a pig. He had the lavish embonpoint of a pig. Also a *porcine* soul. (*The Man Upstairs*, Penguin p. 86)
I pushed round to his office and found him, as usual, up to the *thorax* in bills of replevin and what not. (*Laughing Gas*, Penguin p. 7)
... somebody barged into me and I went *base over apex* into a bush.

(*Laughing Gas*, Penguin p. 176)

It should be added that such extracts gain by being read in their contexts: in the Jeeves/Wooster stories these incongruities often come as climaxes in situations that have been rendered stylistically and otherwise contrastive from the outset.

Granted that stylistic considerations are foremost in this use of native and foreign synonyms, they nevertheless do have semantic ties, *qua* synonyms. But in another type these ties tend to dwindle, so that the principle governing the choice of words becomes, first and foremost, their phonetic similarity, while the message to be conveyed has to adapt itself to this principle — or, to put it differently: there is a tendency to sacrifice almost everything for a fine-looking or fine-sounding phrase.[4] This can of course be done by means of native resources, as in

Televisually, Lord Attlee made his usual *wistful, wispy,* yet *waspish* — only in a nice way — impression. (NP)

But probably the Romance loanwords offer greater scope for the use of this device, which is instanced in the passages quoted below; here, too, one has a suspicion that the phonetically similar words have been lugged in more or less gratuitously:

... the character Colette rigged up for herself ... is still vigorously at all its old *devices* and *vices*. (NP)
If *pagination* is absent (and it is), *vagination* is there in abundance ... (NP)
... subject to the intricate *additions* and *attritions* of film-making ... (NP)

---

[4] In a footnote it is perhaps permissible to call attention to another kind of catalytic effect exercised by Romance loans: it is probably not fortuitously that English uses *sister nation* (cf. French *nation soeur*), while German has *Brudervolk* and Danish *broderfolk;* ultimately it is Latin gender that is at work. Cf. also *He is his own master/she is completely mistress of herself.*

His conscience continued to be busy with the matter. Was he *depraving* Randall? Was he *depriving* Ann? But Randall was *depraved* and Ann *deprived* already. (Iris Murdoch, *An Unofficial Rose*, Chatto & Windus 1962, p. 226).

According to tradition, real farmers can acquire capital in three ways — *patrimony, parsimony, matrimony;* the first being the result of successfully practising the other two. (NP)

It is only the last of the quotations that is reasonably justified as a pithy saying. — This modern congener of euphuism is met with primarily in journalese and in the language of advertising, where the writer's aim is to dazzle and convince the reader through the use of a hard-hitting and effective style.

It must be admitted that particularly the more recondite Romance loans are a two-edged sword; they can be skilfully exploited for informative and stylistic purposes, but only by the competent user. In his autobiography *Good-Bye to All That* (Penguin p. 246) Robert Graves gives a delightful example of the way such words lend themselves to a special kind of donnish humour. Professor Edgeworth opened a conversation by asking T. E. Lawrence: 'Was it very caliginous in the Metropolis?' but his interlocutor was able to give him tit for tat by replying: 'Somewhat caliginous, but not altogether inspissated.' On the other hand there are numerous dangers ahead of those who feel irresistibly attracted by pairs like *ingenious/ingenuous, complement/compliment, precedent/president,* etc., which have been confused for centuries. It may be risky to fall in love with a sonorous word, more particularly if it is a word of foreign extraction. This was what Denis did in Huxley's *Crome Yellow* (Penguin p. 120), with the result that he had to scrap an entire poem on ascertaining that *carminative,* though apparently euphonious enough, does not fit in very well in poetic contexts — apart, perhaps, from a certain kind of modernist poetry. For the fallacy that there is in general an inherent connexion between sound and sense is still widespread.

In 'The Problem of the 'Hard Words' ' *(English Studies* 1953-54, pp. 262-67) Ernst Leisi made the point that the fact of the 'hard words' being less readily understood may contribute to extending the meaning and use of the native vocabulary. In the preceding pages I have tried to give examples showing that there are certain more or less legitimate stylistic endeavours — whether a striving for precision, or for rhetorical and humorous effects — that tend to favour the use of the Romance vocabulary.

A NOTE ON *AT ALL*

Some lexical items are largely restricted to negative contexts,[1] while others have a wider, but still circumscribed, potentiality of occurrence. The status of some of these items seems to be in doubt: take *let alone*, about which *A Grammar of Contemporary English*[2] merely states that it is preceded by a negative. No doubt this is normally the case; but *let alone* also occurs without any preceding negative, for instance in a book written by the prime mover of the *GCE*:

And generations of editors, let alone readers, have been puzzled by Petruchio's [quotation follows]. (Randolph Quirk, *The Linguist and the English Language* ,London, 1974, p. 54).

The point is that *let alone* may be paraphrased not only by 'still less' (as in the *GCE*), but also by 'not to mention' (thus the *OED*, VI, 213).

The pages that follow owe their existence to the observation that *at all* does not, on the surface at least, appear always to behave in accordance with the rules laid down for it in dictionaries and grammars. Not that it is given a lot of comment in the latter; we shall revert to this point later. Some dictionaries contain a rule of thumb governing the use of *at all*. Thus, according to the *OED*, it occurs 'only in negative or interrogative sentences, or conditional clauses',[3] and no doubt this rule accounts for most occurrences of *at all*. Many less detailed grammars of contemporary English make no explicit mention of *at all*; but if we turn to comprehensive works like Poutsma's *Grammar of Late Modern English*,[4] we learn that apart from its use in negative, interrogative, and conditional clauses, *at all* is also found in sentences or clauses 'which are negative or conditional in import'. This formulation accommodates examples like

(1) Two possibles failed to get in at all, since Garth was away. (Iris Murdoch, *An Accidental Man*, Penguin, 1973, p. 117.)

(2) If such an account is acceptable (and it seems to be the preferable one, given the assumption that a V is present at all in the underlying structure of clauses), superficially verbless locative clauses can thus be accommodated in terms of the base rules already proposed. (John M. Anderson, *The Grammar of Case*, Cambridge, 1971, p. 87f.)

[1] For examples, see E. Buyssens, 'Negative Contexts', *English Studies*, XL (1959), 163-9.
[2] Randolph Quirk/Sidney Greenbaum/Geoffrey Leech/Jan Svartvik, *A Grammar of Contemporary English* (abbreviated *GCE*), London, 1972, p. 620.
[3] *OED*, s.v. *all*, 9b; cf. also the *Supplement* to the *OED*, vol. I, 1972, where a non-standard use of *at all* is illustrated.
[4] Part II, Section I, B, Groningen, 1916, p. 1013.

22

In (1) it is easy to produce an explicitly negative transform: '... did not get in at all ...', and the relevant part of (2) may be paraphrased: '... if a V is assumed to be present at all ...'.

The above examples are fairly straightforward; there is no problem in recognizing the negative or conditional import. But there occur many examples of *at all* in which it does not appear so simple to detect the negative or conditional implication, and it may be worthwhile to explore such cases in some detail.

Let us begin by considering *implied negation* as exemplified by the following quotations:

(3) '... You're nice to put up with us at all, sorry if I said anything too strong...' (John Updike, *Rabbit Redux*, Penguin, 1973, p. 49.)

(4) ...after what we've been through, it's nice of Earl to mention us at all. (Walker Gibson, *Tough, Sweet and Stuffy*. An Essay on Modern American Prose Styles, Bloomington, Indiana, 1966, p. 67.)

(5) This habit of vigour ... was the other half of the reason why this call was being paid so promptly, or perhaps at all ... (Kingsley Amis, *The Riverside Villas Murder*, Panther, 1974, p. 29.)

(6) The very fact that the Congress could take place at all indicated that Peking's fractured leadership had come a long way toward resolving its differences. (*Time*, 27 January 1975, p. 10.)

At the first blush no negative element is apparent here. What can it be, then, that conditions the presence of *at all* in these examples? One explanation that suggests itself is that here we have to do with an implied contrast in the form of an imagined negation which, if realized, would contain the items *not* (...) *at all*: underlying (3) there lurks the idea that 'you might not have been willing to put up with us at all'; the negative implication of (4) is: 'Earl might well not have mentioned us at all'; of (5): 'the call might not have been paid at all'; and of (6): 'it might not have been possible for the Congress to take place at all'. If these implied negative formulations are valid, we may generalize by saying that in (3-6) *at all* emphasizes the actual occurrence of an event X while at the same time distinctly suggesting the possibility of the non-occurrence of X.

To shed further light on the potentiality of occurrence of this intensifier in superficially positive sentences, let us consider here a special contextual situation that permits the presence of *at all* with the same negative import; it is illustrated by examples like:

(7) It was notable that Sadat now felt strong enough to talk at all about peace and the limited objectives he seeks. (*Time*, 29 October 1973, p. 20.)

(8) ... I think it is a great achievement that he has managed to write this book at all. (Iris Murdoch, *The Black Prince*, Warner paperback, 1974, p. 406f.)

As far as semantics are concerned, this type may be described as a value-judgment of a fact which is given an emphatic formulation through the employment of *at all*. It may be instructive to compare this with competing formulations. Consider the following type examples:

(a) In the circumstances it was astonishing that he managed to write the book.
(b) In the circumstances it was astonishing that he did manage to write the book.
(c) In the circumstances it was astonishing that he managed to write the book at all.

The content of the subordinate clause of (a) is non-emphatic, while the subordinate clauses of (b) and (c) convey emphasis. In the formulation they are given here, (b) and (c) are semantically close to each other, though hardly completely interchangeable; (c) is more negatively orientated than (b) and may thus carry a negative implication: 'he might well not have managed to write the book (at all)' is suggested more strongly by (c) than by (b). (c) thus has a clear affinity with examples (3-6). But there is a difference. What is noteworthy is the fact that if the *that*-clause is not governed by a sentence containing a value-judgment, only (b) is possible: we do not attest *he managed to write the book at all*. That the governing sentence has to express a value-judgment for *at all* to occur is corroborated by the fact that we register another candidate for stardom in a formulation like *it is a fact that he managed to write the book at all*.[5]

Let us proceed to a different type of implied negation, illustrated by the following:

(9) His fathers had been noble since they had been at all. (Virginia Woolf, *Orlando*, London, 1949, p. 16.)

(10) Note the time it has taken before I have got round to talking about results at all. (David Crystal, *Linguistics*, Pelican, 1971, p. 138.)

(11) Alas, the book was written well before the fruits of Dr David Butler's various researches became at all widely available ... (*New Statesman*, 7 November 1969, p. 643.)

(12) 'Can you get the ship out without the pilot?'
    'Yes. I made a careful study of the river before I knew we would have to have a pilot at all ...' (Richard Condon, *Arigato*, Dell Book, 1974, p. 250.)

Common to (9-12) is the presence of a temporal conjunction. (9) implies that there was a time when *his fathers* were non-existent (this quotation has a somewhat peculiar ring about it owing to the fact that 'existence' and 'non-existence' are absolute concepts that do not normally appear to permit collocation with an intensifier). (10-12) differ slightly from (9) in that they concentrate more on former situations in which the state of things was clearly different from the state of things as it is at the moment of speaking or writing ((10): 'earlier, I didn't at all get round to ...'). Generalizing, we may say about this type that here the contrast is between *an actual* situation in the past and the present situation. — As in the preceding examples, *at all*

[5] Professor R. Derolez suggests that (c) above may also imply that the book written is poor, or short, and the like; that this may indeed be a possibility seems to be borne out by the following quotation: 'It [i.e. a Rubinstein film] does not serve Rubinstein well, but serving him at all makes the film notable' (*Time*, 10 March 1975, p. 2).

might have been left out; when present it is an intensifier, a carrier of emphasis.

Having dealt with implied negation, we may now go on to discuss *implied condition*. In the *GCE*, p. 376f., *at all* is referred to as a non-assertive 'extent adverb' contrasting with assertive *to some extent*: *I can't help at all* vs. *I can help (to some extent)*. In the light of this let us consider the following example:

(13) To the extent that Nixon is at all like L. B. J., he swears, as Johnson did, at least partly in order to show contempt for others ... (*Time*, 20 May 1974, p. 52.)

In this quotation, *to the extent that* is semantically related to *if*, but it should be noted that it is a guarded, non-committal *if*, a downtoner. Likewise, a statement like 'To the extent that this is true, it puts a different complexion on things' will normally suggest doubt about the truth. Similar downtoners are seen in

(14) It would be mistaken to suggest that the image of the teen-age pop-star has been seriously challenged, in adolescent eyes, by that of the student revolutionary, but in so far as this has tended to happen at all I would count it one feather in the cap of secondary education. (James Britton, *Language and Learning*, Pelican, 1972, p. 269.)

(15) Since situations appear to be infinitely various, some linguists have hesitated to embark on a systematic study of the situations which mould the various registers of English. But we may deal again only with an abstract situation, and deal with situation at all only as it affects the form of language. (G. W. Turner, *Stylistics*, Pelican, 1973, p. 167.)

Here the conditional downtoners *in so far as* and *only as* are reinforced by *at all* (which might again have been left out). In (14) and (15) the degree (a slight one) to which a condition is fulfilled determines the result. In

(16) A poem or book or script contains the built-in idea that it is changing something or advancing something by existing at all. (*Language & Literature*, II, 1, Copenhagen, 1973, p. 71.)

it is the lowest possible degree that is suggested, since here the relevant words may be paraphrased 'merely if it exists'; in other words, *a correlation is postulated* between mere existence and the assumed function of the existing poem, etc. Consider further:

(17) ... man's involvement with personal and local identity, with the issues of national politics, with the whole complex web of society, bites deep into language and at the same time conditions in large measure the extent to which one is personally conscious of language at all. (Randolph Quirk, *The English Language and Images of Matter*, London, 1972, p. vii.)

Here again we have to do with an implied condition, but as in (16), it is a condition connoting correlative extent or degree: the extent of one's involvement corresponds to the extent of one's consciousness. — Alternatively, a negative condition might perhaps be implied here: 'unless one is involved ..., one will not at all be personally conscious of language'.

So far we have reviewed some cases of *at all* occurring in sentences suggesting implied negation and condition. It may be asked whether *at all* can be found in superficially assertive sentences which imply a question. It can, although it must be admitted that the example to be given is not very striking, seeing that the presence of *at all* is dependent on the verb *to question*:

(18) Some Pentagon planners question the need for any kind of airlift at all now. (*Time*, 20 January 1975, p. 7.)

It may even be doubtful whether it is question or negation that is implied here, 'import' of one kind or another being admittedly a somewhat slippery concept. Be that as it may, (18) reminds us of the well-known fact that *any* and *at all* are semantically related.[6] This is obvious from examples like:

(19) Those of his acquaintances who cared at all for Ronnie Appleyard and some of that large number who did not, would have admired the way he went into action now. (Kingsley Amis, *I Want It Now*, Panther, 1969, p. 48.)

(20) Whether it [Chinese] is really hard to learn depends in particular on whether we speak a language in the first place which is at all similar to Chinese ... (David Crystal, *Linguistics*, Pelican, 1971, p. 71.)

where the closest paraphrase of *at all* would be *to any extent* or *in any respect*.

(18) above may lead us on to our final point. It is surprising to note that even in as detailed a grammar as the *GCE* no explicit mention is made of the fact that there is frequent collocation between *at all* and the *any* series, not only in negative, interrogative, and conditional clauses, but also in superficially assertive sentences (*GCE*, p. 224). This usage is documented by the following examples, which might easily be multiplied:

(21) With money tight and auto sales plunging, George Nouhan, a partner in a Chevrolet dealership in Hamtramck, Mich., began advertising that he would consider anything, anything at all, as a trade-in on a new car or truck. (*Time*, 13 January 1975, p. 16.)

(22) ... Miss Gomez followed her into the hall, still wanting to speak, to say anything at all, but finding that words would not come to her. (William Trevor, *Miss Gomez and the Brethren*, London, 1971, p. 102.)

(23) For many centuries, the term usury referred to the taking of any interest at all. (*Time*, 10 September 1973, p. 63.)

(24) 'Do you have any idea where Davy would go?'
    'He might go anywhere at all. ....' (Ross Macdonald, *The Instant Enemy*, Fontana, 1972, p. 32.)

The members of the *any* series in themselves denote 'unlimited extent'. As is true of the other uses of *at all* described above, the collocation of *any* and *at all* produces a degree of extra strong emphasis, a point that is perhaps brought home most clearly in (21), where in his endeavour to achieve maximum impact the advertiser proceeds from *anything* to *anything at all*.

[6] Cf. the dialectal or slangy use of *any* = 'at all' listed in the *Supplement* to the *OED*, s.v. *any*, 7b.

The analyses suggested above are deliberately tentative since I am not fully satisfied that they are all of them adequate. The method of paraphrasing may in some cases be objectionable, not least because double paraphrases seem a possibility for some examples. Would a TG grammarian posit a negative – conditional – interrogative – emphatic element in deep structure conditioning the occurrence of *at all* in surface structure? Such a solution in my view would only be a solution in name. Nor would equating *at all* with its semantic near-cognates, German *überhaupt* and Danish *overhovedet*, be any solution. In these circumstances paraphrasing appears to be the least objectionable procedure. But let this note end with an appeal to the insight of native speakers of English.

ASSEVERATIVE *IF* AND ITS CONGENERS

What will here be termed 'asseverative *if*' is the use of *if* found in the well-known colloquial idiom *She is forty if she is a day*. Perhaps not everyone would call this expression an idiom;[1] however, I shall leave out theoretical considerations here, sticking to the assumption made by A. P. Cowie & R. Mackin[2] that idiomatic expressions may 'span sentences of various structural types'. Asseverative *if* seems to have been largely neglected in the description of English: to my knowledge it has not been dealt with in the major histories of English by Poutsma, Jespersen, and Visser, and it is interesting to note what the G. & C. Merriam Company, Publishers of Merriam-Webster Reference Books, wrote to me after I had asked them for information about asseverative *if*: 'Our files do not readily produce any examples of this usage, in part because it is more commonly found in speech, in part because the various forms of the expression have no common lexical items except *if* and our files are lexical' (letter of May 6, 1976). In other words, this use of *if* is liable to be neglected by grammarians as well as by compilers of dictionaries. I have, however, found a number of examples in the *O.E.D.* and its supplementary volumes. My concern in this article will be with the development of the idiom and with what I take to be some of its congeners.

First a brief presentation of the idiom in its contemporary forms. It most frequently occurs in variants like *She is forty if she is a day*, *It costs £ 10,000 if (it costs) a penny*, and *If I've said it once I've said it a hundred times*. At the first blush such sayings appear to be quite illogical; but this is because an element has been skipped. For the chain of 'reasoning' appears to be something like this: 'You will grant me that she is a day old (that it costs a penny, that I've said it once); and if you do that, as indeed you must, I am justified in asserting that she is (at least) forty, etc.'. Not impeccable reasoning, to be sure; rather, these are assertions that operate under cover of logic, as it were; for presumably they draw strength from the many cases in which there is a valid inference from a premise to a conclusion, e.g. *If you mix yellow and blue you get green*. The sharp contrast between *a day* and *forty*, etc., suggests that it would be absurd to deny the assertion. The *if* idiom implies 'at least so and so much', etc., but it is racier than a formulation containing *at least*.

In the variants that are met with in contemporary English, asseverative *if* does not appear to be much more than a couple of hundred years old;

---

[1] See the discussion of idiom status in Adam Makkai, *Idiom Structure in English*, Janua Linguarum, Series Maior, 48 (The Hague & Paris, 1972).
[2] *The Oxford Dictionary of Current Idiomatic English*, Vol. 1 (Oxford, 1975), p. vii.

28

but I would suggest that it has a number of somewhat older congeners. In the first place it may be noted that there are several proverbial expressions dating back to Early Modern English which reveal a logic (or pseudo-logic) somewhat akin to the kind of logic seen in the use of asseverative *if*; for instance:

You may see by a bit what the bread is.
(M. P. Tilley, *A Dictionary of the Proverbs in England in the Sixteenth and Seventeenth Centuries*, Ann Arbor, 1966, B 421).
He that chastens one, chastens twenty.
(*The Oxford Dictionary of English Proverbs*, third edition, Oxford, 1970, p. 116).

In such cases, what holds for a fragment or a single individual is asserted to hold for the whole or for a great number (cf. also the proverb *In for a penny, in for a pound* with its special implication). Experience, such proverbs teach us, warrants a qualitative or quantitative extrapolation from known cases to other, presumably similar, cases. Compare further a nursery rhyme formulation like

... When she was good she was very, very good,
But when she was bad she was horrid ...
(*The Puffin Book of Nursery Rhymes*, Penguin, 1963, p. 18).

which postulates an extrapolation to a very high degree. Without asserting that formulations like those above actually paved the way for the *if* idiom, it may nevertheless be relevant to note that before the emergence of asseverative *if* in its modern form there were popular locutions that had one important 'logical' element in common with the *if* idiom.

In Elizabethan English we may find other cognates of our idiom. Let us consider Shakespeare's sonnet 116:

If this be error, and upon me prov'd,
I never writ, nor no man ever lov'd.

We note here that the content of the *if* clause must be rejected out of hand since, if it were accepted, the conclusion would be patently absurd. A similar formulation is employed by Ben Jonson in *Every Man In His Humour*:

I am a Jew if I know what to say ...
(*Ben Jonson's Plays*, ed. F. E. Schelling, Everyman I, p. 25).

which may be compared with the idiomatic assertion ending ... *or I'm a Dutchman* found in contemporary English. What is denied here is the validity of drawing an inference from premise (protasis) to conclusion (apodosis): it does not make sense to say that I never wrote, that I am a Jew, etc., and consequently the truth value of the content of the premise must be rejected. We may note a related pseudo-logical argument in the idiom apparently created by Shakespeare: *nothing if not* followed by a descriptive adjective:

O, gentle Lady, do not put me too 't,
For I am nothing if not Criticall.
(*Othello* 2.1.120-1)

This idiom, which is still very much alive, assumes that it is obvious to the meanest intelligence that the critical quality is present, and if anybody would be so rash as to deny this, it would be tantamount to denying the person concerned any other quality; if he is not critical (or generous, etc.), it might as well be asserted that he is nothing.[3]

The types discussed above are negatively orientated: if one accepts the truth of the premise, one is led into absurdity by having to accept a conclusion that is contrary to fact and to common sense. But in Elizabethan English we also find asseverative *if* clauses, i.e. clauses that serve to emphasize the truth of an assertion:

If I stand here, I saw him.
(*Macbeth* 3.4.73)

which might be paraphrased: 'If you accept that I stand here, you must also accept that I saw him'. Here, again, we have to do with an appeal not to logic but to common sense, although — as in the preceding cases — the assertion is accommodated in a seemingly logical form.

Although the uses of *if* illustrated so far do involve a pseudo-logical element, they are still a far cry from the modern idiom, which is used to assert that at least a specified age, amount, etc. is present. It is interesting to note, however, that in Elizabethan English there occurs a use of *as well as* (*O.E.D. well* V.20) which only on the surface means 'in the same degree, as much as':

... certaine propheticall rymes, which might be construed two or three wayes as well as to that one whereunto the rebelles applied it ...
(George Puttenham, *The Arte of English Poesie* [1589], Scolar Press Facsimile, 1968, p. 218)
In a night & a day would he haue yarkt vp a pamphlet as well as in seauen yeare ...
(*Strange News* [1593], The Works of Thomas Nashe, ed. R. B. McKerrow, Oxford, 1966, vol. I, p. 287)
... her land, sir *George*, is as well worth a hundred pound a yeare as one penny ...
(*Jack of Newberie* [1597], The Works of Thomas Deloney, ed. F. O. Mann, Oxford, 1912, p. 65)

Even in the first quotation it is not a matter of indifference whether one chooses *two or three wayes* or *that one*; the interpretation is slanted in the direction of the former possibility, and *as well as* approaches the sense of 'rather than'. In the last two quotations it is obvious that the discrepancy in time or money is exploited to point to *a night and a day* and *a hundred pound* as the natural choices, which are mentioned first.

---

[3] A similar kind of logic underlies the use of *if anything*, current since the nineteenth century: *If anything, the situation is worse now than a year ago.*

Two examples from the seventeenth century seem relevant, both containing the sequence *as good as*, which is employed to point a contrast. The first is the forerunner of the proverb that now has the wording *A miss is as good as a mile*:

An ynche in a misse is as good as an ell.
(William Camden, *Remaines of a greater worke concerning Britaine*, 1614, *Prov.* 303).

i.e. if you miss your mark, it is irrelevant *how* wide of the mark you are. The second example is from a mid-seventeenth-century trial:

... for that I must tell you again, and once is as good as if I had told you a thousand times over ...
(*The Tryal of Lieutenant Colonel John Lilburn* ... *1649* ... *Being exactly Pen'd and taken in Short-Hand* ... by Theodorus Varax, quoted from *The Oxford Book of English Talk*, ed. James Sutherland, Oxford, 1953, p. 115).

The first example I have found of an *if* formulation used to assert 'at least such and such an age' is from Swift:

I swear, she's no chicken; she's on the wrong side of thirty, if she be a day.
(*A Compleat Collection of Genteel and Ingenious Conversation* [before 1738], *The Prose Works of Jonathan Swift*, Bohn's Standard Library, vol. XI, 1907, p. 245).

It is probably significant that this should appear in a work which satirizes the clichés of the fashionable wits of the time. I have searched in vain for the idiom in the Restoration dramatists. From the eighteenth century two further examples may be cited:

... my friend Mundy then, who is worth nine thousand if he's worth a farthing.
(Henry Mackenzie, *The Man of Feeling* [1771], The Norton Library, 1958, p. 19).
Who? Mrs. Evergreen? O Lord! she's six-and-fifty if she's an hour!
(R. B. Sheridan, *The School for Scandal*, *The Dramatic Works of R. B. Sheridan*, ed. Cecil Price, Oxford, 1973, vol. I, p. 378).

While in the eighteenth century the idiom appears to be limited to conveying asseverations about age and amounts of money, we shall see that in the course of the nineteenth century it widens its semantic field so as to comprise the same spheres of measurement as it covers in contemporary English.

In nineteenth-century literature there is a fairly generous sprinkling of examples; as will be seen from the selection of instances I subjoin below, asseverative *if* often crops up in the rendering of direct speech. The colloquial tone is unmistakable, more particularly in the Jane Austen quotations:

'... If I have spoke once to Rebecca about that carpet, I am sure I have spoke at least a dozen times; have not I, Betsey?'
(Jane Austen, *Mansfield Park* [1814], ed. R. W. Chapman, Oxford, 1948, p. 440).
'I do not know the distance.' Her brother told her that it was twenty-three miles.
'*Three*-and-twenty!' cried Thorpe; 'five-and-twenty if it is an inch.'
(Jane Austen, *Northanger Abbey* [1818], Collins, 1962, p. 42).

'She's seventeen if she's a day, though he is the very first sweetheart she has had.'
(W. M. Thackeray, *Catherine*, i, *Fraser's Mag.* May 609/2 [1839]).
'... I have heard him, a hundred times if I have heard him once, say to regular cracks-men ...'
(Charles Dickens, *Great Expectations* [1860-1], O.U.P., 1949, Ch. xxv, p. 218).
'... I'll warrant, that if so be I've spent one hour in making hoops for that barrel, I've spent fifty, first and last.'
(Thomas Hardy, *Under the Greenwood Tree* [1872], Macmillan, 1961, Part One, Ch. 2, p. 20).
'... He'll be worth ten thousand pounds, if a penny ...'
(Thomas Hardy, *The Trumpet-Major* [1880], Macmillan, 1962, Ch. viii, p. 67).
He measured six feet two, if an inch; he weighed eighteen stone, if a pound.
(*The Illustrated London News*, 5.7.1884, 18/1).

In twentieth-century English the *if* idiom is quite frequent, particularly in (the rendering of) spoken English. Before we proceed to an exemplification of its typical variants, used to assert that what applies in the case under discussion is 'at least such and such a number of times' or 'at least a specified age, amount of money, distance, height, or length, and weight', it may be relevant to point out that there exists a related *if* idiom which does not, however, indicate size, measurement, or the like, illustrated by quotations such as

'I'd do it for you if I'd do it for anyone ...'
(Henry Cecil, *Friends at Court*, Penguin, 1962, p. 32).
'If you believe that, you'll believe anything ...'
(John Braine, *The Crying Game*, Pan, 1970, p. 34).

It should also be noted that in such examples the content of the *if* clause is regarded as more or less hypothetical, not as an inescapable fact; nevertheless, this idiom shares with the 'weights and measures' idiom an element of extrapolation.

Normally the indication of size, etc. that is asserted to hold precedes the *if* clause. The only twentieth-century variant in which the order of the clauses does not seem to matter is the one in which *once* is contrasted with an indefinite and large number of times; thus we find both

'I've spoken to him about it a hundred times if I've spoken once ...'
(Sinclair Lewis, *Main Street*, Penguin, 1953, p. 199).

and

If Dickens mentions her 'wholesome brown fingers' and 'her honest sunburnt face' once, he mentions them 20 times.
(*The Listener* 29.1.1976, p. 113).

In this variant the round numbers employed to contrast with *once* are generally *ten, a dozen, fifty, a hundred*, or *a thousand*, and these most often contain an element of exaggeration. This is not usually true of the indications of age, length, etc. that appear in the other variants contrasting with a low or the lowest unit of measurement. Let us now illustrate these other variants.

Age:

'She must be eighty-five if she's a day, said Thorpe at last.
(Frederick Forsyth, *The Dogs of War*, London, 1974, p. 184).
'The trouble with Pongo's Uncle Fred … is that, though sixty if a day, he becomes on arriving in London as young as he feels …'
(P. G. Wodehouse, *Uncle Fred in the Springtime*, London, 1939, p. 50).

As appears from the last example, the subject and verb of the *if* clause may be ellipted. — Normally in this variant it is a person's (comparatively great) age that is contrasted with *a day*. The contrasting of a previous century with *a day*, as in the following quotation, is unusual:

[about a painting] 'She's so beautiful!' said Alison. 'Who'd want to cover her up?
'Sixteenth century, if it's a day,' said Roger.
(Source unknown).

Amounts of money:
The items contrasted are a large amount and *a penny*:

The war dragged on. Nicholas had been heard to say that it would cost three hundred millions if it cost a penny before they'd done with it!
(John Galsworthy, *In Chancery*, Penguin, 1962, p. 277).
'He earns £ 20,000 a year if he earns a penny …'
(C. P. Snow, *The Light and the Dark*, Penguin, 1962, p. 58).

Distance, height, length:

'By the time they … cross this headland — it's half a mile if it's an inch — …'
(Alistair MacLean, *Night Without End*, Fontana, 1968, p. 204).
'Why, it's a mile up if it's a yard' [a kite]
(W. Somerset Maugham, 'The Kite', *Modern English Short Stories*, Second Series, O.U.P., 1958, p. 27).
… a mountain of a man …, six foot four if an inch … //
(Alistair MacLean, *The Secret Ways*, Fontana, 1963, p. 109).

As will be seen, not only *mile* and *inch*, but also *mile* and *yard* may be contrasted.

Weight:
Here the contrast is conveyed by *pounds* and *an ounce*:

… I saw a big one [sc. a salmon] in the Bridge pool, thirty pounds if he was an ounce …
(John Buchan, *Castle Gay*, Pan, 1967, p. 222).
'There's a dirty great fish in this Chyne here would turn your guts over for you. Pounds if he's an ounce, he is …'
(Ngaio Marsh, *Scales of Justice*, Fontana, 1969, p. 81).

The last example is noteworthy in that the weight asserted to hold is not expounded by a concrete number: apparently the speaker considers it sufficient to contrast different units of measurement. This is another example showing that language-users are to some extent free to ring the changes on the idiom, though apparently no need has been felt for expansion into the spheres of square and cubic measure or of nautical measure.

The idiom dealt with here belongs among those that allow permutations; the formula

> He is x if he is y
> It weighs x if it weighs y; etc.

permits a number of different exponents of x and y. Thus it forms a parallel to an idiom like *at the drop of a hat*, which in recent years has spawned several semantically related variants: *at the flick of a switch* (or *finger*, or *wrist*), *at the press* (or *push*, or *touch*) *of a button*, *at the twist of a twig*, to mention those most frequently used, and this idiom seems still to be growing. Will the same turn out to be true of asseverative *if*? When metrication has run its full course in Britain, it will be interesting to see whether we shall find asseverative *if* translated into *kilometres* and *metres*.

PREPOSITION + X + COMPLEMENT

It is normally taken for granted that a preposition and its complement are closely knit. Let us quote, as typical of what many grammars say on the subject, the following statement from *A Grammar of Contemporary English*: 'A prepositional phrase ... consists of a preposition followed by a prepositional complement ...'[1] There is no cause for disputing that this is the main rule; but it has a number of exceptions,[2] and it will be the purpose of this article to examine some of those cases in which an X intervenes between preposition and complement.[3]

To begin with it may be pointed out, however, that there occur a number of prepositional set phrases which do not permit the intercalation of adverbials between preposition and complement; these phrases are phonetically closely knit and may be considered semantically incompatible with this kind of modification. Examples are: *at bottom, at last, by night, by now, in fact, in theory, on occasion, on the make, with cause*, and many others. If their complements are occasionally modified, it is an adjective that intervenes: *at long last, in actual fact, for bloody ever, with good cause*. — It is obvious, however, that modification of such phrases by means of preposed or postposed adverbials is possible: *at least in theory, in theory at least*; but we do not attest **in at least theory*.

Prepositional phrases, especially those that express time and place, can be modified as regards degree and measure: '*just* inside the garage', '*right* off the path' (*A Grammar of Contemporary English*, p. 333). It is a moot point whether in such cases the adverb modifies the preposition or the prepositional phrase as a whole; Professor Quirk and his associates incline to the latter view (*op. cit.*, p. 278, p. 334). But while in the examples just given the adverb can only appear before the preposition, there are other instances of modification in which the modifier occurs (a) before or (b) after the preposition — in X position:

---

[1] R. Quirk, S. Greenbaum, G. Leech, J. Svartvik, *A Grammar of Contemporary English* (London, 1972), p. 299.

[2] These do not seem to have called forth much comment so far. In criticizing Jespersen's *A Modern English Grammar* III 13.91ff, Gerhard Dietrich (*Adverb oder Präposition?* [Halle, 1960], p. 26) observes 'dass der Einschub eines Satzgliedes nicht nur nach Adverbien, sondern bisweilen auch nach eindeutigen Präpositionen zu beobachten ist'; it will be my concern to examine how 'bisweilen' may be interpreted.

[3] I shall disregard here the type of word-order found for instance in relative and interrogative clauses (*This is the book I told you of. -- What is this in aid of?*), confining myself to dealing with those cases in which the sequence preposition — X — complement occurs. Nor shall I discuss those cases in which the exponent of X is *and/or* + a co-ordinate preposition (*over and above this, for or against the death penalty*).

(a) First the great bogey, at least to the other side, of nationalisation. (*The Listener* 6.5.76, p. 556)

(b) The dilemma exists on at least two levels. (George Steiner, *After Babel*, OUP 1975, p. 134)

(a) ... a creative use of language ... that is apparent even in very young children. (Peter Farb, *Word Play*, Bantam Books 1975, p. 119)

(b) Wexford was well aware of the guilt one can feel for even thinking ill of a man ... (Ruth Rendell, *Murder Being Once Done*, Arrow Books 1975, p. 143)

(a) The powers of government may have been tolerable when exercised in the limited manner, say, of 1911 ... (*The Listener* 21.10.76, p. 490)

(b) A Viennese performance of, say, 'Lulu' ... (*The Listener* 29.4.76, p. 544)

The difference seems slight, but it may be noted that the (b) cases, in which only the complement is modified, tend to convey the stylistic effect of being more precise and bookish than the (a) cases. This — a desire for precision — is one of the factors that favour the choice of X position for the adverbial, but it is not the only one. Below we shall consider some others; but first it may be useful to comment briefly on the exponence of X.

The most frequent exponents of X are adverbials of various types: *at least, at the back, on the one hand, one day, say*, etc.; but sometimes we find sentences in X position:

'... but how my son, at the ripe age of thirty-eight, with, unless things have changed very much, a very free choice among the women of England, can have settled on — I suppose I must call her so — *Beryl* ....' He left the sentence eloquently unfinished. (Evelyn Waugh, *Brideshead Revisited*, Penguin 1951, p. 302)

This is an attempt at rendering spoken English with its characteristic spontaneity. A rather different example is the following, in which the writer makes effective use of sentence-insertion in order to appeal to the reader:

... a magic 'lifestone' is dropped into her pretty young lap by, would you believe it, a Wicked Old Witch. (*The Listener* 11.11.76, p. 626)

A sentence in X position may, however, also be employed in a more formal style for purposes of condensation:

Most of them had endearing questions directed to the then Leader of the Opposition, mostly challenging him to say where he stood in relation to, and would he condemn, some industrial situation, speech, demonstration. (Harold Wilson, *The Governance of Britain*, Sphere Books 1977, p. 174)

Occasionally the X position may be filled by a somewhat unorthodox parenthesis that would normally take the form of a postmodification of the complement:

Appointed by (no relation) President Johnson to be one of the seven Federal Communication Commissioners, he distinguished himself by ... (*The Listener* 17.3.77, p. 328)

To return to the factors favouring X position. Sometimes this appears to have been chosen because it offers the best solution to a rhythmical problem since any other word-order would produce a rather awkward sentence rhythm. This is true of examples like

The commercial companies' handouts all carry a 'Copyright Notice' from Independent Television Publications Ltd with, among warnings, one that reads:... (*The Listener* 11.3.76, p. 306)

... the place opened up to become a dozen rooms, with — at the back — a view into the courtyard of a dilapidated mosque. (Len Deighton, *Twinkle, Twinkle, Little Spy*, Panther Books 1977, p. 208)

Beyond that was a wide sun-dazzle of sea with away to the right the sharp, green sugar-loaf shapes of the Vedras, lying about a mile off shore. (Victor Canning, *The Python Project*, Pan Books 1969, p. 234)

The examples just given suggest at the same time that not infrequently rhythmical considerations are inextricably bound up with another problem: the writer's decision as to which of two items of information to provide first. Among the prepositions, *with* and *without* appear to accept adverbials in X position most readily, without any awkwardness; indeed, the order *without, however* ... may be said to be the norm:

... a feathery colloquy of the bamboos was clearly audible, with sometimes a collision of the stiff masts ... (Patrick White, *Voss*, Penguin 1960, p. 54)

The Kings of France and England agreed upon a joint Crusade, without however ceasing their immediate strife. (Winston Churchill, *A History of the English-Speaking Peoples*, Cassell 1974, 1, p. 167)

But the same may be true of other prepositions, especially in comparatively brief statements like

But she never gave up hope of, one day, being able to see. (*The Listener* 10.6.76, p. 730)

where it does not matter very much rhythmically or semantically whether the adverbial *one day* is placed as above or at the end. Much the same is true of the example that follows, although a slightly smoother reading would have resulted if the intercalated items after *with* had been placed last:

Pavel comes out of Russia into Britain to seek refuge with, as his credentials, Siberian diamonds and a message about diamonds. (*The Listener* 30.9.76, p. 412)

But if a writer insists on inserting comments or reservations here and now, in mid-prepositional phrase, although normal word-order would prefer them either before or after, the result is somewhat mannered:

... his proposals would have the effect of — under a written constitution — castrating the power of the House of Commons as we know it. (*The Listener* 28.10.76, p. 526)

Later, ... the desire to speak to Clifford, the memory of, in spite of everything, his wisdom, and of, however self-mocked, his affection, made him appear providentially as a last resort. (Iris Murdoch, *A Word Child*, Penguin 1975, p. 380f) and we reach the height of artificiality if the insertion is excessively long, as in

... one (or more) of the lexemes has been added or lost with (of necessity, if we discount for the moment the possibility of synonymy in the earlier or later system) some consequential change ... (John Lyons, *Semantics*, CUP 1977, 1, p. 255)

As mentioned above, X position is statistically not the most frequent. Consequently, it is often the exponent of markedness. The construction may be used as an attention-catching device: the reader is forced to stop short in mid-prepositional phrase by the X, which in this function may be termed an interrupter. The break is often indicated by means of commas, dashes, or parentheses. It is the function of the interrupter to make the reader pay particular attention, here and now, to some aspect of the context. Let us now proceed to an examination of the semantic conditions under which the interrupter generally operates.

As will have already appeared, the exponents of interrupters may be place or time adverbials. They may also be degree adverbials; an example is seen in

... such a thing ... would ruin the good relations which the British Government has developed with the Republic of Ireland since the advent to power there of, in particular, Garret Fitzgerald ... (*The Listener* 15.4.76, p. 459)

It was pointed out above that the choice of X position may convey precision. A similar stamp of precision and orderliness is conveyed by pairs of correlative adverbials in X position; for instance:

... the two opposing answers ... arise from the tension between, on the one hand, the almost exclusive use of proper names to perform the speech of reference, and, on the other hand, the means and preconditions for performing this speech act ... (John R. Searle, *Speech Acts*, CUP 1969, p. 163)

Rosalind Ashe writes a rich, stylish prose, and is particularly adept at charging the country house setting with, first, peace and beauty, and, then, menace and horror. (*The Listener* 17.6.76, p. 790)

It is obvious that the generous use of commas here adds to the impression that this is an orderly presentation of the facts.

The items that herald exemplification may occur in X position:

God ... governs it [the world] both directly by the eternal laws, and indirectly through (for instance) the angels ... (Basil Willey, *The Seventeenth Century Background*, Doubleday Anchor Books 1953, p. 22)

A Viennese performance of, say, 'Lulu' would have sustained the atmosphere so carefully created ... (*The Listener* 29.4.76, p. 544)

Other standard interrupters used in this function are *among other things, for example, let us say*, and *e.g.*

When comparisons are made to function as interrupters, as in

Men stood in a queue at some doctor's table waiting for TAB, battle-hard combat troops with, like himself, their arms bare ... (William Haggard, *The Arena*, Penguin 1966, p. 154)

To every owner, cockfighting is a fine sport with, like boxing or hare-coursing, set rules. (*The Listener* 26.2.76, p. 236)

the result is a somewhat unusual word-order produced by the insertion keeping the reader in suspense.

The function of the interrupter, as has been said, is often to direct the reader's attention to a particular feature of the context. The feature that is focussed on may either precede or follow the X, or, to put it differently: interrupters may occur in both anaphorical and cataphorical functions, most frequently the latter.

Let us first consider anaphorical reference. Here the only function of the interrupter appears to be that of providing a metalinguistic comment on or interpretation of an immediately preceding word:

Obscenities are synonymous with, i.e. have the same meaning as, their clinical equivalents. (John R. Searle, *Speech Acts*, CUP 1969, p. 155)

... we could do with — when I say we, I mean the British trade union movement — we could do with assistance from other trade union movements ... (*The Listener* 14.4.77, p. 481)

He was one of the few peers with a territorial title who actually possessed land in (or to be exact in his case, within three miles of) the place from which the title came. (C. P. Snow, *In Their Wisdom*, Penguin 1977, p. 58f)

The comment in the last example amounts to self-correction.

Most interrupters are, however, cataphorical: they invite the reader to concentrate his attention on some aspect of the immediate sequel. They may provide a metalinguistic comment on the wording adopted by the writer himself, sometimes striking an apologetic note:

... radio actors who ... manage to communicate in their performances an enormous amount of, for want of a better word, humanity. (*The Listener* 13.5.76, p. 615)

The entelechy of forms out of, as it were, a 'pre-setting' of potentialities necessitates a logic of future statements ... (George Steiner, *After Babel*, OUP 1975, p. 142)

The creation of a Prom atmosphere is intended as a blow against — to pick among many meaningful clichés — the gentility principle ... (*The Listener* 8.4.76, p. 440)

Or they may serve to underline the fact that the one who is responsible for the formulation that follows is not the writer, but somebody else; sometimes it is indicated that we have to do with an actual quotation:

That system with, as Emile Benveniste emphasizes, its referral only to the subject and not to the object ... makes up the locale, the 'time-space' of our cultural identity. (George Steiner, *After Babel*, OUP 1975, p. 131)

His mind had set and developed at an unduly early age, without, as Coleridge said, 'the ungainliness or the promise of a growing intellect'. (Winston Churchill, *A History of the English-Speaking Peoples*, Cassell 1974, 3, p. 205)

(46)

While the examples of cataphorical interrupters given above illustrate a metalinguistic function, i.e., the interrupters focus on the choice of words, this is not invariably so. In other cases the function of the interrupter is to comment not so much on the wording, but rather on the content of the sequel. Thus we note the writer's personal comment in

I hoped ... that it was because ... I'd acquired some of the characteristics of — let's be frank — a natural gentleman. (Thomas Hinde, *Games of Chance*, Corgi Books 1967, p. 180)

Przhevalsky was ... an explorer-conquistador on a gigantic scale, moving through central Asia during the 1870s and 80s with (a typical manifest this) '23 camels, two-and-a-half hundredweight of sugar ...' (*The Listener* 3.6.76, p. 716)

Or the comment may take the form of a cautious formulation that emphasizes the subjective element:

Then, of course, someone would sing straight into a microphone at the shattering proximity of, to my ears, two inches. (*The Listener* 15.1.76, p. 55)

... a planning decision in, I think, Clitheroe ... (Harold Wilson, *The Governance of Britain*, Sphere Books 1977, p. 22)

The preceding account has been confined to those cases in which the interrupter appears immediately after the preposition. In the present discussion it may be of some interest to consider gerundial constructions briefly. In these, the interrupter may occur between the gerund 'subject' and the rest of the gerund if a writer feels that, owing to the overall arrangement of the sentence, this is the only convenient or indeed possible place in which to provide information that throws light on the construction as a whole:

... there would have been a considerable risk of his government, simply because it was a Labour government, being vulnerable to the accusation of actually enjoying seeing Britain's role diminish ... (*The Listener* 25.3.76, p. 354)

It was upsetting to think of Martindale, who shared my office, giving my drafts a casual sift through. (Thomas Hinde, *Games of Chance*, Corgi Books 1967, p. 155)

This is a suspended construction: the formulation can only be correctly interpreted at the end of the passage. It may be noted that in this type the 'subject' of the gerund is invariably in the common case.

It is obvious that in spoken English the normally strong bond between preposition and complement can always be broken by a hesitation signal like *well*:

'... Look at Pascal, look at well, anybody ...' (John Le Carré, *The Naive and Sentimental Lover*, Pan Books 1977, p. 60)

and it is not difficult to find examples of anacoluthon in which the complement of the preposition is missing:

'I thought it was all in aid of —' (Iris Murdoch, *An Accidental Man*, Penguin 1973, p. 136)

In a couple of cases the omission of the complement has even become institutionalised; compare examples like

If they have it they spend it. If they don't they go without. (John Fowles, *The Collector*, Panther Books 1976, p. 221)

I could go on writing arguments for and against all night. (*Ibid.*, p. 230)

To these may be added the colloquial use of *considering* = 'in view of the circumstances' and the elliptical expressions *a cuppa* (i.e. normally tea) and *a pinta* (i.e. normally milk); compare also the American English slang term *a gofer* (= *go-for*), 'an errand-boy'.

Many prepositions have developed from adverbs[4] with the result that English has a number of syntactic homonyms ('They went *up*' / 'They went *up* the hill') which may be either adverbs or prepositions.[5] As Gerhard Dietrich points out,[6] it is not always easy to decide whether it is preferable to operate with 'adverbs' or with 'prepositions used absolutely'; this would seem to depend largely on how one views the concept 'ellipsis'. One of the criteria employed by Jespersen to distinguish between adverb and preposition is to say that the presence of an adverbial in X position makes the preceding syntactic homonym an adverb.[7] I hope I have shown here that the sequence: preposition — X — complement, although certainly a minority construction, is not *quantité négligeable* in contemporary English. The bond between preposition and complement is not always indissoluble.

---

[4] See for instance Tauno F. Mustanoja, *A Middle English Syntax* (Helsinki, 1960), p. 346.

[5] Dwight Bolinger, *The Phrasal Verb in English* (Cambridge, Mass., 1971), p. 27ff.

[6] *Op. cit.*, p. 25f.

[7] Bolinger, *op. cit.*, p. 29, criticizes Jespersen for inconsistency in his application of this criterion, and denies its validity.

CO-ORDINATE PREPOSITIONS
WITH A SINGLE COMPLEMENT

I. Introduction

The phenomenon to be dealt with in this paper may be illustrated by examples like *up and down the road* and *for or against the death penalty*. This is a construction which to my knowledge has been largely neglected both in historical grammars and in descriptions of contemporary English. I have found no references to it in Visser[1] or Mustanoja[2]. Jespersen[3] notes briefly that "The same regimen may be dependent on two or more prepositions in the same sentence". Poutsma[4] gives a few examples of co-ordinate prepositions like *over and above* and *up and down*, but does not analyse the construction in detail. Randolph Quirk and his associates[5] devote less than half a page to a discussion of 'Ellipsis of complement of prepositional phrase'. Those scholars who have written monographs on prepositions[6] at most offer sporadic comments on the co-ordination of prepositions. It would seem, then, that this neglected field stands in need of some elucidation.

When I began examining the problem, it was intuitively obvious to me that in contemporary English the occurrence of co-ordinate prepositions is considerably more frequent in some styles than in others. On closer examination it turned out that legal texts — and other texts of a similar technical character — present particularly numerous examples of prepositional co-ordination, unlike ordinary, non-technical prose, in which the incidence is not very high. In order to substantiate this impression I undertook a limited statistical analysis, the result of which should of course not be given undue importance; nevertheless it can hardly be doubted that it suggests a characteristic stylistic difference. In the first 150

1. *An Historical Syntax of the English Language*, vols. I–III, Leiden 1963–73.
2. *A Middle English Syntax*, Helsinki 1960.
3. *A Modern English Grammar*, vol. VII, Copenhagen 1949, 2.36.
4. *A Grammar of Late Modern English*, Groningen 1916–19.
5. R. Quirk, S. Greenbaum, G. Leech, J. Svartvik, *A Grammar of Contemporary English*, Longman 1972, 9.90.
6. A Brahde, *Studier over de engelske Præpositioner*, Copenhagen 1919; V. Brøndal, *Præpositionernes Theori*, Copenhagen 1940; N. Bøgholm, *English Prepositions*, Copenhagen 1920; K.-G. Lindkvist, *Studies on the Local Sense of the Prepositions* in, at, on, *and to* in Modern English, Lund 1950; H. E. Torkildsen, *De engelske Præpositioner*, Kristiania 1902.

pages of a modern novel[7] there occur just two examples (both of the type *with or without X*), whereas an examination of 150 pages of legal texts[8] yields 82 examples. These figures would seem to warrant the hypothesis that the natural breeding ground of co-ordinate prepositions is legal style (and related styles).

It is well known that the scholar to whom this volume is dedicated is profoundly interested not only in modern English, but also in the history of the language, an interest that has resulted in important contributions on his part to both fields; he would no doubt subscribe to the view that many phenomena occurring in modern English are understood better if seen through the perspective of their historical development. It seems fitting, therefore, to try to shed some light on both the diachronic and the synchronic aspects of prepositional co-ordination.

II. Historical Sketch

Old English. In view of its stylistic distribution in modern English, it would be reasonable to assume that prepositional co-ordination originates in legal style — laws, wills, charters, etc. — and has spread from there to non-technical parlance. An examination of Old English legal language — and for that matter, of any other kind of Old English — shows, however, that the elliptical construction is non-existent there. Not that there is not sometimes a need to express concepts like *before and after X* and *to and from X*; but when such a need is felt, two other constructions are resorted to: either the complement is repeated, as in

> ... ge be heora life ge æfter heora life ... (Grant to Worcester Monastery, quoted from A. J. Wyatt, *An Anglo-Saxon Reader*, Cambridge 1939, p. 112)

> 7 ic wylle, þæt ælc man se griðes wyrðe to gemote 7 fram gemote ... (Cnuts Erlasse und Gesetzbuch, in F. Liebermann, *Die Gesetze der Angelsachsen*, vol. 1, I, Halle 1903, p. 366)

or we find the construction: preposition + complement + an adverb which may be formally identical with a preposition:

> ... ge binnan byrg ge butan ... (Grant to Worcester Monastery, quoted from Wyatt, *op. cit.* p. 111)

> ... seofon dagas to eastrum ond VII ofer ... (Das Gesetzbuch der Könige Ælfred — Ine, quoted from Liebermann, *op. cit.* p. 78)

---

7. Len Deighton, *Twinkle, Twinkle, Little Spy*, Panther 1977.
8. *The Sex Discrimination Act 1975*, Chapter 65; *The Oil Taxation Act 1975*, Chapter 22; *The Freshwater and Salmon Fisheries (Scotland) Act 1976*, Chapter 22.

Middle English. During most of the Middle English period examples of the elliptical construction are few and far between. I have come across a couple of examples from the early fourteenth century:[9]

> Al þat hys boue and vnder molde . . . (*The Poems of William of Shoreham*, EETS e.s. 86, 1902, p. 115 (*c.* 1325))

> A squorde sulde stike ouerthwert þorou and þorou þine awen hert. (*Cursor Mundi* 24381, EETS, o.s. 68, 1878 (early fourteenth century))

But in the fourteenth century we normally find the same solutions as were employed in Old English; this may be illustrated from Chaucer:

> Thanne was he byscorned, that oonly shoulde han been honoured in alle thynges and of alle thynges. (Robinson, *op. cit.* p. 235)

> . . . swiche as speken faire byforn folk, and wikkidly bihynde . . . (*ibid.* p. 248)

It may be added that in this period a concept like *from or to X* may be expressed by means of compound adverbs:

> þer ys a welle þat non streem eorneþ þar–fram noþer þer–to . . . (John of Trevisa, quoted from *Specimens of Early English*, vol. II, ed. Morris & Skeat, Oxford 1889, p. 239)

It is only when we come down to the fifteenth century that we begin to find a sprinkling of examples of the elliptical construction. Although it is probably commoner to find the complement repeated or an adverb used, co-ordinate prepositions do crop up rather frequently, particularly in legal texts like the following:

> . . . I, the saide Nicholas Charleton, ordeyne, assigne, and be–queth be this testament, to þe saide Iohn my wyf, the *termys* and state comyng of & in all the ten*ement* with thappurten[au]nt3 that I dwell ynne . . . (*The Fifty Earliest English Wills*, ed. F. J. Furnivall, EETS o.s. 78, 1882, p. 115 (1439))

> . . . þe seyd Anneys hathe grauntyd *and* lete to ferme to þe seyd Will*iam* Palm*er* a pece of londe, outetake þe medwe in *and* of þe same pece . . . (Indenture of lease 1446, quoted from Norman Davis, *Paston Letters and Papers of the Fifteenth Century*, Part I, Oxford 1971, p. 29)

Besides *in and of*, the edition of the Paston Letters contains examples of the conjuncts *of and in* (pp. 208, 411), *of or in* (p. 209), *of and for* (p. 411), *of or for* (p. 195), *of and vppon* (p. 209), and *over and a–boue* (p. 195).

Reginald Pecock has a strong predilection for co–ordinating his prepositions; in fact the main types current in contemporary English are

---

9. Possibly there is another example in Chaucer's *Astrolabe*: ". . . inward and over the zodiak" (*The Works of Geoffrey Chaucer*, ed. F. N. Robinson, OUP 1957, p. 560); however, the OED gives only one example of *inward* in a prepositional function.

present in Pecock's work. His chief motive for employing the construction appears to have been his wish to convey emphasis, as in

> ... not for and bi ignoraunce ... (*The Folewer to the Donet,* ed. E. V. Hitchcock, EETS o.s. 164, 1924, p. 19)

> ... þe seid inward sensitive comoun witt may haue his natural wirchyng about, vpon and anentis þo colouris ... (*ibid.* pp. 27f)

> ... except what he bi argument in resoun dryuyþ and concludiþ of such text, may be open y-nouȝ to ech clerk which wole go bi and bi ech processe ... (*ibid.* p. 9)

where the conjuncts are semantically close or identical; but he also employs co-ordination when a referential distinction is to be made, for instance antithesis:

> ... what is to be seid of beestis soulis þat þei ben bifore and aftir her bodies or no, y kanne not fynde eni mensioun in hooli scripture. (*ibid.* p. 19)

Caxton's penchant for rhetorical doublets is well known, and it also extends to prepositional pairs like the following:

> ... the prouoste told to hym ... how his lady ... had borne, & as yet bare suche a displeasure for & by thoccasyon of him ... (*Blanchardyn and Eglantine,* ed. L. Kellner, EETS e.s. 58, 1890, p. 156)

The period after 1500. Concerning this period I shall confine myself to comparatively brief comments. Prepositional co-ordination outside technical style cannot be said to become widespread until the present century. Some collocations are natural enough in non-technical style (for instance the type *before and/or after X*), but most examples occur in legal and related styles.

Shakespeare has the construction a few times, for example:

> O madness of discourse!
> That cause sets up, with, and against itself ...
> (*Troilus and Cressida,* V, ii, 142 ff)

> Captain Macmorris, I beseech you now, will you voutsafe me, look you, a few disputations with you as partly touching or concerning the disciplines of the war ... (*Henry V,* III, ii, 100ff)

> Thy slander hath gone through and through her heart ...
> (*Much Ado About Nothing,* V, i, 68)

Thomas Nashe uses it in a passage that is undoubtedly intended to parody legal style:

> ... a certain kind of an appendix or page, belonging or appertaining in or vnto the confines of the English court .. (*The Unfortunate Traveller,* in The Works of Thomas Nashe, ed. R. B. McKerrow, Oxford 1966, vol. II, p. 209)

The construction crops up early in dictionary definitions (cf. below p. 225):

> *Prendre le vent,* to goe vp, or against, the wind. (Randle Cotgrave, *A dictionarie of the French and English tongues,* 1611, quoted from the OED, s.v. *up*² prep. 4)

It appears in Fuller's *Worthies* (1662):

> This proverb began in the English Borders, when . . . they had little esteem of, and less affection for, a Scotchman. (Quoted from M. P. Tilley, *A Dictionary of the Proverbs in England in the Sixteenth and Seventeenth Centuries,* University of Michigan Press 1966, p. 588)

An instance of legal pleonasm is seen in

> Persons . . . to serve in or upon the Grand Jury. (*Office Clerk of Assize* a vj, 1676, quoted from the OED, s.v. *upon* prep. 1.h)

Philosophers are among the writers that one might assume would favour prepositional co-ordination. An examination of John Locke's *Essay Concerning Human Understanding* (1690) shows that in most cases he repeats the complement; he has, however, a predilection for combining a prepositional verb with a transitive verb, holding the complement in suspense till after the latter (cf. below, p. 223):

> . . . some of these monstrous productions have few or none of those qualities which are supposed to result from and accompany the *essence* of that *species* . . . (Everyman's edition, ed. John W. Yolton, London 1964, vol. II, p. 51)

It would be superfluous to adduce further examples before the twentieth century since in all likelihood they would not add anything new to the picture. In section III I shall attempt a systematic treatment of the elliptical construction as it occurs in contemporary English.

Why did the construction arise? After having now briefly surveyed the history of prepositional co-ordination in English, let us consider the question of its origin.

There were probably several factors at work. One of them may be accounted for by a reference to the general tendency to employ doublets in Middle English, not least in legal language.[10] The doubling of prepositions appears to have been passed over in silence by grammarians, but it seems quite conceivable that the strong general tendency to use semantically related word pairs (chiefly nouns, adjectives, and verbs) spread to the

---

10. See for instance David Mellinkoff, *The Language of the Law,* Boston & Toronto 1963, p. 120; Inna Koskenniemi, *Repetitive Word Pairs in Old and Middle English Prose,* Turku 1968 (concentrating on pairs like *whole and sound* and *answered and said*); Ernst Leisi, *Die tautologischen Wortpaare in Caxtons "Eneydos",* Zürich & New York 1947.

domain of the prepositions. However, as will have already become clear, we find in Middle English not only the type represented by *over and above X*, with an intensifying or emphatic function, but also the type represented by examples like *above and under X* or *before and after X*, employed to convey contrast. The latter type may have spread owing to its formal similarity with the former, but there is not enough evidence to prove this.

Another circumstance that should be considered is the fact that as early as the Old English period, English had binomial adverbials of the type *within and without*, the terms of which were formally identical with prepositions. The OED is somewhat random in its coverage of this type of adverbial (as well as of prepositional co-ordination); but it seems that in most cases such adverbials crop up earlier than the corresponding prepositional pairs. Thus we have the adverbial *wiðinnan & wiðutan* from about 1000 (OED *within* adv. 1), while the corresponding prepositional pair is not attested till 1885 (OED *without* 1). The adverbial *up and down* is from before 1200; the prepositional pair is attested a good two hundred years later, 1412-20. The first OED example of adverbial *off and on* is from 1535, while *off and on* as a prepositional pair is attested from 1708 (in a nautical sense). Normally a distinction is upheld between adverbial *to and fro* and prepositional *to and from;* but the OED records an example of the latter functioning adverbially, *a* 1450 (s.v. *from* B), while the first attested instance of prepositional *to and from* is from 1489 (s.v. *to* prep. 1).[11] Thus the English adverbial construction may have contributed to paving the way for the use of prepositional co-ordination.[12]

The two possible factors considered so far, the predilection for doublets and the model afforded by the adverbial type *within and without*, cannot, however, be viewed as exclusively English factors. The former is a general feature of mediaeval European literature, while the latter has its parallel in a Latin adverbial type.

Classical Latin has a number of adverbials consisting of terms that are in some cases formally identical with prepositions: *ante aut post, extra et intus, supra et subter, supra infra,* and *ultra citrave* (while *pro et contra* is mediaeval). This type, in conjunction with the corresponding English binomial, may have given a fillip to prepositional co-ordination.

---

11. Actually, this date should be 1595: the quotation is from Caxton's *Blanchardyn and Eglantine*, EETS e.s. 58, 1890, p. 211; but from p. 206 the text printed is that of the 1595 edition of the romance. This is one of the rare occasions on which it is possible to catch out the OED in an error of commission.
12. It should be added, however, that in at least one case the prepositional pair is earlier than the adverbial: *through and through* in its prepositional function goes back to the early fourteenth century (cf. the *Cursor Mundi* example on p. 209), while the first OED instance of the adverbial is from Malory's *Morte Darthur*.

In Classical Latin prepositional co-ordination is rare. It may occur in fixed formulas having an official stamp: *cis et uls Tiberim,* and Caesar uses the construction in one passage: *intra extraque munitiones (Bellum Civile* 3.72.2). But normally we find the same state of things as in Old English, either repetition of the complement or the use of an adverb: ... *quae pro lege contraque eam dicta erant; Et in corpore et extra sunt quaedam bona.* Repetition of the complement is preferred even when two prepositions govern the same case: *in caede atque ex caede vivunt.*

In mediaeval times case distinctions tended to break down in some writers of Latin;[13] according to Kr. Nyrop[14] there was a strong tendency in Vulgar Latin to employ the accusative everywhere after prepositions. I have found no examples of this in my examination of legal Latin composed in England, but there do occur instances of prepositional co-ordination. In a schedule to release of lands from 1471 we read: *de et in manerijs ...* (Norman Davis, *Paston Letters,* Part I, p. 439). Another example comes from Sir John Fortescue's *De Laudibus Legum Anglie* (1471):

> Omnes eciam xij[ci] tales latere omnino quicquid actum est per inter vicinos eorum ... (*De Laudibus,* ed. S.B. Chrimes, Cambridge 1942, p. 66; one MS inserts *aut* between *per* and *inter*)

We cannot, however, assume unreservedly that this kind of Latin has influenced English, though the possibility remains.[15] As has been pointed out by Franz Blatt,[16] "It has proved a tenacious error always to give the priority to Latin in cases of structural agreement between Latin and any modern language". It is also possible that English has influenced Latin in this respect, or again that two concurrent tendencies have gone hand in hand.

There remains the question of possible French influence. The oldest example of prepositional co-ordination given by Kr. Nyrop[17] is from 1529. Law French from about 1300 seems only to have the two constructions that are employed in Old English: *od adicion ou sanz adicion, devant le conqueste e apres.*[18] Thus prepositional co-ordination must have

---

13. Cf. the complaint made by Gregory of Tours: "... pro ablativis accusativa, et rursum pro accusativis ablativa ponis" (*Liber de Gloria Beatorum Confessorum,* Migne, *P. L.* lxxi, p. 830).
14. *Grammaire historique de la langue française,* vol. VI, Copenhagen 1930. p. 69.
15. Professor Ernst Dittmer suggests that on German soil the tendency towards doubling may also have been influenced by the use in legal documents of so-called prepositional nouns like *loco et nomine* and *loco et vice* (e.g. *loco et nomine sororum*).
16. "Latin Influence on European Syntax", *Acta Congressus Madvigiani,* vol. V, Copenhagen 1957, p. 34.
17. *Op. cit.,* vol. V, Copenhagen 1925, p. 24.
18. *Year Books of the Reign of King Edward the First,* Years XX and XXI, edited and translated by A. J. Horwood, London 1866, pp. 25 and 103.

appeared in French some time during the fourteenth or fifteenth centuries, but I have no evidence here.

It would seem, then, that with our present knowledge it is impossible to say anything very definite about the origin or origins of prepositional co-ordination.

III. Prepositional Co-ordination in Contemporary English

A. Non-technical Style

Ambiguity. Initially it may be noted that very occasionally one may be in doubt about the syntactic interpretation of a passage; consider the following example:

> ... a rustic throne that commanded a magnificent view of the treetops below and the sea beyond them. (John Fowles, *The French Lieutenant's Woman*, Signet 1970, p. 135)

where it appears impossible to decide whether *below* is an adverb or a preposition co-ordinated with *beyond*. But in the great majority of cases there is no such syntactic ambiguity.

Classification of the material. The chief conjunctions employed to co-ordinate prepositions are *and, but, or, rather than*, and *as well as*. There occur a great many prepositional exponents, including a number of compounds ones, and they convey a variety of semantic relations. With a view to reducing these semantic relations to some degree of order, we may generalize and say that these paired prepositions form a semantic cline: at one pole we find the antithetical conjuncts, at the other pole occasional, rather unpredictable conjuncts, the remaining space being occupied by more or less close semantic neighbours. It must be emphasized, however, that it is hardly possible to fix an absolute dividing line between the last two types. Thus, although *letters from or about Julian* (see below) undoubtedly illustrates occasional co-ordination, and the co-ordinated prepositions in *at or near the summit* (see below) are instances of semantic neighbours, it would be difficult to pigeonhole an example like

> The images that gathered round and above her were emanations, simple risings and gatherings from the soft, full lake of her nature ... (Margaret Drabble, *The Needle's Eye*, Penguin 1976, p. 192)

For although both prepositions denote (figurative) spatiality, they involve different aspects of space; this is a borderline case that has to be classified arbitrarily. — It is often the conjunction employed that determines whether we interpret the terms of a prepositional pair as being antithetical or semantic neighbours: compare *was it before or after the war?* with *both before and after the war*.

Besides the three types referred to above, it may be practical to operate with three semantic groups (which are not, however, to be considered watertight compartments since prepositions from different groups not infrequently combine): (1) *spatial prepositions*, (2) *temporal prepositions*, and (3) more *abstract prepositions*. In all three groups a cline is observable, ranging from antithesis to occasional conjoining.

(1) *Spatial prepositions* (including such prepositions in their figurative applications)

a. At the antithetical end of the cline we register prepositional pairs like *above and/or below, in(to) and out of, inside and outside, on and/or off, off and/or on* (typically with *duty* as complement; the vacillation may be due to the indiscriminate order of the terms in the corresponding binomial adverbial), *to and from, towards and away from,* and *up and down;* for instance:

> The religious impulse is extremely perilous and can degenerate at any moment, inside and outside the Church. (*The Listener* 17.2.1977, p. 207)

> My mother or Jeanette, on the way into or out of the bathroom, would have been immediately on hand to open the door . . . (Keith Waterhouse, *Billy Liar on the Moon,* London 1975, p. 39)

> . . . there are two continuous opposed waves of influence, towards and away from standardization. (T. H. Pear, *English Social Differences,* London 1956, p. 72)

It may be noted that *inside and outside X* seems to be in free variation with *inside X and out;* compare:

> There was a deep nocturnal silence, both inside the house and out . . . (John Fowles, *The Ebony Tower,* Panther 1976, p. 92)

Sometimes one also comes across *within and without X:*

> From every quarter, within and without the Church, the air resounded with attacks on the various orders of clergy. (G. M. Trevelyan, *English Social History,* Longman 1961, p. 41)

which is now slightly archaic.

Above, we noted the indiscriminate order *on and off/off and on.* In the other pairs listed (apart from *above and below* and *up and down*)[19] the sequence of the terms is normally fixed: the first preposition denotes location in, or direction towards, the referent of the complement, while the second preposition denotes location outside, or movement away from, the referent of the complement.[20] This order may, however, be inverted in marked contexts:

---

19. Compare footnote 22.
20. We find a corresponding order in binomial adverbials like *in and out, inside and out(side),* and *to and from;* an exception is *backwards and forwards.*

> Even in places where continuous occupation seems likely, ... the English settlement grew up beside, and not in, the Romano-British town. (Dorothy Whitelock, *The Beginnings of English Society,* Penguin 1945, p. 15)

> ... de Saussure's influence has been away from, rather than towards, the social aspects of language use. (Roger T. Bell, *Sociolinguistics,* London 1976, p. 220)

b. After this exemplification of antithesis it should be emphasized that the bulk of the prepositional pairs of groups (1) are more or less close semantic neighbours: they are used to refer to contiguous points or areas listed in accounts of spatial descriptions, either directional or locational:

> Quint looked at and beyond him (Victor Canning, *The Mask of Memory,* Pan 1976, p. 186)

> While a few professions remain for a long time at or near the summit of the social scale, others move up and down ... (T. H. Pear, *English Social Differences,* London 1956, p. 21)

If the conjunction is *or,* its function differs according to context. It may, as in the immediately preceding example, suggest a reservation ('at least in that neighbourhood'), or it may serve to add an equally valid possibility:

> There is practically no pain or discomfort when the vaccine is put into, or under, the skin ... (*The Listener* 27.5.1976, p. 662)

With *or* in the latter sense we may occasionally register no fewer than four co-ordinate prepositions:

> The artist, like the God of the creation, remains within or behind or beyond or above his handiwork ... (James Joyce, *A Portrait of the Artist as a Young Man,* Signet 1949, p. 168)

If the conjunction is *but,* what is emphasized is separateness in spite of proximity:

> The speech area, which now bears Broca's name, is close by, but separate from, the part of the motor cortex that controls movements of the tongue and larynx. (*The Listener* 9.12.1976, p. 757)

Note the use of commas in some of the examples to stress the equipollent values of the prepositions. — There is at least one prepositional pair in this semantic subgroup that has become institutionalized, viz. *above and beyond* in its figurative employment:

> Some of Brecht's admirers ... must surely wonder ... whether perhaps Brecht wasn't a trifle sly and shifty above and beyond the call of survival. (*The Listener* 6.5.1976, p. 576)

c. At the less organized end of the cline we find prepositional pairs the terms of which are comparatively distant neighbours; they represent semantic categories that are not often conjoined. The best proof of this is that if they are quoted in isolation, it may be difficult to think of suitable contexts for them to appear in: *from or about, to or about, within and between;* here are a couple of examples:

> Would he not have been allowed to use important letters, from or about Julian . . . ? (*The Listener* 15.4.1976, p. 482)
>
> . . . communication within and between languages . . . (George Steiner, *After Babel,* OUP 1975, p. 61)

(2) *Temporal prepositions*

a. When terms like *before* and *after* occur in prepositional co-ordination, it is the context that determines whether they are to be interpreted antithetically or as marking steps in a temporal progression (*b.* below). An example of contrastive prepositions is the following (in which a *but* may be implied):

> . . . decisions which profoundly concern every individual citizen before, not after, the final die is cast. (*The Listener* 11.11.1976, p. 604)

Concerning the order in which the prepositions occur, it is possible to generalize and say that in most cases (i.e. in unmarked contexts), natural chronology is adhered to:[21] what is prior in time comes before what is posterior; this generalization may be said to form a parallel to the one made above for spatial prepositions. In marked contexts, however, natural chronology may be reversed with the result that the prepositions become particularly contrastive:

> Fraser Steel and I were stuck in one of the lifts, happily after, and not before, a recording. (*The Listener* 22.7.1976, p. 74)

b. In most cases conjoined temporal prepositions are employed to indicate contiguous and successive stages in accounts of temporal progression. Among frequently occurring fixed collocations may be mentioned *before and after, before and since, before and during, before, during and after* (see below), *during and after,* and *up to and including.* What these pairs (or triplets) typically convey is an indication of a period or point of time,

---

21. Compare the following statements: "If it is true that the dictates of society impose a more or less arbitrary time perspective on a language, then the acceptance by historically-minded Western societies of a straight line stretching from the past through the present to the future not only has predetermined expressly temporal formulas, such as *before and after, yesterday and today,* and the fuller trinomial *past, present, and future* . . ." (Yakov Malkiel, "Studies in Irreversible Binomials", in *Essays on Linguistic Themes,* Univ. of California Press 1968, p. 342); "In the case of time sequence, the maxim one might invoke is the submaxim of manner 'Be orderly' with the interpretation 'Unless you explicitly mark the time relation, make your narration of events reflect their sequence' " (Ruth M. Kempson, *Presupposition and the Delimitation of Semantics,* CUP 1975, p. 198).

followed by an indication of a subsequent period, or by a reservation as to the exact time:

> ... there is a long roll of great names greatly revered, during and after their lives, in Germany. (*The Listener* 20.5.1976, p. 640)

> This topic had received a great deal of publicity in and around 1970. (D. Crystal & D. Davy, *Advanced Conversational English*, London 1975, p. 65)

> The relation to contraction indicates a date at or very little after 700. (Ritchie Girvan, *Beowulf and the Seventh Century*, London 1971, p. 24)

c. One sometimes notes that a writer's point of view seems to change from static to dynamic in mid-construction, two semantically somewhat unequal yokefellows being conjoined:

> To study meanings, then, in different actual speakers and writers, and in and through historical times, is a deliberate choice. (Raymond Williams, *Keywords*, Fontana 1976, p. 20)

> ... it [speech] amplifies or interferes with the dominant frequency of language in and across time (George Steiner, *After Babel*, OUP 1975, p. 130)

(3) *More abstract prepositions.* This is something of a ragbag in the sense that it is made to contain, besides obvious candidates like *for* and *with*, a number of prepositions from groups (1) and (2) which have largely lost their spatial or temporal associations.

a. In this subgroup there are a few high-frequency antithetical pairs: *for and/or against, in favour of or against,* and *with or without.* In unmarked contexts the order of the prepositions is the one indicated, the positive term preceding the negative;[22] but in a marked context this order may be reversed:

> No sooner was the match declared on than they began taking bets *against,* instead of *for* the Italians. (Lawrence Durrell, *The Best of Antrobus,* London 1974, p. 143)

The collocation *despite or because of* presents a special problem of interpretation. On the surface it expresses an antithesis, but perhaps it would be truer to say that *or because of* conveys an element of tentative self-correction, the speaker disclaiming responsibility for the correct choice:

> Edinburgh, despite or because of its climate, was one of the great intellectual centres of Europe. (*The Listener* 13.1.1977, p. 34)

---

22. Compare the following statement: "... there develops a tendency for one of the two contrasted features to assume the status of a basic or positive trait and for its opposite to signal the lack of that trait ... the stronger partner in an average IE bi- or multi-nomial asserts its superiority synchronically by rushing to occupy the first place" (Y. Malkiel, *op. cit.* pp. 343f).

What speaks in favour of this interpretation is the fact that *because of* is often preceded by a *perhaps* that emphasizes the speaker's uncertainty, *because of* being added as a kind of afterthought to suggest an alternative explanation:

> ... Brecht is more considerable as a poet than as a dramatist, despite (or perhaps because of) the cult of Brecht the theorist of the theatre. (*The Listener* 6.5.1976, p. 576)

Despite or because of may thus be said to take up a borderline position between *a.* and *b.*

b. Here we may list a few examples in which *or* serves to add a second, weaker and less direct, alternative, which is regarded as being roughly equivalent with the first:

> That palace revolution, engineered by, or through, the King's mistress . . . , transformed the government. (*The Listener* 10.6.1976, p. 736)

> It will hardly surprise either idealist or materialist interpreters of the historical process that much history should be made by, or as a result of, men communicating with each other. (*The Listener* 26.8.1976, p. 252)

> From, or corresponding to, appositional adjectives, nouns have occasionally been formed . . . (Valerie Adams, *An Introduction to Modern English Word-Formation,* London 1973, p. 132)

c. When we approach the less organised end of the cline, we note a number of occasional combinations in which the conjoining may sometimes create a rather strained and artificial effect:

> "To think of it, I who have lived for, and practically on, horses . . ." (Lawrence Durrell, *The Best of Antrobus,* London 1974, p. 60)

This effect is due to the fact that the semantic spheres lumped together by the prepositions are disparate; to take but two examples out of many containing mixed semantic categories: in the first we have a combination of 'temporality and irrelevancy', in the second, of 'origin and opposition':

> Paulhan infers a reality of thought previous to or outside words. (George Steiner, *After Babel,* OUP 1975, p. 128)

> French philosophers tend rather to see the meaning of what they are doing . . . as constituted . . . by the relations which they struggle to work out with the history from and against which they emerge. (*The Listener* 27.5.1976, p. 673)

The example that follows is of a different character. With the juxtaposition of *between* and *among* we cannot speak of mixed semantic categories, but the co-occurrence of the two prepositions, foreign to ordinary language, lends a stamp of condensed precision to the passage, a stamp that is indeed suitable for a text treating of scientific matters:

> ... this dichotomy has strong correlations with sociolinguistic factors ... not only in intra- but also inter-group communication, whether the choice be at the stylistic or dialect level of a single language or at the level of choice between or among languages in a multilingual speech community. (Roger T. Bell, *Sociolinguistics,* London 1976, p. 102)

(Strictly speaking, an example like this belongs in section III.B where, however, I have on the whole confined myself to discussing legal style.)

More than two prepositions co-ordinated. Most of the examples listed so far contain prepositional pairs. Above, (2) *b.,* an example of four co-ordinate prepositions was given, but this is exceptional. Normally the number of conjoined prepositions is limited to two, and this seems natural enough in view of the role played by dichotomies in our world picture. But it is not unusual to find three co-ordinated prepositions occurring together. This need not surprise us if the context deals with time, since we may have occasion to describe not only what happened *before and after* a period, but also to include that period itself:

> But we, reading before, during and after that moment, are not dreaming ... (*The Modern Novel,* ed. G. Josipovici, London 1976, p. 35)

This seems, however, to be the only institutionalized temporal triplet in non-technical style (but cf. p. 227). A writer may also feel a need to employ three conjoined prepositions if he wishes to convey an idea of all the relevant stages of a process having been covered in orderly fashion, or of all the possibilities of a situation having been exhausted:

> As yet, although his mind had worked its way into, through and around the problem thousands of times, he had not decided what he would do ... (Joseph Hayes, *The Desperate Hours,* Mayflower 1975, p. 57)

> There are a great many people still alive who worked with, under or over Slim (notably Lord Mountbatten) ... (*The Listener* 2.12.1976, p. 728)

Less usual and predictable and therefore intellectually more demanding is an example like the following, in which disparate semantic categories are lumped together:

> Lexical congruence working through, without, or in defiance of syntactic structure is, of course, the stock machinery of imagery ... (R. Quirk, *The Linguist and the English Language,* London 1974, p. 62)

Intensifying function of co-ordinate prepositions. In the three groups discussed above, we noted three different kinds of semantic relationship holding between the terms: they may contrast (*with or without*); they may approach each other in meaning (*at or near*); or they may belong to disparate semantic spheres (*previous to or outside*). Common to these relationships is the fact that they point to (more or less) different facets of reality. It should be added, however, that in some cases the pairing of prepositions mainly serves the purpose of intensification or emphasis. The pair *over and above* is so well known that it does not need exemplification. Two other combinations, *in and by* and *in and of*, are probably on the way to becoming stereotypes:

> ... the testimony, in and by itself, amounts to a proof. (Basil Willey, *The Eighteenth Century Background*, Beacon Paperback 1961, p. 127)

> ... a lexical unit in and of itself has a very general meaning in that it refers to a class of set ... (William O. Hendricks, *Grammars of Style and Styles of Grammar*, Amsterdam 1976, p. 69)

The combination *over and against* is probably of very recent origin since it is not listed in the dictionaries. Although its meaning seems to be 'in addition to and contrasting with', it is perhaps most reasonable to interpret it first and foremost as an intensifier in examples like

> ... it should be no surprise that there arises, over and against the *vraisemblance* of genre, another level of *vraisemblance* ... (Jonathan Culler, *Structuralist Poetics*, London 1975, p. 148)

> In the opposition Amy/Martha, the novelist develops a theme of English over and against American attitudes. (*English Studies*, vol. 58, 1977, p. 427)

Another comparatively rare intensifier (though attested as early as the fourteenth century, cf. p. 209) is the type in which a preposition is co-ordinated with itself;[23] in this type the conjunction is invariably *and*, the reduplicated preposition is most frequently *round*, although others also occur, and what is conveyed is the idea of a repeated, protracted and sometimes laborious process:

> Hazel ... sat ... looking out at the silent, rippling veils of rain that drifted across and across the little valley between the two copses. (Richard Adams, *Watership Down*, Penguin 1976, p. 78)

> You look up the highway and it is straight for miles, coming at you, with the black line down the center coming at and at you ... (Robert Penn Warren, *All the King's Men*, New York 1946, p. 3)

> "... I felt I could sum this stuff up and get it out of the way so we didn't need to spend a lot of time going over and over it." (Malcolm Bradbury, *The History Man*, London 1975, p. 132)

> He wore his new green corduroys .. and a College scarf round and round his neck. (Frederich Raphael, *The Glittering Prizes*, Penguin 1976, p. 26)

> Afterwards ... they walked up and up a flinty path, half-smothered in broom and furze. (Vladimir Nabokov, *Laughter in the Dark*, Penguin 1969, p. 74)

---

23. Compare adverbials like *again and again, over and over,* and the intensifying function of the repeated verb in: "... the deep satisfaction that glowed and glowed inside him ..." (H. R. F. Keating, *Inspector Ghote Trusts the Heart*, Penguin 1976, p. 85).

A different kind of reduplication is seen if a writer considers it necessary to place particular emphasis on a preposition or to modify it in some way. In such cases the procedure adopted is to repeat the preposition with a suitable qualification:

> ... private transactions ... can be good or bad according to (and only according to) the human warmth and understanding with which they are invested. (*The Listener* 15.1.1976, p. 56)

> It seems to have been a quiet, stable, 'respectable' home environment, though there were tensions below — just below — the marital surface. (*The Listener* 30.9.1976, p. 402)

> A short biography can only hope to present the course of the poet's life in such a way as will send readers to, or back to, the poems ... (*The Listener* 28.10.1976, p. 544)

Other patterns. Besides the syntactic pattern dealt with so far, there are other patterns in which a similar ellipsis of the prepositional complement occurs. We may begin by considering the pattern

$$\text{noun}_1 - \text{prep}_1 - \text{conj} - \text{noun}_2 - \text{prep}_2 - \text{compl}$$

Let us stick to our rough threefold semantic division, giving first an example of contrast or antithesis:

> A close examination of styles of speech reveals a penchant for or an avoidance of the following ... (Peter Farb, *Word Play*, Bantam 1975, p. 145)

Next an example of semantic neighbours:

> The book illustrates ... how a woman's state can distort ... her view of, and attitude towards, other people. (*The Listener* 20.5.1976, p. 654)

Finally, as an instance of the comparative absence of semantic agreement between the prepositions, we may adduce the following quotation which, containing three parallel nouns and prepositions, is characteristic of the rather heavy bookish style:

> In practice, readers will have no difficulty in drawing a line that separates books in which interest in a [*sic*] nature of, motives for, and results of, a crime is at the heart of a story from those where the criminal interest is a subsidiary one. (Julian Symons, *Bloody Murder*, Penguin 1974, pp. 10f)

Occasionally the construction may accommodate mild joking, as in

> The three best-known names of the modern period are, to the man in and woman on the street, Oscar Wilde, Dylan Thomas and Brendan Behan. (Anthony Burgess, *Urgent Copy*, Penguin 1973, p. 98)

And rhetorical self-correction, an apparent search for *les mots propres*, is seen in the following quotation:

> ... his acquaintance with death, love, his own talents and a need for — a mystical obsession with — the idea of Israel has turned him from a dreamer to a hardened realist. (*The Listener* 29.4.1976, p. 549)

That this construction tends to make rather heavy demands on the writer is suggested by the fact that it sometimes leads to slovenly formulations like those given below:[24]

> ... an important new book club ... has just been launched to meet the increasing interest and growing demand for books on every aspect of the arts ... (*The Listener* 30.9.1976, p. 393)

> There'd been an obsessive love of and pride in the place then. Since then nobody'd had love or pride in it. (Lionel Davidson, *Smith's Gazelle*, Penguin 1977, pp. 39f)

Further patterns exhibiting the same feature of ellipsis are the following:

$$\text{vb}_1 - \text{prep}_1 - \text{conj} - \text{vb}_2 - \text{prep}_2 - \text{compl, and}$$

$$\text{adj}_1 - \text{prep}_1 - \text{conj} - \text{adj}_2 - \text{prep}_2 - \text{compl, as in}$$

> we cannot assume that a student who does not join in or contribute to discussion in seminars is simply unaware of, neglectful of or resistant to any responsibility in this direction. (*The Times Higher Education Supplement* 7.6.1974, p. 6)

Finally, it may be noted that since prepositional verbs are syntactically and semantically equivalent with transitive verbs, the two kinds of verbs may appear together in co-ordinated constructions, involving ellipsis of the complement if the prepositional verb precedes the transitive verb:

> We live under, and in fact accept, the rule of law. (Julian Symons, *Bloody Murder*, Penguin 1974, p. 14)

> Next month he will appear in and direct a stage-show ... (*The Listener* 22.4.1976, p. 497)

Punctuation. Above (p. 216) it was pointed out that the ellipsis produced by the conjoining of two prepositions often carries with it the use of commas to separate off the second item from the first. This of course implies a pause, and it means that the two parallel items are deliberately given separate and equipollent status. This punctuational procedure is typical of somewhat formal style, and it is interesting to note that the same procedure is adhered to in some cases where the transitive verb is followed by the prepositional verb; for instance:

> ... someone who can settle down to earn, and live with, respect. (*The Listener* 20.5.1976, p. 649)

Factors favouring non-ellipsis. After we have now surveyed the elliptical construction in its various manifestations, it is perhaps not superfluous to remark that a number of factors favour non-ellipsis.

---

24. A warning against such usage is found for instance in a prescriptive treatment like Porter G. Perrin's *Writer's Guide and Index to English*, Scott, Foresman and Co. 1942, p. 661.

(1) In the first place, repetition of the complement lends greater weight to a statement than does omission; it was probably not by accident that Theodore Parker in his speech at the Anti–Slavery Convention in 1850 chose the formulation "a government of all the people, by all the people, for all the people" (*The Oxford Dictionary of Quotations*, 1962, p. 373; almost the same formulation as in Lincoln's celebrated Gettysburg Address, 1863). — Although both *in and out of season* and *in season and out of season* occur, the latter formulation tends to be preferred if great emphasis is intended. — There is probably a different reason for the repetition of the complement in an example like

> ... the Year Books, the reports of cases in the King's courts that were written by practitioners for practitioners. (H. D. Hazeltine in *Sir John Fortescue: De Laudibus Legum Anglie,* ed. S. B. Chrimes, Cambridge 1942, pp. xl f)

For although both occurrences of *practitioners* refer to the same broad category, what is meant is 'by some practitioners for other members of the same category'. In other words, this example may be compared with set phrases like *from point to point* and *from time to time,* which also contain different referents.

(2) Secondly there is the problem, already touched upon, of the semantic compatibility of the two prepositions. In

> "Was he educated before the war or by it?" (Anthony Price, *Other Paths to Glory,* Coronet 1976, p. 37)

it is reasonable to assume that the writer avoided ellipsis because he felt that the two prepositions belong to different semantic spheres.

(3) In the third place, the weight of the prepositional complement may sometimes be of importance. Let us consider the following example:

> Noble argues that for many children, television is a positive benefit, that they learn from it, relax with it, fantasize through it ... (*The Listener* 16.9.1976, p. 327)

Here it would seem that the writer considered the complement to be too lightweight for ellipsis; had he chosen it, a rhythmically rather awkward imbalance would have resulted. It should be added, however, that if the prepositional pair is of the high–frequency type, ellipsis is a distinct possibility even if the complement is for instance *it*: thus "Is he for (it) or against it?" In such cases the choice of construction depends on the degree of emphasis one wants to convey.

(4) Finally, the interval separating the two prepositions is of importance:

the farther they are apart, the more probable it is that the complement will be repeated. Compare:

> It was not a particularly interesting brief, he suspected, though inevitably he would get interested in it, once he had started on it. (Margaret Drabble, *The Needle's Eye,* Penguin 1976, pp. 212f)

in which the factors already mentioned may have been influential, although the main reason for non–ellipsis appears to be the distance between the prepositions. If ellipsis is resorted to in spite of the conjuncts being far apart, the result is a somewhat heavy and artificial word–order:

> ... I am writing in (just as I have assumed some of the vocabulary and "voice" of) a convention universally accepted at the time of my story ... (John Fowles, *The French Lieutenant's Woman,* Signet 1970, p. 80)

B. Legal Style

As already mentioned, ellipsis of the prepositional complement is of high frequency in legal style, and in styles of a related character: it is well known that we find the same phenomenon for instance in dictionary definitions. The verb *drub* is explained thus in the *Concise Oxford Dictionary:* "beat (notion) *into, out of,* person" (OUP 1976, p. 318), and *angry* is "... resentful (*at, about,* thing; *at, with,* person) ..." (*ibid.* p. 36). If elliptical constructions are style markers, it is, however, not only owing to their high frequency in legal texts, but also because such texts contain a number of special elliptical constructions that do not — except as quotations — occur in non–technical literature. Let us proceed now to a brief analysis of the elliptical construction in legal texts.

The first point to be made is that in legal texts — whether Acts of Parliament or law treatises — we find all the types discussed above under *A.* There is no need to say more about them; instead, let us consider usage that is normally confined to legal literature.

Legal formulations may be said to be dominated by two stylistic principles that in theory would seem to militate against each other: on the one hand there is the principle of explicitness and exhaustiveness, on the other hand the principle of concision. A legal text should ideally deal with all the relevant aspects of a problem, but it should do so in the briefest possible manner. Sometimes a third principle is in operation as well, viz. a rhetorical principle dictated by the legislators' wish to imbue their text with great dignity and persuasiveness. But although in theory we may distinguish between these principles, in actual fact they are fused; they all tend to produce the same result, the widespread employment of elliptical constructions, and together they contribute to creating the flavour so characteristic of legal texts. Let us exemplify.

First we may consider the rhetorical use of doublets. A good example of this is the formula that opens all Acts of Parliament: "Be it enacted by the Queen's most Excellent Majesty, by and with the advice and consent of the Lords Spiritual and Temporal, and Commons ..." Here we note how the doubling of the prepositions is paralleled by the two–item complement, doubling being a pervasive marker of legal style: cf. set phrases like *null and void, pains and penalties, if and to the extent that* ..., etc. *By* and *with* are identical in meaning; compare David Mellinkoff's comment: "Were it not that the phrase is traditional, either of the words alone could do the job ..." (*op. cit.* [note 10 above] p. 347). Thus the only reason for the presence of both prepositions is a wish to lend dignity and emphasis to the formula. A similar example is the collocation *save and except.* Mellinkoff lists conjuncts like *for and during the term of* (p. 234), *for and in consideration of* (p. 278), and even *in lieu, in place, instead, and in substitution of* (p. 122). Non–technical language has comparatively few parallels (cf. above, pp. 220-22). Occasionally the archaic flavour of such locutions is reinforced by the use of an obsolete preposition, as in

> if X gave land unto and to the use of B in trust for C, B was the legal owner of the land ... (William Geldart, *Elements of English Law,* OUP 1975, p. 26)

The layman may often be in doubt as to whether a doubling is mere rhetoric or is intended to convey a referential differentiation. What, for instance, are we to make of the following:

> The expenditure allowable under this section for any oilfield does not include ... any expenditure wholly or partly depending on or determined by reference to the quantity, value or proceeds of, or the profits from, oil won from the field ... (*Oil Taxation Act 1975,* p. 8)

Is a distinction being made here between *proceeds* of and *profits from?*[25] It is less difficult to understand the distinction made in

> But a corporation created by or in pursuance of an Act of Parliament is subject to the rule that ... (William Geldart, *Elements of English Law,* OUP 1975, p. 71)

where *in pursuance of* appears to refer to the indirect consequences that may arise. Cf. further expressions like *by or under an Act* (*Sex Discrimination Act 1975,* p. 32) and *under or by virtue of this Act* (*ibid.* p. 57). A similar interpretation presumably applies to a formulation like *pensions to or in respect of special constables* (*ibid.* p. 13), where one may envisage

---

25. There may be a technical difference. According to *Jowitt's Dictionary of English Law* (second edition, London 1977, pp. 1438 and 1442), *proceeds* is "the sum, amount, or value of land, investments, or goods, etc., sold, or converted into money", while *profit* is defined as "advantage or gain in money or in money's worth". I am much obliged to Lektor Inge Gorm Hansen for drawing my attention to these definitions (the interpretation of which must be left to the specialist).

in respect of making allowance for a constable's dependant(s).

With the last two examples we have approached the very large group of co-ordinate prepositions in which the terms are semantic neighbours, their employment being dictated by a wish for exhaustiveness and precision. As mentioned, we meet with the same types in legal style as in non-legal texts. But over and above this, there are specific legal features.

For one thing, the conjuncts occurring in legal texts sometimes strike one as being unequal yokefellows; this is true of examples like

> ... the storing of oil as part of or in conjunction with the operation of an oil refinery ... (*Oil Taxation Act 1975*, p. 22)

> ... carrying out works for, or acquiring an asset or an interest in an asset to be used for the purpose of, substantially improving the rate at which oil can be won ... (*ibid.* pp. 8f).

Next, in some formulations we witness the principles of exhaustiveness and of concision as it were struggling for supremacy, the result being a somewhat laborious heaping up of terms:

> The Secretary of State may make and, when made, revoke and vary regulations respecting the time, manner and conditions within, in, and under which claims are to be made .. (Halsbury's *Laws of England,* vol. 30, London 1959, p. 87)

where *time* goes with *within, manner* with *in,* and *conditions* with *under.*

Another circumstance that makes legal texts less accessible to the lay reader is the tendency to combine the ellipsis of a prepositional complement with other forms of ellipsis:

> ... so much, if any, as the participator may specify of, or of the unused balance of, any amount available for use ... (*Oil Taxation Act 1975,* p. 51)

> ... in relation to expenditure incurred in the acquisition of, or of an interest in, an asset. (*Ibid.* p. 52)

A number of collocations characteristic of legal or technical style appear quite frequently outside this style whenever there is a need for them; this applies for instance to *up to and including.* But it is hardly true of the corresponding locution exemplified below, which appears to be confined to legal style:

> ... each earlier claim period back to and including that in which the expenditure was incurred. (*Ibid.* p. 11)

The co-ordination of antithetic prepositions is common in legal parlance. Typical examples are:

> ... civil proceedings by or against the Crown ... (*Sex Discrimination Act 1975,* p. 58)

> ... certain sales to or by petroleum companies ... (*Oil Taxation Act 1975,* p. 64)

Such collocations are unusual in ordinary language. The layman who reads the last example will receive a slight shock since he has his expectation disappointed: he is used to *to or from*. It is peculiarities like these (peculiarities from the layman's point of view, that is) which contribute to creating the special flavour. But it goes without saying that co-ordinate prepositions are only one feature of legal style, albeit a most important one. They operate in conjunction with other parallelisms, with repetitions, and with technical terms, and they often do so in a somewhat heavy sentence structure. Let a final example suffice:

> For the purposes of this subsection the relevant accounting period, in relation to any petroleum revenue tax paid by a company, is the accounting period of the company in or at the end of which the chargeable period for which that tax was charged ends. (*Oil Taxation Act 1975*, p. 29)

Co-ordinate prepositions with a single complement occur in a number of other languages: Danish, Swedish, German, French, Italian, and Russian. No doubt the list could be extended, but it suffices to show how widespread is this construction. The striking thing is that it was non-existent 700 years ago. As has been shown, the first English examples appear in the fourteenth century, but it is only in the following century that the construction really begins to gain ground. The same is true of Danish and German.[26] Fifteenth-century Danish diplomas contain a number of antithetical co-ordinate prepositions, while particularly the Middle Danish Bible translation has rather numerous examples of the co-ordination of semantic neighbours. On German soil the construction is met with after *c.* 1450, both the antithetical and the tautologous types being represented. Official documents in Latin have examples of prepositional co-ordination from about 1350. The construction begins to crop up, then, at roughly the same time in different languages. At this point it is tempting to venture to supplement the tentative explanation of origin offered above by suggesting as an additional possible source the European intellectual climate fostered by a factor like Scholasticism; further research is, however, needed to prove this hypothesis. Thus English is far from unique in having the construction, although there does seem to be one subtype that is specifically English, namely that in which a preposition co-ordinates with itself: *a scarf round and round his neck.*[27]

---

26. I am very grateful to the following friends and colleagues for providing me with information: Professor Poul Lindegård Hjorth and lektor Allan Karker (Danish); Professor Ernst Dittmer (German); Dr. Poul Skårup (French).
27. Dr. J. Oresnik, of Ljubljana, informs me that Slovenian has a corresponding type.

FROM POSTMODIFICATION TO PREMODIFICATION

In contemporary English we often find variation between postmodification and premodification in the nominal group in examples like *a movie made for TV / a made-for-TV movie;*[1] *a studio humming with activity / a humming-with- activity studio;*[2] and at least in American English a formulation like *a plan to fall back on* may alternatively be referred to as *a fallback plan.*[3,4] The choice between such variants is determined by style. The premodified constructions have been on the increase in recent years and are perhaps to be met with most frequently in journalese and related styles. I am not going to discuss the types I have just exemplified; I simply mention them here in order to point out that they may be seen as additional examples of the complementary constructions that form my topic: postmodification as in *the rate of growth* vs. premodification as in *the growth rate.* In other words I shall confine myself to the type of postmodification which consists of a preposition and its complement, and the premodification that may correspond to it.

In his book on word-formation H. Marchand states: "In present-day English, any substantive may be used to determine another substantive..."[5] This appears to be rather too categorical a statement, seeing that in numerous cases only a postmodified construction is available; we may adduce examples like *an article of faith, the centre of gravity, feet of clay, a head of state, a man-of-war, the outbreak of war, a rule of thumb, a sense of humour,* and *a state of siege,* and this list might easily be extended. In most cases the preposition is *of,* but one might add examples like *a man about town* and *a maid in waiting.* It is possible that some of my examples should be considered compounds – cf. the final stress in for instance *man-of-war.* However, there is a cline between free syntactic combinations and compounds, and "there is no clear-cut distinction between the two types of combinations."[6]

Why is it that postmodification is the only possibility for expressions like *rule of thumb* and *prisoner-of-war*? If they are resistant to transformation,[7] it is probably because they have come to be felt as very firmly entrenched set phrases, so entrenched that postmodification sometimes becomes the model for new formations: it is suggestive that the old-established term *prisoner-of-war* is the model of a fairly recent formation like *prisoner of conscience* (used in Amnesty International contexts).

In most cases, however, there are two constructions available: one with postmodification, which I shall refer to as the *A* construction, and a corresponding one having premodification, the *B* construction. It goes without saying that I shall only deal with those cases in which there is identity of denotation (though not of explicitness) between the constructions; thus examples like *a glass of wine* vs. *a wine-glass* and *a box of matches* vs. *a matchbox* are outside my concern. I shall consider the variation found in examples like *English for special purposes* vs. *special purpose English, the teaching of foreign languages* vs. *foreign language teaching, cancer of the stomach* vs. *stomach cancer, the balance of terror* vs. *the terror balance,* and *a tax on gifts* vs. *a gifts tax.*[8]

As will be seen, the change from A to B may have a number of consequences. The definite article is deleted: corresponding to *officials in the Pentagon* we have *Pentagon officials.* If the prepositional complement is a plural noun, it often becomes a singular in the B construction: *foreign language teaching;* but sometimes the plural form is retained: *a gifts tax, the civil rights movement.* As will have appeared, the preposition is often deleted, but obviously it cannot be dispensed with in examples like *his behind-the-scenes activity,*[9] *on-the-record interviews,*[10] *on-the-scene observations,*[11] and *under-the-table perquisites.*[12] The article is also retained here. Sometimes there is vacillation: *a duty officer* vs. *three on-duty soldiers.* In a few cases a preposition is replaced by a prefix. Thus, corresponding to *demonstrations against the Shah* we may find *anti-Shah demonstrations;*[13] compare also *a pre-breakfast session*[14] and *the postwar period.*

The semantic function of the attributive noun in the B construction corresponds to that of a classifying adjective. This is perhaps seen most clearly if we compare adjectival constructions that compete with B at least on the surface. In *a surprising attack* the adjective is gradable, while the attributive noun in *a surprise visit* is not. There is semantic differentiation: *surprise* as a premodifier obligatorily conveys a temporal element, approximately 'sudden, without prior notice', so that what *a surprise attack*[15] first of all suggests is the idea of an attack that comes unannounced, while no temporal element necessarily attaches to the adjective *surprising.* Thus a nominal premodifier indicates the category to which the head noun belongs, and this category may be explicitly or implicitly contrasted with different categories. A wife may have *husband trouble,*[16] a girl, *boyfriend trouble,* just as an editor may have *author trouble.*[17] We may compare *a surprise attack* with a *naval attack,* and *audience fatigue* with *metal fatigue.* A *disaster area* is of course an area in which conditions are or may become disastrous; but it is first and foremost a categorising expression that may be implicitly contrasted with, say, *a development area.* Variants like *a giant steamer* and *a gigantic steamer* appear to be used indiscriminately; but here again I submit that we have to do with a corresponding difference, which becomes quite obvious given the proper headword: *the giant emu* and *the giant panda* are zoological terms that denote category, so that we might have, for instance, *an unusually small giant panda* without any semantic conflict arising between *small* and *giant.* If this is correct, it means that by using the expression *a giant steamer* we assign the referent to a definite category,[18] while *gigantic* would merely suggest enormous size. – There are, however, instances where the two variants appear to be completely synonymous: according to Webster (1961) *a sympathetic strike* equals *a sympathy strike.*

The semantic scope of postmodifications is probably unlimited, but there are perhaps three well-defined semantic fields that lend themselves with particular frequency to premodification, namely locative and temporal indications and indications of size; for instance: *a village in Sussex – a Sussex village; the Crash in*

1929 – the 1929 Crash; a slim volume of 134 pages – a slim (134 pages) volume.[19]

What are the circumstances under which premodification may occur, and are there any constraints on its use?

In their discussion of the problem Randolph Quirk and his associates[20] make two points:

(a) It is only if the prepositions of the postmodified A construction belong to the most central group that transformation to B is possible. Thus we have alternative formulations like *work in the docks* and *dock work*, while an example like *work near the docks* does not lend itself to a similar transformation, nor does the sequence *the green light above the door*. There is undoubtedly something in this, though it is not quite clear to me what is meant by 'most central'.

(b) If the postmodification conveys 'relative impermanence' it cannot become a premodifier. Thus, while we have both *the table in the corner* and *the corner table*, there is no B construction corresponding to *the girl in the corner*, since "Premodification confers relative permanence which befits the assignment to a corner of a table or even a waitress, but not a girl as such".[21] No doubt this is true as far as it goes, and perhaps it is impossible to delimit the difference between permanence and impermanence more precisely. Anyhow, that a breach of this rule of thumb may lead to striking stylistic results should appear from the following example. In Anthony Burgess's novel *Inside Mr Enderby* the main character is warned while flying to Rome: "Your ticket does not entitle you to undisputed monopolization of the john." We are told that the man who issues this warning is an American , who is subsequently referred to as "the American who had ousted Enderby from the john"; this is further reduced to "the American from the john", and finally, some 10 pages later, we read: "An American, not the john one, poised his camera to shoot."[22] Here the normal limits of premodification have clearly been transgressed, the result being a stylistically striking formulation.

The above remarks may be supplemented by a consideration of the rôle played by the 'given' – 'new' principle in the choice between A and B. In 'Points of Modern English Syntax' N. E. Osselton expresses the view that if we compare an A formulation like *the cost of beans* with the subsequent B formulation *bean costs*, we are led to the conclusion that *beans* in *the cost of beans* has been given end position for the sake of contrast or emphasis: *beans* in *the cost of beans* is the news carrier, but this is no longer the case in the subsequent formulation *bean costs*.[23] If this is correct – and I believe it is – a parallel is established between the (unmarked) given – new order of sentences and of nominal groups. However, I believe that both the traditionalist stylistician and the modern text grammarian would add something to this; they would stress that there are three factors which determine the conventional and acceptable use of anaphora: 1. unambiguousness, 2. a principle of economy (or laziness), and 3. variation. As for the first factor, unambiguousness, we have already touched on the deletion or non-deletion of prepositions in the change from A to B: a preposition is retained in a B construction if its deletion would entail ambiguity or loss of necessary information: *behind-the-scenes activities*. But some measure of indeterminacy is tolerated: both *a path in the jungle* and *a path through the jungle* have *a jungle path* as their transform. As for the principle of economy, the rule is: do not provide more information than is necessary.[24] Now the A construction is the typical 'first-mention' variant, which tends to be replaced by the shorter and less explicit B construction at 'second mention' (or 'further mention'). Once a full reference has been given, there is no need for explicitness at later stages. There are well-known parallels elsewhere: pronominalization, the use of abbreviations at further mention, and the use of short forms like *felt* for *felt hat, quake* for *earthquake,* and *Sunday* for *Sunday paper.*[25]

Let me give a few examples of the change from A to B. At first mention we may find *the rate of interest,* at second mention *the interest rate;*[26] similarly, *a declaration of nullity* is followed by *a nullity declaration;*[27] *the probability of a response* becomes *response probability;*[28] *slips of the tongue* becomes *tongue-slips;*[29] *the hostile relationship between mother and daughter* becomes *the knotty mother-daughter relationship;*[30] and *restraints on prices and wages* becomes *wage and price restraint.*[31]

A special case in which the principle of economy is operative is presented by headlinese: here the headline will often contain the B variant while the fuller A variant follows in the text. We may find for instance *Department Heads* in the headline, followed by *the heads of the departments* in the text.

Sometimes the change from A to B may give the impression of being a more or less mechanical procedure; and while, as has been pointed out, the typical change is from A to B, one may occasionally find the inverse order. Here I am afraid we have to drag in the elusive factor of random variation, which may do duty as a rag bag to account for the cases that do not fit into our neat scheme. How else can we explain the following? "A rustle in the earpiece. Her *impatience sigh,* unlike her *sigh of frustration,* is not so sharp. The *impatience sigh* begins with a liquid click in the roof of the mouth..." (my italics).[32]

The title of my paper may suggest a chronological progression from postmodification to premodification, and that is indeed intentional. For it is a fact that over a long period now – and particularly in the present century – the B construction has been on the increase.

Let me give a few historical examples, testified to by the OED: *some person of Quality* is attested from 1625, while the first example of *quality* as a premodifier is from 1706: *Your Quality Lady.* The OED has *field of battle* from 1718, *battlefield* from 1812; *rate of exchange* from 1727, *exchange rate* from 1896; *book of reference* from 1836, *reference Library* from 1858. – A fossilized example is afforded by the word *rigmarole,* which was originally *Roll of Ragman,* then *Ragman('s) roll,* ending up as *rigmarole.*

So, although not a few A constructions seem indestructible, the historical development is on the whole clear enough, showing increased scope for premodification. It is interesting, then, to note that there is a parallel between the diachronic development and the typical distribution of A and B variants in contemporary English texts. But it should be emphasized that that is not the whole story; for in contemporary English the B construction has become so widespread that it is often chosen as the *only* construction, without any preceding A construction; compare recently formed concepts and corresponding B constructions like *consumer durables, income tax,* and *welfare state.* Thus the transformational relation between A and B is only partial.

The spread of premodification has called forth the wrath of prescriptivists like A. P. Herbert, and H. W. Fowler.[33] Sir Alan speaks of "Cannibal English", the 'real' adjectives being swallowed up by nouns, and Fowler refers to "... a monstrous abuse of our ancient and valuable right to use nouns as attributive adjectives". This "corruption" causes sentences to "stumble along painfully and obscurely in synthetic lumps instead of running easily and lucidly with analytical grace", as will be seen, a somewhat emotional condemnation. I have tried to show that as *wholesale* condemnation it is hardly justified. On the other hand there is no denying that the B construction *is* abused by some. If one finds this kind of premodification used to excess in, for instance, scientific and technical literature, it is due, I think, to a feeling among authors of such literature that this mode of expression somehow confers prestige.[34] And I note with interest that this is also the view taken by Kenneth Hudson in his *The Jargon of the Professions* (1978). Here, by way of conclusion, is Hudson's statement:

Why go for the compressed, unnatural form, which the human brain cannot handle, instead of something more expanded and more logical? The answer, apart from sheer ignorance and clumsiness, can only be an ever-present impulse to prove that one is not as other men. If the outside world uses prepositions, the expert must leave them out. Two nouns glued together – 'cue utilisation', 'person perception', 'tract interrelationships', 'word swarm' – are proof of academic quality.[35]

Notes

1. "... her heavily advertised made-for-TV movie..." Time Magazine 7.10.74, p. 59.
2. "We all know about the busily involved, humming-with-activity studio..." The Listener 16.9.76, p. 330.
3. "...the U.S. had no fallback plans..." Time Magazine 12.3.79, p. 31.
4. What has sentence form in an article is often nominalized in headlines; cf. the following example from The Observer, 4.2.79, p. 1: headline *Holy war threat by Khomeini.* The text that follows has: "Ayatollah Khomeini warned yesterday that he might have to launch a holy war..."
5. Marchand, H. 1969. The Categories and Types of Present-Day English Word-Formation. Munich, 2nd ed., p. 23.
6. van Roey, J. "A note on Noun + Noun Combinations in Modern English". English Studies 1964, p. 52.
7. Incidentally, this is also a pedagogical problem. Danish has compounds like *frimærkesamling* and *digtsamling.* The first corresponds to *stamp collection,* and this analogy tricks some Danes into forming* *poem collection.*
8. New Statesman 8.8.69, col. 166.
9. "In truth they have been giving him some behind-the-scenes help." Time Magazine 20.11.78, p. 22.
10. Time Magazine 27.11.78, p. 24.
11. Time Magazine 27.11.78, p. 9.
12. Time Magazine 27.11.78, p. 25.
13. Cf. " the anti-Shah protesters", Time Magazine 4.12.78, p. 50.
14. Time Magazine 3.12.73, p. 33.
15. Other combinations are *surprise award, surprise bestseller, surprise choice, surprise decision, surprise gift, surprise initiative,* and *surprise move.*

16. "She was having husband trouble and needed taking out of herself." Bainbridge, Beryl. 1978. Injury Time. London: Fontana, p. 16.
17. "... he [T.S. Eliot] said: 'Tell me, as one editor to another, do you have much author trouble?'" The Oxford Book of Literary Anecdotes, ed. James Sutherland. London. 1975, p. 441.
18. Cf. "... giant corporations ... middle-size companies..." Time Magazine 5.3.79, p. 41.
19. Time Magazine 14.7.75, p. 9.
20. Quirk/Greenbaum/Leech/Svartvik. 1972. A Grammar of Contemporary English. London: Longman, p. 915.
21. Quirk/Greenbaum. 1973. A University Grammar of English. London: Longman, p. 400.
22. 1973. Harmondsworth: Penguin, pp. 124ff.
23. English Studies 1975, pp. 148-9.
24. These two factors correspond to H. P. Grice's 'Co-operative Principle', cf. Kempson, Ruth M. 1975. Presupposition and the Delimitation of Semantics. C.U.P., p. 142.
25. Cf. Sørensen, Knud. 1975. Aspects of Modern English Prose Style. Copenhagen: Schønberg, pp. 51ff.
26. New Statesman 7.11.69, col. 656.
27. Sykes, Christopher. 1977. Evelyn Waugh. Harmondsworth: Penguin, p. 188.
28. Terwilliger, R. F. 1968. Meaning and Mind. O.U.P., p. 99.
29. Lyons, John (ed.). 1970. New Horizons in Linguistics. Harmondsworth: Penguin, p. 69.
30. Time Magazine 26.2.79, p. 47.
31. Galbraith, J. K. 1977. The New Industrial State. Pelican pp. 255ff.
32. Le Carré, John. 1977. The Naive and Sentimental Lover. Pan, p. 75.
33. Fowler, H. W. 1965. A Dictionary of Modern English Usage, 2nd ed. revised by Sir Ernest Gowers. Oxford: O.U.P., p. 242; Herbert, A. P. 1959. What a Word! London: Methuen & Co., pp. 145- 6.
34. Sørensen, Knud, op. cit. p. 94.
35. Hudson, Kenneth. 1978. The Jargon of the Professions. London: Macmillan, p. 94.

DETERMINATIVE *THAT OF* VS. ZERO

In order to pinpoint the problem to be dealt with here, let us consider *Beowulf* 1282-4:

	Wæs se gryre lǣssa
efne swā micle,	swā bi eth mægþa cræft,
wīggryre wīfes	be wǣpnedmen ...

This passage is variously handled by translators. R.K. Gordon, in *The Song of Beowulf* (1923:56), reproduces the ellipsis: 'The dread was less by just so much as the strength of women, the war-terror of a woman, is *less than a man ...*', while David Wright's translation (Harmondsworth (Penguin), 1957: 57) has: '... just as the fighting strength of a woman is *not so great as that of an armed man ...*' (my italics). At the first blush the *Beowulf* poet seems to have employed a somewhat slipshod formulation of the comparison: one might have expected the passage to conclude: ... *be wǣpnedmannes (wīggryre)*. However, this kind of construction has existed throughout the history of English. My main concern in this article will be with the elliptical or zero construction as it occurs in contemporary English, in competition with the *that of/those of* construction; but before discussing the modern material, let us take a brief look at a few examples culled from earlier stages of the language.

The comparison involved is often, but by no means always, effected by the presence of *like,* about which the *OED* states (VI, 284, 1.f.): 'Inaccurately const. dative (etc.) instead of ellipt. possessive', giving examples from *c.* 1300 onwards.[1] There are several such elliptical constructions in Chaucer; for instance:

His top was dokked lyk a preest biforn
(*The General Prologue* 590; Robinson: 23).

But of hir song, it was as loude and yerne
As any swalwe sitting on a berne.
(*The Miller's Tale* 3257-8; Robinson: 49).

Shakespeare also employs the construction a number of times, for instance:

Truly, Master Holofernes, the epithets are sweetly varied,
like a scholar at the least ...
(*Love's Labour's Lost* 4.2.8-9).

But in that crystal scales let there be weighed
Your lady's love against some other maid ...
(*Romeo and Juliet* 1.2.99-100).

Burns writes: 'Your locks were like the raven ...' ('John Anderson, my Jo', *Poems,* London (Everyman), 1947: 324), and Dickens in his description of Mrs Podsnap refs to her 'neck and nostrils like a rocking-horse' (*Our Mutual Friend* I, 2, London (Everyman), 1953: 10).

The construction is largely neglected in grammatical treatments of modern English. Poutsma (1926: I. A., Ch. XXIV, 47) rather surprisingly characterizes the *that of* construction as 'decidedly uncongenial to the language', but makes no mention of the zero construction, which also seems to have been passed over in silence by R. Quirk and his associates (1972). On the other hand it is dealt with briefly by Fowler (1965: 336) and by Schibsbye (1970: 213), which latter work devotes a footnote to it:

In a comparative phrase linked by *like* with a possessive pron. + subst. *that of* is sometimes omitted: *his voice rang out like a prophet of the Lord denouncing the ungodly.* This is regarded as slovenly.

In my view 'sometimes' is probably an understatement, modern examples being quite frequent, more particularly in spoken English. It is quite true that the zero construction may often be characterized as slovenly, although other considerations are relevant as well; but of this more anon.

The example adduced by Schibsbye would appear to have four variants:

(1) His voice rang out like the voice of a prophet.
(2) His voice rang out like a prophet's (voice).
(3) His voice rang out like that of a prophet.
(4) His voice rang out like a prophet.

This sort of comparison involves twice two semantic items: a characteristic of A is compared with (or more vaguely related to) a corresponding characteristic of B; alternatively:

$$A's\ x :: B's\ x$$

corresponding to (1), (2), and (3) above. Variant (4) may then be symbolized by the formula

$$A's\ x :: B$$

where the lopsidedness stands out; or, as Fowler puts it (*op. cit*): 'the word governed by *like* must be *in pari materia* with the one to which it is compared.' – The formula should not be interpreted too narrowly: it is not all the examples discussed that are constructed with a genitive or a possessive; but provided the twice two semantic items are somehow present or implicit, the formula seems useful.

Before we proceed to a discussion of variant (4), the zero construction, a few illustrations of and comments on the other variants may be in order.

Here, first, is an illustration of variant (1):

... it [a poem] is acceptable ... because its setting is the setting of a fantasy world ...
(Walter Nash, *Our Experience of Language,* London, 1971: 86).

The repetition of the noun in preference to pronominalization is not very frequent, possibly because such repetition tends to create an air of pedantry. – In (2) it is apparently rare to find the noun repeated (I have no examples). – The choice between (2) and (3) would seem to be determined by two factors. In the first place, where the genitive is ruled out or would at least be awkward, (3) is resorted to:

And the hundreds of plaster models made for these figures give an impression of creative power equal to that of the seventeenth century.
(Kenneth Clark, *Civilisation,* London, 1974: 319).

... there can be said to be more of the Renaissance in his work than in that of any other writer of the age.
(J.B. Priestley, *Literature and Western Man,* London, 1962: 15).

In the second place there is a tendency for those nouns that take the genitive to prefer this in informal style, while the *that of* construction is favoured in formal style: *His income is higher than his brother's/ ... higher than that of his brother.* But this is only a tendency; where both constructions are employed in the same passage, there does not seem much to choose between them:

His career differed from that of Summers in that he had never been charged with any offence involving violence. It resembled Summers's in the fact that he had lived in Sydney since the late sixties ...
(Julian Symons, *The Plot Against Roger Rider,* Harmondsworth (Penguin), 1975: 99).

We now come to variant (4), the zero construction. First it may be noted that it occurs not only with *like,* but also with a number of more or less synonymous items, especially *compared with, identical to/with, similar to, in accordance with, in common with, in keeping with,* and *the same as,* as well as with antonyms of *like* (*different* and *unlike*), for instance:

And then, at the end of the Second World War, we were completely exhausted, and the larders and the linen cupboards were bare, compared with the Germans or the French ...
(*The Listener* 20.5.1976: 630).

I don't know whether geisha are happy. But I do know that their ambitions are the same as most women ...
(*The Listener* 12.6.1975:777).

The population of this eastern quarter was Arab but the feel of the place subtly different from any of the cities that Roscoe had travelled through.
(Andrew Osmond, *Saladin!* London, 1975: 258).

Furthermore the zero construction appears frequently in comparisons mediated by *as ... as,* and it also occurs with comparatives and with verbs that denote a comparison:

Burnley are still hardly being taken as serious contenders for the First Division championship although why not is a mystery because their claims for the title are as valid as any team at present.
(*The Guardian* 29.3.1975: 24).

The origins of English are better known than many other languages because of the number of documents that have survived.
(Peter Farb, *Word-Play,* London (Bantam), 1975: 337).

... since the war they [the Germans] had erected huge studios and were producing films that rivalled the Americans in technical excellence ...
(Robert Graves & Alan Hodge, *The Long Week-End,* Harmondsworth (Penguin), 1971: 133).

What are the factors that favour the occurrence of the zero construction? In the majority of cases it is found in the relaxed style, in passages where its lopsidedness cannot give rise to any misunderstanding, and where the addition of *that of/those of* might actually sound somewhat pedantic. Thus, if a journalist writes:

Of the world's major economies, said the OECD, all except Britain and Italy will enjoy real growth in the second half ...
(*Time Magazine* 4.8.1975: 20).

no mistake is possible: it is obvious that it is the British and Italian economies that are being referred to. And if the author of a scholarly work makes use of a formulation like:

Chemical nomenclature has a morphology which is more complex than that of everyday English, but unlike everyday English it is comparatively regular ...
(Valerie Adams, *An Introduction to Modern English Word-Formation,* London, 1973: 210).

it is probably because she has instinctively shied away from the pedantic-sounding repetition of *that of everyday English.*

The two constructions are in frequent competition, and the tendency appears to be for the zero construction to be employed at second mention:

'... His I.Q. is about thirty points lower than that of a not too agile-minded jellyfish ...'; ... the ninth earl had an I.Q. thirty points lower than a jellyfish ...'
(P.G. Wodehouse, *Full Moon,* Harmondsworth (Penguin), 1975: 134 & 181, the second occurrence harking back to the first).

After a comparative + *than* the zero construction is at least as frequent as the *that of* construction:

... the writing was that of a novelist rather than a playwright ...
(*The Listener* 23.10.1975: 543).

His voice was deep and slow, the accent more like that of an English public school man, which he was, than an African.
(Frederick Forsyth, *The Dogs of War,* London, 1974: 10).

It may be added that the zero construction is particularly frequent if the item following *like,* etc. is qualified by a present participle or a relative clause, the comparison being often loosely attached and of a somewhat imprecise character:

But, as they danced again, Tess saw his expression revert to what it had been earlier that evening, preoccupied, oddly soft or undefined, like a man procrastinating.
(C.P. Snow, *The Malcontents,* Harmondsworth (Penguin), 1975: 183).

(142)

... her head looked like a woman who has just come out of prison or boarding school.
(Doris Lessing, *The Summer Before the Dark,* London (Bantam), 1974: 245).

A similar looseness, typical of extempore speech, characterizes examples like:

He ... knew a great deal of the history and literature of several cultures, especially India.
(*The Listener* 28.4.1977: 551).

What he wants is much more like the situation you have got in the United States ... You can't
have a situation like the United States without having a consensus.
(*The Listener* 28.10.1976: 526).

Another circumstance that probably favours the spread of the zero construction
is the fact that in spoken English there is identity between the plurals and the
genitive plurals of most nouns. If an examiner asks a candidate: 'Is Achebe's use of
proverbs different from other ['raitəz]?' it would be hard to tell whether the
transcribed form is to be *writers* or *writers'*. Numerous such ambiguous examples
may be met with in a magazine like *The Listener,* where the choice between
genitive and zero is a question of the presence or absence of an apostrophe. A
typical example is the following, and in this connexion one may well doubt
whether the speaker's manuscript contained an apostrophe; if it did, it may have
dropped out in the printing:

Well, it may be that the social revolutionaries included politically inactive people, but that
implies a judgment just as reckless as any of the whisky-drinking newshounds, on the Western
front.
(*The Listener* 4.12.1975: 753).

– in other words, the ambiguity of spoken English may lead to the abandoning of
what is after all merely a typographical nicety.

It is a well-documented fact that the longer a construction is, the more probable
are breaches of numerical concord; see on this for instance Juul (1975: 117).
Similarly there is a strong tendency for the zero construction to occur in long
sentences cut in half by parentheses:

But Donald Sinden said: 'I think the most perfect English spoken today, for my ear, is (she may
be a friend of yours, I think she's miraculous) Patricia Hughes, announcer on Radio Three.'
(*The Listener* 13.5.1976: 610).

As was pointed out above, most occurrences of the zero construction are seen to
involve a lopsided comparison if viewed in the cool hindsight of logico-
grammatical analysis. However, in the heat and haste of language generation,
zero constructions are normally unsurprising to the listener or reader provided
they are not seriously ambiguous. This is true of an example like:

The voice I'd heard was Doctor McCabe on the hall telephone.
(Thomas Hinde, *Games of Chance,* London (Corgi), 1967: 142).

although the moment one begins to tamper with language, one may come up with
a doubtful transform like *Who is that voice.* – The fictional rendering of colloquial

speech or thought often involves the avoidance of a cumbrous construction, producing instead a result like the following:

... I could swear Ron's teeth chattered just like that old cat we once had when it saw sparrows fluttering outside the window ...
(Wallace Hildick, *Bracknell's Law,* London, 1976: 168).

It is interesting to note that one may sometimes come across constructions which can be interpreted either as representing the zero construction or as instances of verbal ellipsis; consider the following:

He must have begun carving when style was dominated by the violent twisting rhythms of Cluny and Toulouse; and he has created a style as still and restrained and classical as the Greek sculptors of the sixth century.
(Kenneth Clark, *Civilisation,* London, 1974: 55).

'A style as ... classical as the Greek sculptors created' or 'a style as ... classical as that of the Greek sculptors'? Either would make sense.

In other cases we may find a zero construction which involves the writer's changing his point of view in mid-sentence (unless, of course, he is merely being slipshod); but not much harm is done provided his meaning remains clear. Thus, in the quotation that follows it does not seem to matter a lot whether the reference is to the fate of a person or to that person himself:

If a young girl or boy is kidnapped or driven out, and the thread of the narrative is linked to his or her fate and not to those who remain behind, then the hero of the tale is, in effect, the kidnapped boy or young girl.
(V. Propp, *Morphology of the Folktale,* tr. Laurence Scott: *International Journal of American Linguistics,* 24, 1958: 34).

Sometimes, however, there may be more serious epistemological uncertainty:

Her shadow, reflected on the ceiling, monstrous and overpowering like a witch, seemed part of the heavy curtains ...
(Daphne du Maurier, *The Scapegoat,* London (Pan), 1975: 274).

Was her shadow compared with a witch, or with that of a witch? In this case the question seems barely worth pondering, but possibly the example shows a writer taking refuge in an ambiguous construction, opting for the line of least resistance.

It is time for a final assessment of the zero construction. I hope I have demonstrated that it occurs quite frequently in several varieties of English, although it must be said to be most widespread in informal spoken English and in the rendering of this. It would be too sweeping a statement to assert that the zero construction is invariably slovenly; it would be more resonable to say that its degree of acceptability depends in large measure on the context in which it appears. A genitive construction is sometimes ruled out, and if the language-user is faced with the choice between a *that of* and a zero construction, he may well instinctively avoid the former in some cases because it might have an unduly pedantic effect. A related phenomenon may be seen in one of the uses of *beyond* (cf. the *OED* (I, 842, 10)). A statement like *I went a step beyond Whiston* may be paraphrased 'I went a step beyond the point to which Whiston went', but it would be a pedantic paraphrase; and in many contexts nobody but the diehard pedant would stop to frown on this use of *beyond*.

Note

1. A similar construction occurred in Classical Greek: κόμαι χαρίτεσσιν ὁμοῖαι (*The Iliad* XVIII.51), and it is not infrequent in modern Danish: *en domsprofeti, der ikke står tilbage for de gamle helvedesprædikanter* ...

References

Fowler, H.W. (1965), *A Dictionary of Modern English Usage,* second edition, revised by Sir Ernest Gowers. (Oxford).

Juul, A. (1975), *On Concord of Number in Modern English.* (Publications of the Department of English, University of Copenhagen. Volume 1). (Nova, Copenhagen).

Poutsma, H. (1926), *A Grammar of Late Modern English,* I. (Groningen).

Quirk, R., S. Greenbaum, G. Leech, J. Svartvik (1972), *A Grammar of Contemporary English.* (London).

Robinson, F.N. (ed.) (1957), *The Works of Geoffrey Chaucer,* second edition. (Oxford).

Schibsbye, K. (1970), *A Modern English Grammar,* second edition. (Oxford).

SOME OBSERVATIONS ON PRONOMINALIZATION

Pronominalization may be viewed as, first of all, an economical textual device. But there are limits to its use: where ambiguity might arise, pronominalization tends to be avoided, and there are other constraints on its use. What I shall do in this article is to present some facts, followed by more or less tentative explanations.

My primary concern is with those cases where there is alternation between the sequence *nominal ... coreferential personal or possessive pronoun* and the sequence *pronoun ... nominal*. The principal area of interest here is the *complex* sentence in which a subordinate clause precedes its main clause. As a type example we may take

(1) When *John* came home, *he* had a cup of tea, or
(2) When *he* came home, *John* had a cup of tea

But where the main clause precedes, we normally only have

(3) *John* had a cup of tea when *he* came home

and in a *compound* sentence (consisting of two [or more] main clauses) the nominal also normally has to come first:

(4) *John* came home, and *he* had a cup of tea

In order to account for the difference between complex and compound sentences I adopt John Lyons's suggestion that 'a complex sentence is a grammatically more cohesive unit than a compound sentence'.[1] As for the difference between the two kinds of complex sentence (with the subordinate clause either preceding or following its main clause), I would suggest that there is a greater degree of sentence cohesion where the subordinate clause precedes its main clause than where the reverse is the case. Or, to put it differently: if the subordinate clause comes first, we are forced to be attentive, we are kept in suspense till we have heard or read the main clause; this suspense reflects a special form of cohesion which makes it possible to defer the question of identity (of coreferentiality or non-coreferentiality) till the main clause.

My attention was first drawn to the problem when it struck me that some translations from English into Danish contained somewhat odd-looking examples of pronouns preceding their nominals, in other words cataphoric pronouns. Now cataphoric pronouns are decidedly rare in normal Danish,

[1] John Lyons, *Semantics*, vol. 2, (1977), p. 661.

and it can hardly be doubted that they must be considered anglicisms where they occur to any appreciable extent (as in news-items with English-language sources or in a practically bilingual writer like Karen Blixen [Isak Dinesen]). But how widespread are cataphoric pronouns in English? Prescriptivists discourage their use; thus Fowler: 'The pronoun should seldom precede its principal'[2] and Gowers: 'It is usually better not to allow a pronoun to precede its principal'.[3] Sometimes the existence of cataphoric pronouns is even passed over in complete silence: 'Pronouns ... take their identity from a noun which comes before them, and which they refer to ...'.[4] It is obvious that such prescriptivist pronouncements tell us nothing whatsoever about how widespread the phenomenon is.

In so far as grammarians take up the problem at all, they are not in agreement. While Zandvoort asserts[5] that 'the personal pronouns of the third person are chiefly used anaphorically ...', Schibsbye maintains[6] that 'the personal pronoun very frequently precedes the noun represented ...'

These conflicting statements led me to undertake my own little investigation. The text I chose was J. R. R. Tolkien's *The Lord of the Rings*[7] (which will be supplemented by examples from other texts). An analysis of 50 pages of *Lord* (pp. 662-711) showed that where the order of main and subordinate clauses could be inverted, there were 79 cases of main preceding subordinate clause, as against 96 cases of subordinate preceding main clause. But the majority of these 96 cases are irrelevant from the present point of view, for various reasons:

(a) In some, the same pronoun occurs in both clauses;
(b) Sentences containing first and second person pronouns are of course also irrelevant; and
(c) In many cases there is no coreference between the items of the subordinate clause and those of the main clause.

Of the total of 96 examples with the subordinate clause preceding its main clause, (a), (b), and (c) together account for 80 cases. This leaves 16 relevant instances, and of these there are 10 examples of anaphoric pronouns, 6 of cataphoric pronouns. This corresponds roughly to the distribution over the whole book (1,077 pages), where I have counted 96 examples of anaphoric pronouns as against 65 of cataphoric pronouns. Roughly, then, for every 3 cataphoric pronouns there are 5 anaphoric ones. It would, however, be rash to attach undue importance to these figures; a larger material should be analysed. There are bound to be fluctuations dependent on the idiosyncrasies of individual writers. Here are a few supplementary figures:

[2] H. W. Fowler, *A Dictionary of Modern English Usage*, second ed. revised by Sir Ernest Gowers, (1965), p. 482.
[3] Sir Ernest Gowers, *The Complete Plain Words*, (London, 1954), p. 146.
[4] Donald Hall, *Writing Well*, (1979), p. 315.
[5] R. W. Zandvoort, *A Handbook of English Grammar*, (1957), p. 130.
[6] Knud Schibsbye, *A Modern English Grammar*, (1965), p. 181.
[7] London 1968; henceforth referred to as *Lord*.

	nominal — pronoun	pronoun — nominal
Newsweek 18.2.80	25	13
Time 25.2.80	22	10
N. Monsarrat, The Cruel Sea	5	10
I. Murdoch, The Sea, the Sea	3	7

It is obvious that there is scope for variation, and some writers seem to prefer cataphora to anaphora.

In passing it may be noted that there are other elements that are normally anaphoric but which may very occasionally appear in a cataphoric function: the pro-form *do so*:

As to my own story, I have tried to *do so*, but I cannot swear that I have always *told the truth* ... John Knowler, *Trust an Englishman*, Paladin 1974, p. 8.

the pro-form *one*:

She, too, would have a new name and, if she cared for *one, a new identity*. (source lost).

Compare also the cataphoric use of the 'general noun' *man* in

He had, amazed and delighted at *the man's* civility, given *the London porter* a shilling for carrying his bag nearly fifty yards ... R. Kipling, *The Day's Work*, St Martin's Library 1964, p. 268.

If we compare the complex sentences containing anaphoric pronouns with those containing cataphoric pronouns, it may be noted that there are three types of subordinate clause that predominate, viz. temporal, conditional, and concessive clauses. The distribution is as follows in *Lord*:

	anaphoric	cataphoric
temporal clauses	47	39
conditional clauses	34	3
concessive clauses	11	8

As far as temporal and concessive clauses are concerned, then, there is rough correspondence between the anaphoric and the cataphoric use of the pronouns; but where the subordinate clause is conditional, there is a strong tendency for the nominal to precede its pronoun.

In the majority of cases, no matter whether we have to do with anaphoric or with cataphoric pronouns, the coreferential items fill the subject slot in both clauses; but besides, there is occasional coreference between subject and object or prepositional complement; e.g.

(5) and as *Mr. Baggins* was generous with his money, most people were willing to forgive *him* his oddities ... *Lord*, p. 33.
(6) as *they* went on, ... this feeling of insecurity grew on *all the Company*. *Lord*, p. 401.

To this it should be added that adjectival possessives and genitives present a special case: together with their nominals they may establish *partial coreference* with an item in the other clause; e.g.

(7) When *his eyes* were in turn uncovered, *Frodo* looked up ... *Lord*, p. 368.
(8) Then as the dark hole stood before *him* ..., the thought of Frodo ... smote upon Sam's mind. *Lord*, p. 754.

Occasionally a complex sentence may accommodate *two sets* of coreferential items; e.g.

(9) As *Frodo* was borne towards *them the great pillars* rose like towers to meet *him*. *Lord*, p. 413.

This example may be supplemented by examples from other texts:

(10) In the four days since *he* had last seen *him*, *Sorme* had forgotten many things about *Nunne*. Colin Wilson, *Ritual in the Dark*, (Panther, 1976) p. 127.
(11) ... as *he* reads *it the reader* interacts with *the text* ... M. Coulthard, *An Introduction to Discourse Analysis*, (Longman, 1977), p. 180.

This may be the place to consider whether it is possible to point to any factors that condition the choice between anaphoric and cataphoric pronouns. If prescriptivists discourage the use of cataphora, it is probably because they want to prevent ambiguity, and it is of course true that many formulations containing cataphoric pronouns are ambiguous when considered in isolation; e.g.

(12) That *he* had failed was, of course, obvious to *the Colonel*. Patrick White, *Voss*, (Penguin, 1957), p. 427.

where only the context can tell us whether *he* and *the Colonel* are coreferential; but the attentive reader will hardly be in doubt. The wish to avoid ambiguity may be a factor favouring the use of anaphora, but not the only one.

Let us consider example (11) anew:

(11) ... as *he* reads *it the reader* interacts with *the text* ...

It is not hard to think of alternative formulations:

(11a) as *he* reads *the text the reader* interacts with *it* ...
(11b) as *the reader* reads *the text he* interacts with *it* ...
(11c) as *the reader* reads *it he* interacts with *the text* ...

All these are grammatical, but in my view they are not equally acceptable from a *stylistic* point of view, the last two being less euphonious than the others. *Euphony* is a factor, and *rhythm* is another. Unfortunately, rhythm is a somewhat elusive concept, but I suggest that it was the writer's rhythmical considerations that dictated the following formulation:

(13) It could be claimed that since *they* vary considerably in length *the stanzas in 'Sir Gawain and the Green Knight'* are simply formalized paragraphs. N. F. Blake, *The English Language in Medieval Literature*, (London, 1979), p. 65.

An acceptable rhythm can hardly be separated from a proper *semantic distribution*. I should like to illustrate this by taking a look at a special kind of concessive clause:

(14) Tired as *he* was *Merry* could not sleep. *Lord*, p. 862.
(15) Puzzle as *they* might, *the prisoners* could not make out the function of this building ...B. Aldiss, *Enemies of the System*, (London, 1978), p. 86.
(16) and try as *they* would, *the U-boats* could no longer break through in any decisive sense ... N. Monsarrat, *The Cruel Sea*, (Penguin, 1964), p. 342.

As mentioned before, I am concerned with those cases where there is alternation between anaphora and cataphora, and I am not asserting that it would be impossible to find anaphoric pronouns in the type of example just given, though I have not found any, and my informants query my made-up examples. What I would suggest is that there is a strong tendency for this special kind of concessive clause to have a cataphoric pronoun, and that this may be due to the writer's (perhaps subconscious) endeavour to establish an even semantic distribution over the whole complex sentence. The concessive clause opens with an item that owing to its position is given extra strong emphasis, and therefore the nominal — which I take to be weightier than the pronoun — is placed in the main clause. If this explanation is correct, we may consider the following example in a corresponding light:

(17) If I was after the Ring, I could have it — NOW! *Lord*, p. 187.

Here, each of the two clauses has been assigned its semantic heavyweight, *the Ring* and *NOW*.

The principle of *end-weight* seems to have been operative in an example like

(18) as *they* went on, borne steadily southwards, this feeling of insecurity grew on *all the Company*. *Lord*, p. 401.

An *indefinite nominal* tends to appear first, followed by its anaphoric pronoun:

(19) if *a traveller* followed the road that turned west of Ephel Dúath, *he* would come in time to a crossing ... *Lord*, p. 667.

But we also find cataphoric pronouns, as in

(20) once *he* was in uniform *a man* had to do exactly what he was told ... N. Monsarrat, *The Cruel Sea*, p. 171.

In the last example *a man* is roughly equal to *every man* or *everybody*. Indefinite nominals with this semantic import are readily compatible with a peripheral use of the personal pronouns (as in *Everyone should do what he considers best*). In their central application, however, the personal pronouns are definite — hence probably the oddness of cataphoric *it* in

(150)

(21) Under the bush, so that *it* only became visible when the constable pulled the branches aside, there was *a square of maroon cloth*. Colin Wilson, *The Schoolgirl Murder Case*, (London, 1975), p. 5.

where *a square of* ... has one specific referent.

Some *prepositional phrases* may be said to be roughly equivalent to subordinate clauses. If a sentence is opened by a prepositional phrase containing an item that is coreferential with an item that occurs later in the sentence, the exponency of the first occurrence of that item may vacillate. Consider the example

(22) With *their* conversion to Christianity, *the Vikings* forged new links ... J. Graham-Campbell & D. Kidd, *The Vikings*, (London 1980), p. 58.

When I asked three native informants to comment on a version of (22) that I had tampered with, viz.:

(22a) With *the Vikings'* conversion to Christianity, *they* forged new links ...

comments ranged from 'acceptable' via 'doubtful' to 'unacceptable'; one informant found this version grammatically acceptable but textually doubtful. This is probably as far as we can get towards an explanation: there is nothing ungrammatical about the presence of the nominal in the prepositional phrase, witness authentic examples like

(23) Throughout *Breznev*'s career, *he* has acted in a blunt and unsubtle way ... *Newsweek* 24.3.80, p. 8.
(24) Despite *Thatcher*'s diplomatic style, no one, except the French, denies that *she* has a case. *Time* 31.3.80, p. 12.

where for rhythmical reasons one might well have expected the pronouns to appear first. This seems to be obligatory in an example like

(25) On *his* way to school *John* met a friend

possibly because *on his way* is short and formulaic. By contrast, it is the length and weight of the nominal that forces it into second position in

(26) In *his* only interview with an American reporter last week, *Iranian President Abolhassan Bani Sadr* spelled out his position on the release of the American hostages. *Newsweek* 25.2.80, p. 14.

where the alternative version would definitely be stylistically poorer.

Cataphora alternates with anaphora in *defining relative clauses*. Anaphora is too well-known to call for exemplification, but here are a couple of instances showing cataphora:

(27) The title *he* earned last week is one that *Joe Clark* has coveted since his boyhood days ... *Time* 4.6.79, p. 18.
(28) '... It looks as if the chap who sold *it* gave *the bottle* the usual wipe over before wrapping ...' P. D. James, *Shroud for a Nightingale*, (London, 1971), p. 51.

There is one further sentence-type that calls for brief comment; it consists of the beginning of a main clause, followed by an intercalated subordinate clause and by the rest of the main clause:

(29) I also found, though I was not looking for *it, a touching (too touching) picture of my father* ... Iris Murdoch, *The Sea, the Sea*, (Penguin, 1979), p. 170.
(30) I noticed, because *its* appearance caught my eye, *a letter with a London postmark addressed to Mr C. Arrowby* ... ibid. p. 490.

It may be noted that with this syntactic arrangement cataphora is the only possibility, owing to the length and weight of the object. There appears to be no clash here between the definiteness of the pronoun and the indefiniteness of the nominal.

When a main clause precedes a temporal, conditional, or concessive subordinate clause, there is normally no choice: the nominal appears in the main clause. But very occasionally one may come across a cataphoric personal pronoun in this construction:

(31) There was a note for *him* lying on the hall table when *Dr Bickleigh* came in to lunch. Francis Iles, *Malice Aforethought*, (Penguin, 1979), p. 43.
(32) Like most of her comrades-in-waiting, Betty Kirtley of Little Rock, Ark., merely wants to 'spoil *him* to death' with home cooking when *her hostage son* finally returns. *Newsweek* 25.2.80, p. 18.

It is difficult to account for the cataphoric pronoun in (31); in (32) it is presumably the writer's wish to incorporate a quotation that is responsible for the unusual formulation. Such examples must be considered exceptional.

On the other hand we do find alternation between adjectival possessives and genitives in main clauses followed by object clauses; here are two examples containing cataphoric possessives:

(33) *His* aides believe that *Kennedy* draws most blood when he assails Carter ... *Time* 25.2.80, p. 11.
(34) *Her* lawyer says that *Mrs Wilson* has been caught by the two-year rule ... *The Guardian* 25.2.80, p. 2.

It is difficult to explain the difference here, if any; but in other cases it is obvious that the cataphoric possessive has been placed in the main clause because the alternative formulation would lead to stylistic clumsiness:

(35) We know from *their* names that *some moneyers of Viking coins* were of Frankish or Anglo-Saxon origin ... *The Vikings*, p. 122.

Possessives may also alternate with genitives in simple main clauses; here are a few examples of cataphoric possessives:

(36) Only *her* naval supremacy saved *England* ... A. S. Turberville & F. A. Howe, *Great Britain in the Latest Age*, (London, 1921), p. 5.
(37) The news of *their* inheritance did not elate *the boys* ... John Cheever, *The Wapshot Chronicle*, (New York, 1959), p. 53.
(38) *His* party brings down *Ohira*. Time 26.5.80, p. 21.

Why is it that a cataphoric possessive should often be preferred to a nominal in the genitive in such examples? One suggestion that could be made is that this choice pushes the nominal to or towards the end of the clause, which is normally the area of greatest semantic weight. In other cases a possessive may be preferred to avoid stylistic clumsiness:

(39) One day *his* father took *Colin* with him on a bus to the city. David Storey, *Saville*, (London, 1976), p. 41.

This formulation avoids the not very euphonious alternative: ... *took him with him* ...

A few words about *co-ordinate main clauses*. Here anaphora is the rule:

(40) *John* promised to come, but *he* didn't

In *journalese*, however, and occasionally elsewhere, some writers resort to the trick of placing a personal pronoun with cataphoric function in the first clause, only giving its coreferential nominal in the second. This is particularly often done at the beginning of an article, presumably to arouse the reader's curiosity:

(41) *They* cover Peking and Paris and most points in between. But last week, *the staff of the prestigious, employee-operated newspaper Le Monde* was making news instead of reporting it. *Newsweek* 10.3.80, p. 27.

The formulation of this passage was probably also dictated by the writer's wish to avoid overloading the first clause with an extremely heavy and content-packed subject. A further example:

(42) *He* may not represent the U.S. at the United Nations any more, but that does not mean that *Andrew Young* has slowed his pace ... *Time* 25.2.80, p. 34.

Finally, here is an instance rendering everyday speech:

(43) 'I hate to bring *him* up once more on such a lovely day,' she said, 'but *my husband* actually used to pat me on the head ...' Wilfred Sheed, *Square's Progress*, (London, 1965), p. 166.

A further point that may be relevant here is the following: common to these examples is the fact that there is a contrast between the content of the first and the second clause, manifested through a *but*. It would seem, then, that the presence of such a contrast is one condition of this use of cataphora.

My discussion has concentrated on examples considered in isolation, and that is probably where one ought to start. But it is obvious that since the choice between anaphora and cataphora is largely determined by stylistic — or textual — considerations, one ought also to look at pronominalization as it manifests itself in longer passages, in texts. This approach makes it obvious that operating with degrees of cohesive tolerance is onesided; for if a given text discusses a certain concept or a certain person, the problem is not one of establishing identities — that has already been done. The stylistic problem becomes how to effect a suitable alternation between nominal and pronoun — suitable in at least two respects: monotony should be avoided, and an effective semantic distribution — effective Communicative Dynamism[8] — should be achieved. Here is a longish example showing how a journalist has solved the problem:

Diplomats who have known *him* agree that *Gromyko* has a prodigious mind and a file-cabinet memory. *He* works without notes, but, warns one Western ambassador, *he* is the master of any assignment. 'If you sit down with *him* without doing your homework, you're a dead duck. *He* knows it all and *he*'ll cut you to pieces.' *He* has an excellent if heavily accented command of English, but usually chooses to speak through an interpreter. *He* also has enormous patience; *he* can stonewall on an issue for session after session of negotiations, a practice that is often interpreted correctly as a signal that the Kremlin is simply not ready to move.

What puzzles *his* Western counterparts is the question of just how much *Gromyko* shapes the Soviet Union's foreign affairs, and just how much *he* is chained to policy designed by others. Khrushchev, who often belittled his Foreign Minister, once crudely boasted that if he ordered *Gromyko* to drop his trousers and sit on a cake of ice, *Gromyko* would dutifully oblige. *Time* 26.5.80, p. 11.

The occurrence of a proper name twice at the end of the above quotation may seem strange, and it conveniently takes me to my final point, which is a brief discussion of some cases where *pronominalization is absent*. When the same referent is brought up more than once in the same context, pronominalization is of course the rule. We do not normally find for instance '*John* felt ill, and so *John* stayed in bed'. And yet there are cases where the repetition of a nominal is preferred to pronominalization. As Stig Johansson states: 'Instead of using a personal pronoun to refer to a previous noun phrase, SE [= learned and scientific English] often prefers a repetition of the original noun phrase'.[9] And Gowers points out[10] that — presumably to prevent ambiguity — legal language is more sparing of pronouns than ordinary prose. However, we may also find repetition of nominals outside technical registers, though it must be emphasized that such repetition is the marked choice. But 'marked' in what sense? Dwight Bolinger says about a formulation like '*Mary* wants to eat my soup but *Mary* isn't going to get the chance': 'I suspect that this is a side effect of the repetition of a personal name as a kind of reproof'.[11] I quite agree with Bolinger, but would add to his 'reproof' than in a given context the repetition of personal names may convey ironical overtones as well; cf.

(44) *Mr Crabbe* was dead as mutton, but *Mr Crabbe* continued to write moral stories in rhymed couplets. W. S. Maugham, *The Moon and Sixpence*, (Penguin, 1955), p. 12.

[8] Cf. e. g. F. Daneš, *Papers on Functional Sentence Perspective*, (The Hague, 1974).
[9] Stig Johansson, *Some Aspects of the Vocabulary of Learned and Scientific English*, Gothenburg Studies in English 42 (1978), p. 32.
[10] Op. cit. p. 145.
[11] Dwight Bolinger, *Meaning and Form*, (1977), p. 7.

(45) *Julius II* was not only ambitious for the Catholic Church: he was ambitious for *Julius II*. K. Clark, *Civilization*, (London, 1974), p. 126.

In these examples we have repetition of personal names; but it also occurs with other nominals, and where this is the case, what is conveyed is simply a strong degree of emphasis:

(46) *Death* had been perfectly consistent with *morphia poisoning*, because *death* had been due to *morphia poisoning*. Francis Iles, *Malice Aforethought*, (Penguin, 1979), p. 181.

(47) *Help* was on the way — new weapons, more escorts, more aircraft, but *help* did not come in time ... N. Monsarrat, *The Cruel Sea*, p. 116.

TG grammarians who have written on pronominalization[12] repeatedly make the point that such and such a construction is not equally acceptable to all native speakers of English, and the native informants I asked to comment on some of my examples disagreed in several cases over acceptability. It is obvious that pronominalization constitutes an area of uncertainty. Not only has it been incompletely mapped so far, but even where some mapping has been carried out, there is by no means always a consensus as to acceptability. I believe there is a lot of truth in Bolinger's view[13] that there is no difference in form without some difference in meaning, but even if one accepts this principle, it may not be easy to define the semantic differences involved. While I was working with these problems, I was often reminded of Halliday's statement: 'Language, unlike mathematics, is not clearcut or precise. It is a natural human creation, and, like many other natural human creations, it is inherently messy'.[14]

[12] Among them:
A. Akmajian & R. Jackendoff, 'Coreferentiality and Stress', *Linguistic Inquiry* 1 (1970), pp. 124-6.
D. J. Allerton, 'Deletion and Proform Reduction', *Journal of Linguistics* 11 (1975), pp. 213-37.
Peter Cole, 'Indefiniteness and Anaphoricity', *Language* 50, pp. 665-74.
S. Kuno, 'Functional Sentence Perspective', *Linguistic Inquiry* 3 (1972), p. 302.
R. W. Langacker, 'On Pronominalization and the Chain of Command', in Reibel & Schane (eds), *Modern Studies in English*. Readings in Transformational Grammar, 1969.
R. B. Lees & E. S. Klima, 'Rules for English Pronominalization', *Language* 39 (1963), pp. 17-28.
Paul M. Postal, *Cross-Over Phenomena*, (1971).
J. R. Ross, 'On the Cyclic Nature of English Pronominalization', In Reibel & Schane.
[13] Op. cit., passim.
[14] M. A. K. Halliday, *Language as Social Semiotic*, (London, 1978), p. 203.

THE GROWTH OF CATAPHORIC PERSONAL AND POSSESSIVE PRONOUNS IN ENGLISH

I had better begin with a reservation. The historical development of pronominal cataphora in English seems to have been largely neglected. Consequently, I have tried to examine as many texts as there was time for. I have dirtied myself with data – but probably not sufficient data. Therefore, what I have to present here should be regarded as my provisional findings.

Perhaps it may be useful to start with a brief presentation of pronominal cataphora in contemporary English[1]. There are various types. Let me mention a few that I am *not* going to include in my discussion.

There is the type containing a cataphoric possessive in coreference with a nominal of the same clause: 'Only *her* naval supremacy saved *England*.' This type is at least as old as Shakespeare, who has: 'Call all *his* noble captains to *my lord*'. (*Anthony and Cleopatra* 3.13.189).

There is the sentence type consisting of a *that* clause followed by its main clause: 'That *he* had failed was, of course, obvious to *the Colonel*,' where only the context can tell us whether *he* and *the Colonel* are coreferential.

There is the type that opens with a prepositional phrase containing an item that is coreferential with an item that occurs later in the clause: 'With *their* conversion to Christianity, *the Vikings* forged new links ...' Does this alternate with 'With *the Vikings'* conversion to Christianity, *they* forged new links'? It does, in principle; however, native informants I asked disagreed over the acceptability of the latter formulation. – I mention these types – others might have been added – simply in order to suggest that pronominal cataphora covers a wide (and largely unexplored) field. Here I want to concentrate on another type: the complex sentence construction in which an adverbial subordinate clause precedes its main clause, where nominal and pronoun are coreferential, and there is alternation between anaphoric and cataphoric pronouns. Thus we find alternation between

When *he* came home, *John* had a cup of tea, and
When *John* came home, *he* had a cup of tea.

Further, we find alternation between

When *his* parents arrived, *John* told them what had happened, and
When *John's* parents arrived, *he* told them ...

In the latter pair, an adjectival possessive or a genitive establishes partial coreference with an item in the main clause. Let me add that the most frequent subordinate clauses are temporal, concessive, or conditional, and that I include in my material the expanded type containing sub-clauses governed – or dominated – by one of the two constituent clauses; for instance:

1. ... when *he* entered the large hut ..., I was somewhat afraid that the impatient violence of *my companion* might procure us an indifferent reception. (W. Scott, *Redgauntlet*, p. 132)

After this brief presentation it may be asked what, if anything, we can learn from grammarians about pronominal cataphora. If we turn to the early English grammarians, it is not so strange that we should find them stating without reservation that personal pronouns are anaphoric (to put it in modern terms); for these grammarians were strongly influenced by Latin grammar, which has no exact parallel to the modern English cataphoric construction; and though it did occur, cataphora was decidedly rare in early English. One of the earliest English grammarians, William Lily, states in his *Shorte Introduction of Grammar* of 1567 that (personal) pronouns 'rehearse [= repeat] a thing that was spoken of before'[2], and this statement is frequently repeated over the centuries. Lindley Murray, in his *English Grammar* of 1795, makes the general statement that 'Whatever leaves the mind in any sort of suspense as to the meaning, ought to be avoided with great care'[3]. He may or may not have been thinking of pronominal usage, but elsewhere in his book he introduces a reservation, saying: 'Sometimes, however, when we intend to give weight to a sentence, it is of advantage to suspend the meaning for a little, and then bring it out full at the close'[4]. Here again it does not appear what specific phenomena he has in mind; but later on I hope to show the relevance of this latter statement of Murray's. Even today one may come across a statement like the following: 'Pronouns ... take their identity from a noun which comes before them, and which they refer to ...'[5] – There does exist an extensive TG literature on the subject of cataphora in modern English[6], but I am not sure how much of it I have understood. Two things about it have struck me, however; nowhere does one find any mention of the frequency of cataphora today; and TG grammarians repeatedly make the point that there is no consensus as to acceptability. This corresponds to my own experience, and it means that if one concentrates – as I have done – on those cases where there would seem to be alternation between anaphora and cataphora, one sometimes grows doubtful: pronominalization is an area of uncertainty.

If we turn to contemporary traditional grammarians, we shall find that they are not always in agreement about the frequency of cataphora. Thus Zandvoort states that 'The personal pronouns of the third person are chiefly used anaphorically ...'[7], while Schibsbye maintains that 'the personal pronoun very frequently precedes the noun represented'[8]. While grammarians may thus apparently differ, prescriptivists like Fowler and Gowers agree in discouraging the use of cataphora, probably because it may lead to ambiguity[9].

Before I embark on a diachronic examination of the problem, it should perhaps be pointed out that it is by no means all occurrences of the sentence type I have analysed that are relevant. In the first place, sentences containing first and second person pronouns are of course irrelevant, and so are sentences showing no coreference between items in the two clauses. But even where there is coreference, this has to be manifested by a nominal and a pronoun (or the inverse order); from my point of view it is no good finding two identical pronouns or – occasionally – two identical nominals. Rough statistics from contemporary English suggest that these irrelevant examples constitute some 80 per cent of the total number of complex sentences consisting of a subordinate clause preceding its main clause. Hence the comparative paucity of relevant examples.

Pronominal cataphora is very rare in Old[10] and Middle English. I have come across a single instance in Ælfric:

2. Þa ða *he* into ðam wætere éóde. ða wæs ðæt wæter and ealle wyllspringas gehalgode þurh *cristes* lichaman ... (*Catholic Homilies*, 2nd ser., EETS 1979, p. 22)

Although I haven't been able to trace any source here, Ælfric might well have been translating from Latin, whose sentence construction, if rendered slavishly, might explain the Old English formulation. That this sort of translation *is* a factor to be reckoned with becomes clear from the Old and Middle English renderings of the following passage from the Bible:

3. Et factum est cum accumberet in domo illius multi publicani et peccatores simul discumbebant cum *Iesu* et discipulis eius ... (Mark 2,15, *Vulgate*, ed. R. Weber, 1969)

   And hit gewearð, þa *he* sæt on his huse, þæt manega manfulle sæton mid *þam Hælende* and his leorningcnihtum ... (*The Gospels in West Saxon*, ed. J.W.Bright, 1905-10)

   And it was doon, whanne *he* sat at the mete in his hous, many pupplicans and synful men saten togidere at the mete with *Jhesu* and hise disciplis ... (Wyclif, late version, Forshall-Madden 1850)

In unmarked Latin contexts the subject is implied by the verb, and in a verbatim translation into English a pronominal subject is naturally supplied. Let me add that I have come across a single independent Middle English example:

4. For how *hit* evere be ywonne, but hit wel despeneth,
   Worldly wele ys wykked thyng to hem that hit kepeth.
   (*Piers Plowmann*, C Text, XIII 95-6, Salter & Pearsall p. 124)

However, independent examples of cataphora in Old and Middle English are few and far between. In due course I shall return to the problem of the origin of cataphora, but it would be unnatural not to anticipate a bit here by pointing to one possible source of cataphora in English: slavish Biblical translation from the Latin. But it is interesting to note that the King James version of 1611 treats the Mark passage differently:

And it came to pass, that, as *Jesus* sat at meat in his house, many publicans and sinners sat also together with *Jesus*...

This formulation may be due to a less degree of slavishness.

The cataphoric construction occurs sporadically in early Modern English. Shakespeare has it in a few passages, for instance:

5.   ... 'cause *he* fail'd
His presence at the tyrant's feast, I hear,
Macduff lives in disgrace. (*Macbeth* 3.6.21-3)

6.   But that *it* eats our victuals, I should think
Here were a *fairy* . (*Cymbeline* 3.7.13-4)

It may of course be objected that owing to the exigencies of the metre, poetic examples are not on a par with prose ones; this is true enough, but the objection hardly applies to an example like

7.   When *they* are thirsty, *fools* would fain have drink. (*Love's Labour's Lost* 5.2.372)

For the Modern English period I have examined a number of texts, each comprising 300 pages, with roughly 25-year intervals, to see if there are any significant changes in the relative frequencies of anaphora and cataphora. Here are my findings:

	anaphora	cataphora
Bacon, *The Advancement of Learning* 1605 (268 pp.)	26	0
Hobbes, *Leviathan* 1651	65	6
Locke, *Some Thoughts Concerning Education* 1705	83	18
Swift, *Gulliver's Travels* 1726	24	2
Fielding, *Tom Jones* 1749	97	16
Johnson, *The Rambler* 1750-2	49	0
Gibbon, *Decline and Fall of the Roman Empire* I 1776	115	9
Jane Austen, *Sense and Sensibility* c. 1800	54	6
Scott, *Redgauntlet* 1824	50	7
Dickens, *Dombey and Son* 1848	50	15
Hardy, *Far from the Madding Crowd* 1874	17	11
Butler, *The Way of All Flesh*	73	12
Wells, *The World of William Clissold* 1926	14	4
Waugh, *Men at Arms* 1952	6	9

What, if anything, can we learn from these figures? They hardly suggest any clear development of cataphora in the course of the Modern English period, although it must be said that in the period as a whole they are much more frequent than in the two earlier periods. But in most of these writers cataphora is the minority construction. One point that can be suggested is that the incidence of cataphora seems to depend, first of all, on the individual writer's idiosyncrasy. There appears to be no correlation between frequency and genre. But possibly the material is not large enough.

The above may be supplemented by some figures from contemporary literature. In. J.R.R. Tolkien's *The Lord of the Rings* (nearly 1,100 pages) I have counted 96 examples of anaphoric pronouns as against 65 cataphoric pronouns; roughly, then, for every 5 cases of anaphora there are 3 of cataphora in this sentence type. Some modern novelists actually seem to prefer cataphora. Thus, Nicholas Monsarrat's *The Cruel Sea* (1964) has 5 examples of anaphora, 10 of cataphora, and in Iris Murdoch's *The Sea, the Sea* (1978) the figures are 3 and 7, respectively.

As mentioned, my material only comprises those passages in which – as far as I can judge – a writer might have chosen either anaphora or cataphora, but that does not mean that either construction is always equally acceptable from a stylistic point of view. I shall turn now to some factors that appear to be influential in the choice between the two constructions.

Up till now I have been treating the complex sentence (consisting of a subordinate clause preceding its main clause) as if it occurred in isolation. In many cases this is too simplistic, though one has to begin somewhere. I do, however, want to make the point that if one looks at the larger context, this can often account for the presence of cataphora. Consider the following:

8.   *The beloved son of Marcus* succeeded (A.D. 180) to his father, amidst the acclamations of the senate and armies, and when *he* ascended the throne, *the happy youth* saw round him neither competitor to remove, nor enemies to punish. (Gibbon I p. 77)

This instance of cataphora should not be viewed in isolation, since Gibbon may well have resorted to the construction for the sake of *textual variation* (it goes without saying that a given context might equally well favour anaphora).

If we consider the syntactico-semantic characteristics of nominals that are coreferential with pronouns, a number of points emerge. In the first place, if a nominal functions in the *subject slot,* its likelihood of appearing in a cataphoric construction (i.e., in the main clause) is greater than in other functions. Next, the coreference holding between pronoun and nominal normally presupposes full semantic concord. Now there is a peripheral use of the personal pronouns which makes them readily compatible with indefinite nominals, as in 'Everyone should do as he considers best'. But in their central application the personal pronouns are *definite,* and therefore, in their cataphoric function they are usually coreferential with definite nominals, very often proper names. If, nevertheless, formally indefinite plurals do sometimes appear in construction with cataphoric pronouns, as in

9.   Whether it is that *they* are as much bored with the day [Sunday] as their neighbours ..., *clergymen* are seldom at their best on Sunday evening ... (Butler, *The Way of All Flesh,* p. 109)

it is because they are used generically – here: 'all clergymen'.

We are dealing with factors that are less than absolute – perhaps 'tendencies' would be a better term. One such tendency, to be observed in good writers, is their endeavour to achieve an *effective semantic distribution,* or Communicative Dynamism. The trouble with this criterion is that it is difficult to operate with it in isolation. In the first place it impinges on what I said earlier about textual variation, and it is also bound up with *euphony, rhythm,* and the principle of *end-weight.* But let me exemplify. Consider the following:

10. ... Young as *he* is, *the lad*'s notions of moral rectitude I defy you ever to eradicate. (Fielding, *Tom Jones,* p. 116)

As I see it, the concessive clause here has extra strong emphasis owing to the initial position of the predicative *young,* and that may be the reason why the writer chose to put the lightweight pronoun *he* in a clause that already had enough emphasis, relegating the nominal to the main clause.

Next I give an example showing how the choice of cataphora helps at the same time to produce an attractive rhythm and to place a weighty nominal where it has most impact: near the end of the sentence (this may have been what Lindley Murray was thinking of when he advised writers sometimes to 'suspend the meaning for a little, and then bring it out full at the close'):

11. ... had I not seriously and from my heart believed *it* might be of service, might lessen her regrets, I would not have suffered myself to trouble you with *this account of my family afflictions* ... (Jane Austen, *Sense and Sensibility,* p. 168f.)

Next, let us consider some factors that tend to *block cataphora* – or in other words, to favour anaphora. I have already touched on definiteness as the usual requirement for nouns to occur in cataphoric constructions. Hence the anaphora of

12. when *a great prize* happens to be drawn, the newspapers are presently filled with *it* ... (Fielding, *Tom Jones,* p. 41)

is the expected construction. So, if the definiteness requirement is the norm, it is a bit surprising to find cataphora in

13. ... Miss Nugent never saw him but at breakfast or dinner; and, though she watched for *it* most anxiously, never could find *an opportunity of speaking to him alone* ... (Maria Edgeworth, *The Absentee,* 1812, p. 289)

But it may perhaps be assumed that in this formulation it is the principle of end-weight that is victorious (alternatively one might say that a heavily modified nominal tends *not* to appear in the subordinate clause).

Occasionally, however, one may find cataphora where an indefinite nominal is unmodified – and in a rendering of spoken English:

14. ... If I could have hoped to train *him,* I would have bought *a Lion* instead of that dog, and would have turned him loose upon the first intolerable robber ... (Dickens, *Bleak House,* p. 248)

The only explanation I can think of is that here Dickens deliberately deviates from normal usage in order to heighten dramatic tension.

But too harsh a shock to the reader's expectations is normally avoided, and that is why a nominal that has not been referred to previously usually appears at first mention, in the subordinate clause:

15. when Constantius landed on *the shores of Kent,* he found *them* covered with obedient subjects. (Gibbon I, p. 273)

And since the items that *idioms* consist of normally rub shoulders, this fact sometimes rules out cataphora:

16. when this gentleman made *advances,* as he presently did, Ernest in his forlorn state was delighted to meet *them.* (Butler, *The Way of All Flesh,* p. 240)

It is obvious that in this example the indefiniteness of *advances* further strengthens the case for anaphora.

Over and above this, the prescriptivists' discouragement of cataphora that I have briefly referred to may be taken to contain the salutary warning that where *ambiguity* might arise, the safest choice is anaphora. And the longer a sentence is, the greater will be the risk of ambiguity. Thus, if a description contains two male characters, a writer may (perhaps instinctively) decide to stick to anaphora to prevent confusion; at least that is how I would explain the following quotation:

17. *Peter* charged the provisions with the rapacity of a famished lion; and so well did the diversion engage *him* [Peter], that though, while *my father* stated the case, *he* [Peter] meant to interrupt *his* [my father's] statement, yet he always found more agreeable employment for his mouth... (Scott, *Redgauntlet,* p. 151)

It is time now to return to the problem of the origin of cataphora in English. I have already suggested that one source of the construction may have been slavish translation from Latin. But this applied to Old English and Middle English and more especially to Biblical translation, which was slavish almost by definition.

It is important, however, to call attention to the general Latin influence exerted on English sentence structure particularly in the Renaissance, mainly via translation. As one writer has put it: 'It is impossible to estimate how much the development of sixteenth-century prose was encouraged by the business of translation [i.e. chiefly from Latin], which, beside[s] introducing new words and ideas, itself helped to mould the prose style of the widely read translators'[11]. One outcome of writers being engrossed with translation was that it taught them the habit of holding items in temporary suspense as the sentence moved on[12]. And I believe it is not too far-fetched to imagine that this new syntactic and intellectual habit helped to pave the way for the spread of pronominal cataphora – the kind of construction that requires the reader to wait till the main clause, before the referential identity of the preceding pronoun is revealed.

From these general remarks I now move on to a specific point, to discuss a sentence type that I believe may be relevant to the problem of origin. We find this type exemplified in Shakespeare:

18.　　　　　　　　　　Banquo, *thy soul's flight,*
　　If *it* find Heaven, must find it out tonight. (*Macbeth* 3.1.140f)

This is the construction that has been termed 'nesting' or 'medial branching' or 'mid-branching'[13]. I shall call it *mid-branching.* It normally consists of the subject of the main clause, followed by a subordinate clause, most often a temporal, conditional, or concessive clause, though other types occur; the construction ends with the rest of the main clause, and the pronominal subject of the subordinate clause is coreferential with the subject of the main clause. This mid-branching construction occurs sporadically as early as Old English (in translations from Latin), and it is not rare today; but it had its heyday in the Renaissance, and there can be little doubt that it was largely inspired by the corresponding Latin construction. Let me give an example of a translator transferring such a Latin construction:

19. Galli, et quia interposita nocte a contentione pugnæ *remiserant* animos et quod nec in acie ancipiti usquam *certaverant* proelio nec tum impetu aut vi *capiebant* urbem, sine ira, sine ardore animorum *ingressi* postero die urbem patente Collina porta, in forum *perveniunt...* (Livy's *Roman History* 5.41, rec. Madvig, 1861)

      The Gaules, both for that now *they had rested* from fight a whole night, and so their choler was somewhat cooled, and also because *they had not* in any place *fought* a bloudie and dangerous battell with them, nor even at that time *wan* the cittie by any assault or force, *entred* the morrow after into the cittie, without anger and heat of furious rage, by the gate Collina, standing wide open, and so *passed forward* to the common place of assemblies... (Philemon Hollands's translation, 1600, p. 206)

It may be added that it is not just this particular Latin construction that may produce a mid-branching English sentence, but also for instance the variant in which the place of the subordinate clause is taken by an ablative absolute, as in

20. *Consules* eo anno *agro* tantum Ligurium *populato* ... nulla re memorabili gesta Romam ... *redierunt...* (Livy 45.44)

      The consuls that yeere after *they had* onely *wasted the territories* of the Ligutians [sic], ... having done no memorable service *returned* to Rome... (Holland p. 1232)

The mid-branching construction is, however, not confined to translations from Latin. It was extremely popular in certain kinds of Elizabethan English. I am thinking of the *Euphuistic* style, in which mid-branching serves as a vehicle for parallelism and antithesis; here, for instance, is Lyly:

21. Yet will you commonly object ... that the bavin though it burn bright, is but a blaze, that scalding water if it stand a while turneth almost to ice, that pepper though it be hot in the mouth is cold in the maw... (*Euphues*, quoted from the Norton Anthology, I, p. 855)

It has been aptly said of Lyly's syntax that it 'aims at unravelling the complexities that inhere even in apparently simple things. And if such complexity seems more than a little schematic, it may be recalled that for the first time, in the sixteenth century, native prose was shouldering the burden formerly carried by the learned languages'[14]. But while the mid-branching construction is a Latinism where it translates a similar Latin construction – and probably when used independently by learned writers - it must be added that it can come curiously close to another construction that is definitely native and colloquial. This colloquial type has been described by Otto Jespersen in the following way: 'A speaker begins a sentence with some word which takes a prominent place in his thought, but has not yet made up his mind with regard to its syntactical connexion...'[15]. Jespersen refers to this as *extraposition*, illustrating it with examples like 'verie good orators when they are out, they will spit' (*As You Like It* 4.1.77). In such an example the only difference between the Latin construction and extraposition is that the latter type has a resumptive pronoun (*they*); but if the extraposed item is not the subject, the colloquial tone of the construction is strengthened, e.g.: 'that woman that cannot make her fault her husbands occasion, let her neuer nurse her childe' (*As You Like It* 4.1.77).

But what is the relevance of the mid-branching construction to our problem? As mentioned, mid-branching occurs today, but it has declined appreciably over the last three centuries; for one thing, Euphuistic parallel structure went out of fashion (though it still lives to some extent in a writer like Dr Johnson); for another, it was perhaps felt that the strong topicalization conveyed by the nominal appearing in initial position was stylistically adequate only in rare cases. However, there was still a need for hypotactic sentence arrangement, and I hope that it is not too fanciful to assume that many a mid-branching construction was replaced by – or transformed into – the sequence subordinate clause ... main clause, with either anaphora or cataphora, so that

The General, after *he* had inspected the troops, gave orders for attack

became *either*

After *the General* had inspected the troops, *he* gave orders...

or

After *he* had inspected the troops, *the General* gave orders...

– the choice between anaphora and cataphora depending on the factors that I have tried to account for.

There is one source of influence that can probably be ruled out. Until about a year ago I had suspected that one of the reasons for the existence of pronominal cataphora in contemporary English was influence from French. However, there turned out to be no literature on developments in French, so I got in touch with a Romance colleague, Dr. Povl Skårup, who was very interested in the problem and undertook a limited investigation spanning the period from Old French to the present day, imposing the strict conditions on himself that he only considered cases where the referent of the pronoun had not been previously mentioned in the context, and only those cases where pronoun and nominal fill the subject slot. He came up with a result that was surprising to both of us: this cataphoric construction only begins to appear in French about 1830, and the fact that the construction is common in modern French may well be due to influence from English, one of the possible channels of transfer being Walter Scott, whose novels – in translation – were very popular in France about 1830[16]. I have checked a French translation of Scott, and it turns out that in some passages the translator does transfer Scott's cataphoric construction[17].

Summing up my tentative conclusions, I would say that in Old and Middle English, pronominal cataphora is at most nascent; it occurs sporadically in translations from Latin, but its independent status is doubtful. In the Renaissance we note a widespread Latinization of English sentence structure, a general result of which is an increased cohesive tolerance, an increased ability among language-users to hold a period, a complex sentence, in suspense. Different sentence constructions make different demands on language-users as far as cohesion is concerned: it is relevant to point out here that the construction consisting of main clause plus subordinate clause (where only anaphora is normally possible) is less demanding than the construction in which the subordinate clause precedes its main clause[18]. And in the latter construction, cataphora is more demanding than anaphora. So much for the general syntactic influence from Latin. A specific outcome of this influence is the spread of the mid-branching sentence type that was common both in translated literature and in Euphuistic writings. When Euphuism declined, I assume that the mid-branching construction was in many cases replaced by the sequence subordinate clause ... main clause, with either anaphora or cataphora (the same suggestion has been made for French by Povl Skårup, who points to the affinity between the two constructions).

In his *Principles of Diachronic Syntax*[19] David Lightfoot lists among what he calls 'extra-grammatical causes of change', the factors of *foreign influence* and *expressivity*. If these factors are applied to the present problem, we may say that foreign influence – indirect influence, since Latin has nothing exactly parallel to English pronominal cataphora – is the first factor that makes itself felt: it paves the way for the spread of a certain syntactic mould. Once this step has been reached, expressivity begins to manifest itself, as I have tried to suggest, in the stylistic exploitation of pronominal cataphora. In French, cataphora is characteristic of literary style (Povl Skårup), and the same is true of English (although occasional examples do occur in spoken English). In most English writers cataphora is less frequent than anaphora; but, although I am not a native speaker of English, I venture to submit that cataphora is not so rare that it is felt as a striking minority construction. In the course of the Modern English period, then, cataphora may be said to have established a secure niche for itself in English.

Notes

1. Cf. my article in *English Studies*, Some Observations on Pronominalization' (1981, p. 146-55).
2. Quoted from Emma Vorlat, *The Development of English Grammatical Theory 1586-1737*, Leuven University Press 1975, p. 186.
3. Scolar Press Facsimile, Menston 1968, p. 191.
4. ibid., p. 205.
5. Donald Hall, *Writing Well*, Little, Brown & Co. 1979, p. 315.
6. A. Akmajian & R. Jackendoff, 'Coreferentiality and Stress', *Linguistic Inquiry* 1 (1970), p. 124-6.
   D.J. Allerton, 'Deletion and Proform Reduction', *Journal of Linguistics* 11 (1975), p. 213-37.
   Peter Cole, 'Indefiniteness and Anaphoricity', *Language* 50, p. 665-74.
   S. Kuno, 'Functional Sentence Perspective', *Linguistic Inquiry* 3 (1972), p. 302.
   R.W. Langacker, 'On Pronominalization and the Chain of Command', in Reibel & Schane (eds), *Modern Studies in English*. Readings in Transformational Grammar, 1969.

R.B. Lees & E.S. Klima 'Rules for English Pronominalization', *Language* 39 (1963), p. 17-28.

Paul M. Postal, *Cross-Over Phenomena*, Holt, Rinehart & Winston, 1971.

J.R. Ross, 'On the Cyclic Nature of English Pronominalization', in Reibel & Schane.

7. R.W. Zandvoort, *A Handbook of English Grammar*, Longman 1957, p. 130.

8. Knud Schibsbye, *A Modern English Grammar*, OUP 1965, p. 181.

9. H.W. Fowler, *A Dictionary of Modern English Usage*, 2nd ed. revised by Sir Ernest Gowers, OUP 1965, p. 482. Sir Ernest Gowers, *The Complete Plain Words*, London 1954, p. 146.

10. Although they do show cataphora, the following two examples from poetry do not fall within the type studied here:

> Hwæþre þæt gegongeð, þeah þe hit sy greote beþeaht,
> lic mid lame, þæt hit sceal life onfon.
> (*Judgement Day* I, 98-9)

> 'Sigel' semannum symble biþ on hihte,
> ðonn hi hine feriaþ ofer fisces beþ,
> oþ hi brimhengest bringeþ to lande.
> (*Rune Poem* 45-8)

11. James Winny, *Elizabethan Prose Translation*, CUP 1960, p. XX.

12. Franz Blatt, 'Latin Influence on European Syntax', *Travaux du Cercle Linguistique de Copenhague*, vol. XI, p. 56.

13. R. Quirk et al., *A Grammar of Contemporary English*, Longman, 1972, p. 793. Walter Nash, *Designs in Prose*, Longman 1980, p. 116f.

14. J.A. Barish, 'The Prose Style of John Lyly', *ELH* XXIII, 1956, p. 27.

15. *A Modern English Grammar* VII, 1949, p. 233.

16. Cf. Povl Skårup, '"Quand il le sut, Hector reprit espoir"', (PRÉ)-PUBLICATIONS, Romansk Institut, Aarhus University, No. 61, Nov. 1980, p. 28-46. For convenience I quote his summary: 'La construction "Quand il le sut, Hector reprit espoir", où les deux sujets sont coréférentiels et où le pronom ne renvoie pas à ce qui précède mais au nom qui suit, ne semble pas apparaître avant 1830 (Le Rouge et le Noir, par Stendhal), en suivant de près les premiers exemples d'autres cas d'un pronom renvoyant à un nom qui suit dans une proposition suivante. Ce phénomène peut être d'origine purement française, mais il peut également être une imitation de l'anglais (Walter Scott)'.

17. Scott's *Quentin Durward* was published in 1823. I quote from the Collins edition (n.d.). A translation by Louis Vivien appeared in 1838 ('traduction nouvelle'), so there may have been a previous translation. I subjoin a couple of examples.

Scott p. 388. The instant her guests had departed, Mother Mabel took the opportunity to read a long practical lecture to Trudchen...

Vivien p. 355. Dès que ses hôtes furent éloignés, la mère Mabel saisit cette occasion de débiter à Trudchen une longue leçon de morale...

Scott p. 320. While he was tracing the 'letters blake' of the ditty so congenial to his own situation, Quentin was interrupted by a touch on the shoulder...

Vivien p. 282. Tandis qu'il restait les yeux fixés sur les lettres gothiques de cette inscription si fort en rapport avec sa propre situation, Quentin se sentit toucher sur l'épaule...

Scott p. 31. I hastened to answer that, though they might differ from those of my own, I had every possible respect for the religious rules of every Christian community.

Vivien p. XXX. Je me hâtai de répondre que quoiqu'ils pussent différer de ceux de la mienne, j'avais tout le respect possible pour les règlements religieux de chaque communauté chrétienne..

18. Cf. John Lyons, *Semantics*, Vol. 2, 1977, p. 661.

19. CUP 1979, p. 381ff.

THE DISTRIBUTIVE PLURAL AND ITS LIMITS

The term 'the distributive plural' is hardly fully established in grammatical literature, though it does occur,[1] but it conveniently captures the numerical concord that usually obtains in cases like the following:

She shook her head / They shook their heads
He lost his life / They lost their lives
He was made a fool of / They were made fools of

Thus, if two people are referred to, they are assumed to have a head each and a life each, etc., and this is manifested linguistically. Other constructions involving plurality also normally manifest this through plural forms: we speak of 'the late OE and early ME periods', 'the First and Second World Wars', and 'her first and second fingers'. I shall refrain from trying to formalize the concept of the distributive plural, but shall simply say that it normally occurs in modern English when a plural nominal is in construction with another nominal that also denotes plurality.

In the types referred to above there is a fairly strong tendency for the distributive plural to occur. Thus material and immaterial 'possessions' belonging to more than one will be manifested by a plural form: 'A kestrel hovered close to the tops of the pines...';[2] '...their frequently grim revolutionary careers'.[3] Sometimes the plural concept is underlined by adjectives like *various* and *separate*: '...people who ... always maintained a certain secrecy about their various pasts...';[4] '...the two managers heaved their separate sighs of relief...'.[5] If the subject is plural, there is likewise a marked tendency for the predicative to be in the plural: 'His dignity, his particular cleverness, his power were for the Count guarantees of stability, proofs of meaning'.[6] However, it will have appeared already from the title of this paper and from the reservations suggested (in the form of adverbs like *usually* and *normally*) that the matter is not quite simple, and various grammarians guard themselves with similar reservations. Thus R. W. Zandvoort states that 'Concord of number is mostly observed in English...';[7] according to G. Scheurweghs 'There is usually concord in number between the subject and the nouns of inherent possession';[8] and Knud Schibsbye states that [in cases where the plural might be expected] 'The singular is

---

[1] Cf. K. Schibsbye, *A Modern English Grammar*, London 1970, p. 107.
[2] Victor Canning, *The Finger of Saturn*, Pan 1975, p. 14.
[3] *Time* 14.5.1984, p. 14.
[4-5] Margaret Simpson, *Sorry Wrong Number*, London 1973, p. 42 & p. 63.
[6] Iris Murdoch, *Nuns and Soldiers*, Penguin 1981, p. 19.
[7] *A Handbook of English Grammar*, London 1957, p. 263.
[8] *Present-Day English Syntax*, London 1961, p. 11.

... sometimes used'.[9] G. H. Vallins even voices what in my opinion is an unduly defeatist attitude when he discusses the question: 'Do we say "The men and women shook their head", as if they had one head between them, or "The men and women shook their heads", as if they had half-a-dozen heads each? ... There is no rule: the reader has to use his own discretion.'[10] It is true that once one begins looking for examples of the distributive plural, it becomes obvious that this is an area of divided usage. I believe, however, that the general rule is for the plural to occur in the cases mentioned, but that there are a number of factors that tend to block its use. In the following pages I shall endeavour to shed some light on these blocking factors which, incidentally, may not always be easy to distinguish from each other; some of them may work together.

The first factor to be considered is a commonsensical one, namely the speaker's or writer's wish to avoid ambiguity. In a quotation like:

They were discontented always with what government they had...; but few of them honestly thought out a working alternative...[11]

it is the writer's intention to convey the idea that few of these people bothered about a single alternative; a plural form here might be taken to mean that each of those concerned contemplated or refrained from contemplating more alternatives than one. In an account of presidential elections in the United States we read that 'the individuals who hope to be chosen as party candidate have to build up their own funds';[12] there is only one candidate for each party. In impromptu (and surreptitiously recorded) speech one may overhear somebody saying: 'What I think we need you see is rooms with a table',[13] i.e. a number of rooms, each with its table; the plural *tables* might give rise to misunderstanding.

In other cases the choice between singular and plural hinges on the fact that a word may have an uncountable sense denoting a process and a countable sense denoting non-process. Thus, if we find the singular *organization* in 'the national and international organization of the trade',[14] it is because it is meant to refer to the process of organizing, while in the same context the plural *organizations* would be interpreted as meaning 'organized bodies'. Conversely, if we read that 'Asquith did not hesitate to ... demand the resignations of all Ministers',[15] it is probable that the plural form means 'documents stating the writers' intention to resign', while 'the resignation of all Ministers' would refer to their act of resigning. The noun *attention* is an uncountable when it means 'directing one's thoughts to', while the plural form *attentions* means 'kind or polite acts'. That is why we find the singular in 'Milestones [a magazine section]

[9] Op. cit., p. 107.
[10] *Good English*, Pan 1960, p. 163.
[11] T. E. Lawrence, *Seven Pillars of Wisdom*, Penguin 1962, p. 343.
[12] Peter Bromhead, *Life in Modern America*, London 1970, p. 84.
[13] Jan Svartvik/Randolph Quirk, *A Corpus of English Conversation*, Lund 1980, p. 828.
[14] S. H. Steinberg, *Five Hundred Years of Printing*, Pelican 1961, p. 46.
[15] W. S. Churchill, *Great Contemporaries*, London 1947, p. 14.

has continued to command the attention of both the discerning and the disputatious'.[16] In such cases, then, plural forms are avoided for pragmatic reasons.

As far as exclusively uncountable nouns are concerned, the language-user has no choice, for such nouns have no plural. By definition, an uncountable noun cannot appear with the indefinite article or in the plural, while a countable noun may take the indefinite article and may be pluralized. Now countable and uncountable nouns sometimes appear together in contexts that require the distributive plural, and in such cases they behave differently, for instance in an example like:

He attacked the Malthusian argument that the sufferings of the poor were caused by their early marriages and excessive fertility...[17]

— *fertility* being an uncountable noun. Many other nouns that are members of this class behave in the same way: even if they refer to several individuals, they appear in the singular. Thus, if we have occasion to refer to people who are proud, we speak of their *pride*. Of newspaper readers in the past we learn that 'This need for [typographical] economy ... put a heavy strain on their eyesight'.[18] Even if a number of people testify, the nominalization of this becomes 'The testimony of aides and servants',[19] and it is the same form that refers to the *fame* of one great man and to the *fame* of several great men. But membership of the class of uncountables is arbitrary; for while *fame* is an uncountable, its synonym *reputation* is a countable that may often be seen in a distributive plural function, as in 'the reputations of these two distinguished medical men'.[20] Indeed it is characteristic of English that many abstract nouns behave in a similar way, so that if there is occasion to speak of a number of people, one may find references to their *backgrounds*, their *dispositions,* their *enthusiasms*, their *imaginations*, their better *judgements*, etc.

The problem of deciding whether a noun is countable or uncountable is, however, rather a tricky one. It is true that some dictionaries, like the *Oxford Advanced Learner's Dictionary of Current English* and the *Longman Dictionary of Contemporary English*, give much information about the problem; but the information they provide does not always tally with actual contemporary usage. However, it is hardly to be expected that dictionaries of comparatively modest compass can keep fully abreast of all recent developments — and the countability of nouns *is* an area that is undergoing change. For instance it is by no means rare these days to find nouns like *anger, nonsense,* and *progress* in a countable function, though they are characterized as uncountables in grammars. Recent examples of their new function are: 'an anger that they can

[16] *Time* 18.6.1984, p. 5.
[17] E. P. Thompson, *The Making of the English Working Class,* Penguin 1979, p. 680.
[18] S. H. Steinberg, op. cit., p. 322.
[19] *Time* 16.5.1983, p. 14.
[20] Richard Gordon, *The Medical Witness,* London 1971, p. 106.

do nothing about';[21] 'Black angers roiled behind her frowning eyes';[22] 'You are picking up my remarks and trying to make a nonsense of them...';[23] 'a steady progress towards enlightenment'.[24] Some of these examples are probably at the limits of normal usage, and sometimes it would seem that contextual pressure is at work. Thus the noun *thirst* does not normally appear in the plural, but it does in '...North European Gentiles with flabby paunches and serious thirsts',[25] probably because it is in parallel construction with the countable plural *paunches*. Such unconventional plurals may even occur without any contextual support. One novel reports on 'the deepest inner angers of these men',[26] and in another novel one reads that 'They had talked about their childhoods'.[27] The existence of such examples suggests that countability has fuzzy edges.

There is a further point that calls for comment in connection with countability. This is a point that grammarians appear to have overlooked, but which does receive some attention from dictionary-compilers. There exists a sub-class of nouns that may be characterized by their ability to appear with the indefinite article while they rarely if ever occur in the plural. In one respect, then, they behave as countables, in another as uncountables. These countable *singularia tantum* are noteworthy in a discussion of the distributive plural precisely because, owing to their conformity with the behaviour of countables in the singular, they might be expected by the unwary foreigner to undergo pluralization in suitable contexts. But usually they do not. Here are a few examples:

We had a meeting and gave our ideas a good airing.[28]

The poets who achieved outward and visible success during their lifetime can be counted on the fingers of one hand.[29]

...artisans were willing ... to risk their livelihood to put experiments to the test.[30]

At least as striking is the way writers have shifted their linguistic stance...[31]

Some people with disordered minds become a prey to fears of being murdered.[32]

Here the nouns *airing, lifetime, livelihood, stance,* and *prey* are representatives of the sub-class, and the nouns *disgrace* and *nuisance* behave in the same way: 'These slums are a disgrace'; 'Pearls are a nuisance'; the sub-class also contains

[21] *The Listener* 31.7.1975, p. 153.
[22] James Jones, *A Touch of Danger,* Fontana 1974, p. 130.
[23] William Trevor, *The Old Boys,* London 1964, p. 11.
[24] *The Times Higher Education Supplement* 21.9.1973, p. 17.
[25] William Styron, *Sophie's Choice,* Bantam 1980, p. 238.
[26] Alan Seymour, *The One Day of the Year,* Sphere Books 1969, p. 126.
[27] Iris Murdoch, *An Accidental Man,* Penguin 1973, p. 427.
[28] *The Longman Dictionary of Contemporary English,* 1978, p. 20.
[29] S. H. Steinberg, op. cit., p. 341.
[30] E. P. Thompson, op. cit., p. 911.
[31] Randolph Quirk, *Style and Communication in the English Language,* London 1982, p. 27.
[32] *The Longman Dictionary of Contemporary English,* p. 866.

a number of deverbal nouns, for instance *hash* and *say*: '...There are plenty of gals around who make a perfect hash of it';[33] '...pacifist speakers were usually allowed to have their say along with everyone else'.[34] It is all the more surprising to note that the noun *education,* which is yet another member of this sub-class (in fact the *English Pronouncing Dictionary* gives no plural -*s* ending for it) may nevertheless occur in a distributive plural function, at least in American English: 'colleges across the country are responding ... to help students pay for their educations'.[35]

So much for the problem of countability. Let us proceed to a discussion of the blocking factor that may be termed fossilization, by which is meant that a great many set phrases, often hackneyed and more or less dead metaphors, tend to appear with their nouns in the singular, no matter whether there is singular or plural reference. Typical examples are: 'most of Britain's allies kept a low profile during the ordeal';[36] 'a great many young entrepreneurs ... certainly hoped to make their pile';[37] 'The three eldest, Rose, Marigold and Violet, ... come in to lend a hand';[38] 'the poor were at the end of their tether';[39] 'we must be on our guard'.[40] Many of these more or less faded metaphors have anatomical terms as their objects or complements: 'The neighbours are going to keep an eye on things';[41] 'They [the police] turned a blind eye to motorists who had had one too many';[42] 'Most professional politicians look upon this demand with a jaundiced eye';[43] 'We did not want to get egg on our face a second year running';[44] 'They're too scared to lift a finger';[45] 'the clients legally don't have a leg to stand on';[46] 'They're all off their rocker';[47] 'Mor and Nan had ... taken Tim ... under their wing'.[48]

In some of these set phrases we note the sequence preposition + possessive pronoun + singular noun: *off their rocker, under their wing.* It may be added that there is a tendency for the sequence preposition + possessive + plural noun to contrast with the sequence preposition + definite article + singular noun, also in plural contexts, as illustrated in the following quotations:

[33] John Le Carré, *The Little Drummer Girl,* Pan 1984, p. 100.
[34] Cowie/Mackin/McCaig, *The Oxford Dictionary of Current Idiomatic English,*Vol. 2, 1983, p. 273.
[35] *The New York Times* 14.11.1982, section 12, p. 3.
[36] *Time* 7.5.1984, p. 11.
[37] E. J. Hobsbawm, *Industry and Empire,* Pelican 1978, p. 276.
[38] P. D. James, *Unnatural Causes,* Sphere Books 1984, p. 127.
[39] E. J. Hobsbawm, op. cit., p. 91.
[40] Karl R. Popper, *Conjectures and Refutations,* London 1963, p. 30.
[41] Honor Tracy, *In a Year of Grace,* London 1975, p. 207.
[42] Julian Symons, *A Three Pipe Problem* London 1975, p. 9.
[43] Vera Böiken, *American Civics,* Copenhagen 1983, p. 178.
[44] *The Observer* 9.8.1981, p. 4.
[45] Richard Gordon, *The Medical Witness,* London 1971, p. 18.
[46] *The Observer* 9.8.1981, p. 17.
[47] A TV programme, New York 10.11.1982.
[48] Iris Murdoch, *The Sandcastle,* Penguin 1961, p. 57.

We were in this thing now, up to our necks.[49]

... people who are up to the neck in current problems...[49α]

There seems to be a mechanism at work in accordance with which a possessive pronoun co-occurs with the plural, the definite article with the singular. But sometimes there is a clear difference. If we compare 'people who speak through their noses' with 'people who pay through the nose', it is obvious that the former expression is to be interpreted literally, while the latter is a fossilized idiom. However, if we examine some of the numerous other idioms of which *nose* forms a part, it is not so easy to find a clear pattern of distribution between singular and plural. Here, first, are examples with singular *nose*:

... we are not going to be led by the nose...[50]

The police pulled them [homeless alcoholics] in whenever they got up the public's nose too much.[51]

The crowds who always have a nose for personality[52]

You boys on Channel Five want to keep your nose clean, now don't you?[53]

As far as the last idiom is concerned, the *Longman Dictionary of English Idioms* recommends pluralization where appropriate, and it would seem that the singular of the example quoted here is characteristic of very relaxed spoken language. According to the *Longman Dictionary* we should expect invariability in the following: 'to have one's nose in a book'; 'to be no skin off someone's nose'; 'to turn one's nose up'; and 'to thumb one's nose at'. However, the *Longman Dictionary* turns out to be not entirely reliable, since the last idiom mentioned *can* undergo pluralization: 'They are already thumbing their snotty, aristocratic noses at us'.[54] Instances of the plural are also found in the following:

The English neighbours would ... look down their noses...[55]

...this public system of education, at which they hold their noses.[56]

Getting their noses really down to business.[57]

Bataille wants to rub our noses in the idea of the continuous.[58]

According to the *Longman Dictionary* there are yet other locutions that prefer the plural (for instance 'they are cutting off their noses to spite their faces' and 'the money was stolen from under their very noses'), so that the plural idioms

[49] E. B. White, 'The Hour of Letdown', in Vera Böiken, *American Short Stories*, Copenhagen 1983, p. 148.
[49α] *A Supplement to the OED*, s.v. *neck*, sb., 3.e. (1935).
[50] *The Longman Dictionary of English Idioms*, 1979, p. 234.
[51-58] quoted from *A Supplement to the Oxford English Dictionary*, Vol. II, *H–N*, 1976, s.v. *nose*.

outnumber the singular ones, probably because the plural expressions have retained some degree of vividness.

Above I commented adversely on the reliability of the *Longman Dictionary of English Idioms,* but I hasten to add that in general it is reliable; it records standard usage, and if occasionally one comes across deviations from this standard, it must be taken to mean that there is some scope for going beyond the normal limits if a writer or speaker wants to achieve freshness and vividness. Let me briefly exemplify such deviations. According to the *Longman Dictionary* the idiom 'to be at a loose end' is invariable; but the distributive plural also occurs 'Both of us were at loose ends'.[59] Again, we are informed by the same dictionary that 'a free hand' is invariably found in this form; the plural can, however, occur, as in 'The state governments had completely free hands in deciding how to use their share of the money'.[60] It may also be somewhat surprising to find plurals in the following quotations:

'... I like these people. They have better senses of humor than the people in Ohio'.[61]

Ornamental initials and woodcuts therefore make their appearances simultaneously with books printed from movable type.[62]

Most complex prepositional phrases, like *in the case of, at the disposal of, at the expense of,* and *with the exception of,* are normally invariable; that is to say that the noun of the phrase is in the singular also when followed by a noun in the plural: 'at the expense of the German and Dutch Nazis'.[63] Very occasionally one may, however, find the noun of the prepositional phrase agreeing in number with a following plural complement, as in 'The technostructure in the cases of both public and private ownership'.[64] Again, a sequence like *in the form of* will normally be invariable even if followed by a plural noun: 'the preponderance of their strategic forces is in the form of large ICBMs';[65] but exceptions occur, especially when the noun is premodified: 'those wealthy retired people, who often prefer to keep their riches in the tangible forms of gold and jewelry'.[66]

A final point that is relevant to a discussion of fossilization concerns the condensed construction that is illustrated by 'Three men came marching along, *pipe in mouth* and *sword in hand*'. This is Jespersen's example,[67] in connection with which he calls attention to the use of the singular. When the construction occurs in a cliché-like function, the singular is indeed obligatory: 'They went cap in hand to their boss',[68] where *cap in hand* means 'humbly'. In other cases

---

[59] H. G. Wells, *The World of William Clissold,* London 1926, III, p. 376.
[60] Vera Böiken, *American Civics,* Copenhagen 1983, p. 271.
[61] John Updike, *Rabbit is Rich,* Fawcett Crest, New York 1981, p. 313.
[62] S. H. Steinberg, op. cit., p. 158.
[63] S. H. Steinberg, op. cit., p. 302.
[64] J. K. Galbraith, *The New Industrial State,* Pelican 1972, p. 113.
[65] *Time* 25.6.1984, p. 17.
[66] R. L. Maurice/K. Follett, *The Gentlemen of 16 July,* Pinnacle Books 1982, p. 40.
[67] *A Modern English Grammar,* Vol. II, 4.36.
[68] *The Longman Dictionary of English Idioms,* p. xii.

we may, however, find the plural: 'crack drill squads ... stood at attention, bayonets fixed'.[69]

Incidentally, one may find curious and substandard evidence of the force of formulaic invariability in an unorthodox plural form like 'those two *son of a bitches*'.[70] The orthodox plurals are *sons of a bitch*[71] and *sons of bitches*.[72]

Let us now turn to the blocking factor that may be termed singularization and which may in some cases account for the absence of the distributive plural. The term singularization is used by J. Forsyth in his account of aspect in Russian, where he employs it in the sense of 'the presentation of a recurrent action ... by selecting one occasion, one complete performance, and holding this up as a sample of the recurrent phenomenon. This practice of quoting an instance may conveniently be called 'singularisation' of a multiple action'.[73] Before we proceed to discuss the relevance of this concept to the non-occurrence of the distributive plural, it may be useful to show briefly how it can be employed to explain a peculiarity in the use of the English progressive.

Repeated or habitual action is normally expressed through the use of the simple tenses, and the notion of habit may be reinforced by an adverb like *always,* as in 'He always smoked while he shaved'. This is the normal, neutral, and unmarked formulation. Now the interesting thing is that occasionally one may come across a formulation like 'He always smoked while he *was shaving'*.[74] Here the opening main clause refers to habitual action, but in the subordinate clause the writer suddenly adopts a singularizing point of view: a single occasion (*while he was shaving*) is selected and held up as a sample of the recurrent phenomenon. In other words, there is a change of viewpoint in mid-construction.

This kind of change has a parallel in some cases where the distributive plural is absent. Instances of singularization may be seen in examples like 'Most of them needed a haircut';[75] 'I don't have many friends, Kirsten said, giggling. They get mad at me. They can't take a joke';[76] 'They die in bed at a ripe old age'.[77] The assignment of such examples to the singularizing type may perhaps be queried by some: why not say instead that in 'They die at a ripe old age' we have a case of fossilization, of sticking to the singular formula 'a ripe old age'? Or why not say that the singular in 'They can't take a joke' owes its presence to the speaker's wish to avoid ambiguity? To which I can only reply that these interpretations are not impossible, but that to me such examples above all convey a change of viewpoint, a switch from a plural to a singular focus. There

---

[69] *Time,* 7.5.1984, p. 20.

[70] John O'Hara, 'Graven Image', in Vera Böiken, *American Short Stories,* Copenhagen 1983, p. 73.

[71] T. E. Lawrence, op. cit., p. 457.

[72] William Saroyan, *The Adventures of Wesley Jackson,* Four Square Books 1961, p. 43.

[73] *A Grammar of Aspect,* CUP 1970, p. 174.

[74] K. Follett, *The Key to Rebecca,* Signet Books 1980, p. 18.

[75] Carson McCullers, *The Heart is a Lonely Hunter,* Penguin 1964, p. 195.

[76] Joyce Carol Oates, *Angel of Light,* London 1981, p. 110.

[77] Lawrence Sanders, *The Third Deadly Sin,* Berkley Books 1982, p. 58.

appears to be more room for doubt about the interpretation of examples like 'the witches have vanished like a bubble'[78] and 'The strain of more than a day in the tunnel ... had screwed their nerves up tight as a drum'.[79] Are *like a bubble* and *tight as a drum* to be taken as invariable formulas or as singularizing expressions? Be that as it may, I believe there are other examples that lend themselves most naturally to a singularizing interpretation. Here are a few examples: 'All morons hate it when you call them a moron';[80] 'most who call themselves "socialist" are in fact committed to one of these things rather than another';[81] "But surely you must be sorry for the people who are hanged?" "Why should I be? They have committed a crime, and they deserve their punishment";[82] 'There are ... earlier examples of an author preferring one publisher to another'.[83] Perhaps one might add in this context a few idiomatic expressions that favour the singular: 'Many were taken prisoner'; 'They were held hostage'; 'They fell victim(s) to the conqueror's rage'.

As mentioned at the beginning, the distributive plural normally occurs in the type 'the 18th and 19th centuries', where the conjunction *and* has an additive value. However, if the conjunction is *or*, with a disjunctive value, the singular is sometimes found, the two items being singled out one at a time: 'most of these [villages] were probably deserted by the fourth or the fifth century';[84] 'as early as the twelfth or thirteenth century';[85] it does not seem to matter whether the definite article is repeated or not.

If the subject is in the plural, there is a tendency for the predicative to be in the plural too, as in 'churches were the only independent avenues for political and labor dissent'.[86] However, it is by no means rare for the singularizing factor to make itself felt. In such cases the writer, having introduced his plural subject, switches over to a singularizing focus on the predicative: 'These vehicles have come to be a status symbol';[87] 'Moscow's difficulties with the Poles were a sign of trouble and decay';[88] 'Jokes ... are a useful pointer to possible colloquialism'.[89]

In passing it may be noted that it is not very common to find a singular subject followed by a plural predicative, as in 'The most valuable result of his visit to his native country had been the friendships which he formed with French patrons'[90] or 'One particularly successful buy was two small cane chairs'.[91]

[78] *Macbeth*, Arden, edited by K. Muir, London 1951, p. 17.
[79] R. L. Maurice/K. Follett, *The Gentlemen of 16 July*, Pinnacle Books 1982, p. 92 f.
[80] J. D. Salinger, *The Catcher in the Rye*, Penguin 1959, p. 48.
[81] *The London Review of Books*, 1–14 March 1984, p. 3.
[82] Richard Gordon, *The Medical Witness*, London 1971, p. 60 f.
[83] S. H. Steinberg, op. cit., p. 296.
[84] W. G. Hoskins, *The Making of the English Landscape*, Pelican 1970, p. 51.
[85] W. G. Hoskins, op. cit., p. 274.
[86] *Time* 14.5.1984, p. 10.
[87] *Time* 26.3.1984, p. 23.
[88] *Time* 9.4.1984, p. 24.
[89] G. L. Brook, *The Language of Shakespeare*, London 1976, p. 33.
[90] *Encyclopedia Britannica*, 1961, vol. 18, p. 383.
[91] P. D. James, *Innocent Blood*, Sphere Books 1981, p. 118.

Singularization selects one occasion, one complete performance, and holds this up as a sample of a recurrent phenomenon. It has been argued by F. T. Wood that the singular occurs in another function as well. According to Wood, 'When a plural noun is what we may call a "generalising plural", i.e. when it denotes not a specific plurality but the whole of a species or a group generally, so that what is said of all applies to each one, the tendency is to employ a singular for any characteristic attributed to the species...',[92] and he illustrates this point with the example 'Ostriches bury their *head* in the sand'. This is a statement that characterizes the whole species; but if we were speaking of specific ostriches, the formulation would be 'The ostriches buried their *heads* in the sand'. This is a tendency, but no more than that; in fact, a counterexample is provided by the *Longman Dictionary of English Idioms* which, in explanation of the ostrich idiom, states as follows: 'Referring to the belief that OSTRICH-ES bury their heads in the sand when they are in danger...'.[93] The tendency may perhaps account for the singulars found in examples like 'Readers should return to their proper place volumes ... which they may have had occasion to use';[94] 'the three leaders chosen since the war were elected in their own right before becoming leader';[95] 'lexicographers are now in the position of sorcerer's apprentice...'[96]

I have tried to identify a number of factors that tend to block the use of the distributive plural: the wish to avoid ambiguity; the fact that uncountables are invariably in the singular; the existence of a sub-class of countable nouns that prefer the singular; fossilization, or the force of invariability; and singularization. If the relevance of these factors is accepted, and if there is agreement about how to identify them (which may not always be easy), there should be no need for the defeatism of a G. H. Vallins. It must be added, however that over-optimism is equally out of place. For the fact is that, depending on the style used, English accepts or at least tolerates several types of numerical to-ing and fro-ing. In the nursery rhyme

> Cherry ripe, cherry ripe, ripe I say.
> Full and fair ones — come and buy.[97]

we move from the singular to the plural, and a similar change is characteristic of colloquial speech and of attempts to render it:

You mean he says stuff like his wife doesn't understand him, Jocasta said. That can be boring. Usually their wife understands them backwards, that's the problem.[98]

But an abrupt switch into the plural can occur even in definititions found in scholarly works:

---

[92] 'Singular or Plural? A Question of Concord'. *Moderna Språk* 51, 1957, p. 289.
[93] *The Longman Dictionary of English Idioms*, p. 152.
[94] The British Library, *Notes for Readers*, 1981.
[95] Harold Wilson, *The Governance of Britain*, Sphere Books 1977, p. 192.
[96] Randolph Quirk, *Style and Communication in the English Language*, London 1982, p. 87.
[97] Quoted from M. A. K. Halliday/R. Hasan, *Cohesion in English*, London 1976, p. 91.
[98] Margaret Atwood, *Bodily Harm*, Seal Books 1981, p.154.

By a symbolic structure I mean those structures which ... are built upon a symbolic framework.[99]

A language can express anything required of it; they differ in the sort of situational features compulsorily brought to notice by the grammatical system...[100]

This move from the singular to the plural also accommodates the kind of humorous exaggeration that we find in

'I don't want to become like Sandy, a sort of playboy, keeping a tart in a flat and —' — 'I don't imagine Sandy kept tarts in flats!'[101]

All these are instances of generalization. The inverse shift, from plural to singular, can sometimes be explained by the fact that an entire species may be referred to either through the use of the indefinite plural or the definite singular, and this may lead to a formulation like the following, taken from the *Encyclopedia Britannica*:

Ostriches are unique in possessing only two toes..., thus distinguishing it from the ostrichlike rhea of South America.[102]

More often, however, this plural-to-singular shift is characteristic of improvised speech. In a surreptitiously recorded conversation one may hear one of the participants say

but I like the abstract ones [paintings] because you keep seeing it in a new different way.[103]

And in an article from *The Listener* a speaker is reported as stating that '...panellists [in those games where the audience is privy to the answer at the start] are more valued for their willingness to make a fool of themselves'.[104] In their *Advanced Conversational English*[105] Crystal and Davy quote the following formulation: '...they knew they just had to put their dressing gown on' and comment:

the concord rules of colloquial English are much more flexible than in more formal varieties. Here, A obviously means *gowns* (one for each child), but the context is so clear that she does not bother to use the plural form.

Novelists, too, who try to render colloquial speech may offer striking instances of numerical to-ing and fro-ing, for instance

'We both had a parson for a dad. It's an unhappy start for a boy. If they're sincere you despise them as a fool: if they're not you write them off as a hypocrite.'[106]

[99] Pamela Gradon, *Form and Style in Early English Literature*, London 1971, p. 96.
[100] R. H. Robins, *General Linguistics*, London 1971, p. 271.
[101] Iris Murdoch, *Henry and Cato*, Triad Panther 1977, p. 135.
[102] Vol. 16, 1961, p. 959.
[103] Jan Svartvik/Randolph Quirk, *A Corpus of English Conversation*, Lund 1980, p. 208.
[104] *The Listener* 16.12.1976, p. 783.
[105] Longman 1977, p. 52 & p. 55. I owe this reference to Arne Juul.
[106] P. D. James, *Unnatural Causes*, Sphere Books 1984, p. 143.

It is more surprising to note this sort of discord in what one would assume is premeditated prose. Thus one reads in an advertisement that 'Candidates must have two years of experience as ... a secretary',[107] and the editor of a collection of short stories states in the introduction that 'these stories do have three things in common. They can serve as a good readable story that will repay close examination'.[108] Such numerical clashes must be put down to lack of forethought, and the factors at work in such examples seem to be either fossilization or singularization.

Sometimes, however, such a clash may be exploited stylistically. Thus, if a writer wants to insist on the dual nature of a collective noun, he may resort to a formulation like

... a side room, one of those out-of-sight chambers churches have where the choir puts itself into robes...[109]

This example comes from John Updike, and since there is great reluctance in American English to treat collectives as plurals as far as verbal concord is concerned, this may in part account for the numerical clash of 'the choir puts itself into robes', though it may also be the writer's intention to stress the unitary behaviour of a group. That is, however, something that must be left to the reader's interpretation. But sometimes the reader is told explicitly that a writer departs from the norm for a specific reason. This is true of the following quotation:

... when their eye was drawn — they were unmarried sisters, with everything in common, and had, in regard to some things, one eye between them — when their eye was drawn by a once-quite-familiar name to an obscure paragraph in their daily paper, their hearts (or their heart) stopped.[110]

The last examples demonstrate the fact that certain styles may show an unorthodox distribution of singular and plural. It is hardly surprising that we should come across instances of numerical to-ing and fro-ing in spoken language, though it is striking that the same may be true of what one would assume was well-groomed language. A further cause of deviation from the standard language is the careful writer's deliberate violation of the norm, made in order to shock the reader into unconventional interpretations.

As for the blocking factors, it must be said that they do not always work in the contexts where they might be expected to: it is not always possible to predict whether an expected distributive plural will be blocked or not. In the same novel one reads first: 'they've all got bad consciences'[111] and later 'they've all got a bad conscience',[112] which suggests how slight a difference there may be between the two formulations. Those who try to legislate about matters linguistic and stylistic realize that the distribution of singular and plural consti-

[107] *SUNY-B Inside* 26.8.1982, p. 2.
[108] Vera Böiken, *American Short Stories*, Copenhagen 1983, p. 7.
[109] John Updike, *Rabbit is Rich*, Fawcett Crest, New York 1981, p. 218 f.
[110] Elizabeth Bowen, *Look at all those Roses,* London 1951, p. 101.
[111-112] P. D. James, *The Black Tower*, London 1975, p. 31 & p. 141.

tutes an area of divided usage. Thus, in the introduction to the *Longman Dictionary of English Idioms* it is pointed out that 'Often when the subject of the verb in idioms is plural, any other noun in the idiom may also become plural', and that the usual formulation is, say, *they were laughing up their sleeves*. The comment goes on: 'In actual speech, such a noun may be left in the singular...., but it is usually better to use the plural form'.[113] The vagueness of this prescriptive statement is suggestive.

Sometimes idiomaticity leaves the speaker no choice. If we consider a handful of verbs — *cross, change, exchange, switch* — that imply the presence of two items or individuals, we note that some of them require plural objects: 'He crossed paths / swords with me'; 'John exchanged hats with Peter'; 'He switched positions'. In a number of cases the verb *change* behaves in the same way: it is 'to change hands / owners / places / seats / trains', while in other cases a singular object is obligatory: 'to change colour / direction / step', and there is vacillation between 'change gear' and 'change gears'. The fact that usage has here sanctioned the plural in some cases, the singular in others, may serve to remind us of the other areas of vacillation discussed above.

We shall have to live with some cases of divided usage, but I do not believe that it is necessary to share the pessimism of a G. H. Vallins. We do find some vacillation, but not anarchy.

---

[113] *The Longman Dictionary of English Idioms*, p. xi f.

II
LITERARY STYLISTICS

SUBJECTIVE NARRATION IN *BLEAK HOUSE*

In narrating his story an author has several stylistic media at his disposal: he may use Direct Speech (D.), Indirect Speech (I.), Report (R.), or Free Indirect Speech (FIS.). This fourfold division is identical with the one found in B. Fehr's treatment,[1] except that his *Substitutionary Speech* is here termed Free Indirect Speech (= *style indirect libre, erlebte Rede*[2]). The first two terms are probably unambiguous; it should be superfluous to remark that I., and FIS. comprise both speech and thought. By R. is here understood an author's largely objective narration of the events of his story. The term FIS. has caused some ambiguity and will be discussed below. The present article is particularly concerned with the relations between I. and FIS.

The reason for the uncertainty as regards FIS. is that it is not always easy to delimit it clearly, for instance in imperceptible transitions from I. to FIS. or in cases where R. and FIS. coincide formally. Several writers mention this difficulty; thus W. Bühler[3] says: 'Oft finden sich Fälle, in denen I. in E. übergeht; da beide Ausdrucksweisen, was den Wortkörper anbelangt, einander sehr nahe, ja oft identisch miteinander sind, so hält es in manchen Stellen sehr schwer, sie mit Sicherheit zu scheiden.' E. Lerch[4] speaks of 'ein unentwirrbares... Ineinander von Bericht und Redewiedergabe', and F. Karpf[5] emphasizes that what is apparently 'Tatsachenbericht' may in fact prove to be 'Wiedergabe von Reden und Gedanken'. In L. Spitzer's opinion[6], FIS. is pre-eminently characterized by being intonation and imitation, so that difficulties of interpretation only arise in its written form: 'Durch die schriftliche Fixierung entsteht erst das Äquivoke der Ausdrucksweise'.

FIS. is generally defined as being independent of any governing sentence of the type 'he said'. Although Bühler shrinks from defining FIS. explicitly, he seems in most cases to take the above definition for granted, but in doubtful instances he introduces another criterion: that of 'Erlebtheit' or subjectivity: 'Wenn eine Gestalt stark im Vordergrunde steht und mit ihrer Persönlichkeit einen grossen Teil der Handlung bestimmt, so werden wir in einem Zweifelsfalle eher auf E. als auf bloss indirekte Wiedergabe durch I. schliessen' (*op. cit.,* p. 85). Now there is general agreement as to the stylistic tone inherent in FIS.: it is characterized as more vivid and emotional than I. and at the same time as more subdued than D., but as will be demonstrated below, this does not always hold true; for I. may be as subjective and emotional as FIS. (at least in some writers), so that the element of subjectivity is not a sound criterion of FIS.; the only valid criterion would seem to be that of formal independence.

The element of subjectivity characteristic of FIS. has led some writers astray, terminologically as well as towards the pitfall set for all students of stylistics: that of over-interpretation. Thus O. Funke[7] says of the shifted tenses in FIS. and I.: 'Diese versetzten Tempora fungieren aber nicht bloss temporal, sondern vor allem modal; man sollte in solchen Fällen von *modalem praeteritum* oder *praeteritum obliquum* sprechen ...' Of course one realizes what Funke means, but it seems inadvisable to speak of mood in connexion with a language that has long ago discarded any extensive use of the subjunctive, and one gets a suspicion that here is a case of squinting grammar when one bears in mind that the author's native language is German. This suspicion is corroborated when one reads Günther's remarks on Bavarian I. in the indicative: 'Steht, wie im Bayrisch-Österreichischen, auch die konjunktionslose Rede im Indikativ ("Sie sagt, sie liebt die Freundinnen mehr als die Männer ..."), so wird dieser konjunktivisch empfunden'.[8] Against Bühler's book the general objection can be raised that he reads too much into the occurrences of FIS.; after citing examples from various contexts he proceeds to enumerate the several uses of FIS., arriving at a very large number. Thus FIS. is said to be a highly suitable medium for expressing e.g. contrasts, differentiation, *Andeutung verworrener Lage, Verhüllung der Gedanken, Unzufriedenheit, abwehrendes Ausweichen, Unwesentlichkeit, geheime Motive, Pläne*, etc., a really formidable array of uses that might be continued *ad infinitum*. Of course FIS. may be found in contexts containing all these elements, but so may D., I., and R.; in other words, Bühler over-interprets FIS. in the light of the context.

That the element of subjectivity and emotion is not a trait peculiar to FIS., but may also occur in I., is a point that has so far received scant recognition. The general opinion seems to be that FIS. takes over some of the characteristics of D., while in the case of I. this happens only occasionally – in Karpf's formulation: 'Ausserdem teilt die ER mit der DR das Festhalten von bestimmten, hauptsächlich gefühlsmässigen Elementen, die ein ganz objektiver Berichterstatter in der IR nur irgendwie weitläufig umschreiben könnte oder ganz fallen lassen müsste...' (*op. cit.*, p. 229f). If that statement is correct, it will be the purpose of the following pages to show that at least the author of *Bleak House* is a most subjective reporter. This novel,[9] which initiates the copious use which Dickens made of FIS. in his later work, may presumably be considered representative of his later style.

Several passages in *Bleak House* are permeated by a peculiar impressionistic tone, of which the reader receives a foretaste already in the opening lines of the book:

London. Michaelmas Term lately over, and the Lord Chancellor sitting in Lincoln's Inn Hall. Implacable November weather. As much mud in the streets as if the waters had but newly retired from the face of the earth...

This peculiar atmosphere is created by several factors: the lapidary style, encompassing a wide range of objects at great speed; the preponderant use of the present tense, and of FIS., both making for actualization and vividness; and an unusual kind of I. which approaches FIS. in many respects. The stylistic difference normally obtaining between the two media is here largely effaced, so that it is possible to list a number of parallel cases of FIS. and I. striking the same subjective note:

One of the devices contributing towards the vividness of FIS. is frequent borrowing from D. Such loans may occur without any special indication, or they may be placed in inverted commas. The vacillating typographical practice does not seem to be of any consequence. In I., too, quotations from D. are not infrequently met with:

FIS.: Mrs. Rouncewell is not quite sure as to that. Heaven forbid that she should say a syllable in dispraise of any member of that excellent family; above all, of my Lady, whom the whole world admires; but if my Lady would only be 'a little more free', not quite so cold and distant, Mrs. Rouncewell thinks she would be more affable. (p.157.)

I.: 'Are those the fever-houses, Darby?' Mr. Bucket coolly asks, as he turns his bull's-eye on a line of stinking ruins.
Darby replies that 'all them are,' and further that in all, for months and months, the people 'have been down by dozens,' and have been carried out, dead and dying 'like sheep with the rot.' (p. 311.)

Another vivifying characteristic of FIS.: it is not unusual for a person speaking in FIS. to address people directly; such direct appeal also occurs in I.:

FIS.: Now, Mrs. Piper – what have you got to say about this?
Why, Mrs. Piper has a good deal to say, chiefly in parentheses and without punctuation, but not much to tell. Mrs. Piper lives in the court (which her husband is a cabinet-maker), and it has long been well beknown among the neighbours counting from the day next but one before the half-baptising of Alexander James Piper aged eighteen months and four days old on accounts of not being expected to live such was the sufferings gentlemen of that child in his gums) as the Plaintive – so Mrs. Piper insists on calling the deceased – was reported to have sold himself. (p. 147.)

I.: She began piteously declaring that she didn't mean any harm, she didn't mean any harm, Mrs. Snagsby! (p. 809.)

The former quotation is a mixture of Mrs. Piper's story and the author's comments, but somehow the transition to direct address is not felt to be so abrupt as in I. In the following quotation there is a complete leap form I. to D., indicated by means of inverted commas:

At last come the Coroner and his inquiry, like as before, except that the Coroner cherishes this case as being out of the common way, and tells the gentlemen of the Jury, in his private capacity, that 'that would seem to be an unlucky house next door, gentlemen, a destined house; but so we sometimes find it, and these are mysteries we can't account for!' (p. 468-469.)

Interjections, asseverations, etc., properly belonging to D., may be reproduced both in FIS. and in I. with the effect that the reader is tricked into hearing more clearly the actual words uttered (even though the first quotation below is probably a case of reported reflection, not speech).

FIS.: And here Mrs. Snagsby is seized with an inspiration.
He has no respect for Mr. Chadband. No, to be sure, and he wouldn't have, of course... Why

did he never come? Because he was told not to come. Who told him not to come? Who? Ha, ha! Mrs. Snagsby sees it all. (p. 356.)

I.: (Mr. Snagsby loving) ... to remark (if in good spirits) that there were old times once, and that you'd find a stone coffin or two, now, under that chapel, he'll be bound, if you was to dig for it. (p. 130.)

In FIS. we find the peculiar kind of syntactically independent questions which, compared with direct questions, are only characterized by the shifting of tense and person:

Would she go with me? Yes, Ada thought she had better go with me. Should we go now? (p. 694.)

Compare also the following quotation, instancing a wide-spread way of conveying a message:

... 'but it's a gentleman, miss, and his compliments, and will you please to come without saying anything about it.' (p. 519.)

If the speaker is in the first person, there need be no deviation from D.:

...I began to get older, and to ask myself why should I ever write? (p. 749.)

In I. we find, of course, the ordinary dependent question with a conjunction and normal word-order, but the less dragging independent questions are also very frequent:

She clung round my neck... saying what should she do without me! (p. 698.)

In the quotation below there is a curious contamination of the two types of question, probably caused by the rather long parenthetical remark:

... And I considered whether, if it should signify any one of these meanings, which was so very likely, could I quite answer for myself? (p. 516.)

As will have appeared from some of the examples adduced, the speaker in FIS. may be linguistically characterized as vulgar; this is also extremely frequent in I., and the stylistic effect is similar to the one resulting from the adoption of interjections, etc.:

Jo suddenly comes out of his resignation, and excitedly declares, addressing the woman, that he never known about the young lady, that he never heern about it, that he never went fur to hurt her, that he would sooner have hurt his own self, that he'd sooner have had his unfortnet ed chopped off than ever gone a-nigh her, and that she wos wery good to him, she wos. (p. 633.)

Other linguistic idiosyncrasies may find expression in FIS. as well as in I.:

FIS.: (A French maid speaking)
Ha, ha, ha! She, Hortense, been in my Lady's service since five years, and always kept at the distance, and this doll, this puppet, caressed – absolutely caressed – by my Lady on the moment of her arriving at the house. (p. 158.)

I.: Sir Leicester is majestically wroth... The debilitated cousin holds that it's – sort of thing that's sure tapn slong votes – giv'n – Mob. (p. 570.)

116   (4-5)

F. Karpf has gone into the problem of the intonation of FIS.[10] and after consulting prominent British phoneticians arrives at the conclusion that the intonation of FIS. is exactly identical with the one used in actual conversation. This result tallies well with Spitzer's emphasizing of imitation as an all-important element of FIS. (I may add that my own observation of Danish corroborates Karpf's conclusion.) Now it is of course almost impossible to convey in print the intonation of a statement; there is, however, the use of italics or capitals to indicate emphasis, which is closely bound up with intonation. First an example in FIS.:

'...If your ladyship would wish to have the boy produced in corroboration of this statement, I can lay my hand upon him at any time.'
  The wretched boy is nothing to my Lady, and she does *not* wish to have him produced. (p. 408.)

In I., too, this typographical device occurs, and in such cases it is probably permissible to conclude that the intonation approaches D.:

...he feels that it is in his nature to be an unimprovable reprobate, and that it's no good *his* trying to keep awake, for *he* won't never know nothink. (p. 361.)

A final point that calls for comment in this comparison of FIS. and I. is Dickens's use of 'situational words'. In principle, English possesses two sets of words (adverbs, pronouns, and a few adjectives) indicating time and place, the 'here-and-now' words, and the 'there-and-then' words,[11] whose use is determined by the attitude of the speaker or writer. The words of the former category are used with reference to the present time and place, thus making for greater vividness, those of the latter group are used with the connotation of distance in time or place and strike a more objective note. In theory, then, we may expect to come across 'here-and-now' words primarily in FIS., 'there-and-then' words primarily in I., but it should be added that the difference is far from being clear-cut, although the following quotation affords an instance:

My guardian called me into his room next morning, and then I told him what had been left untold *on the previous night*. There was nothing to be done, he said, but to keep the secret, and to avoid another such encounter as that of *yesterday*. (p. 607; my italics.)

But in view of Dickens's peculiar I. it is not surprising that we should find *to-morrow morning,* which is properly a 'here-and-now' phrase, in I.:

Mr. Bucket (still grave) inquires if to-morrow morning, now, would suit... (p. 720.)

Shiftings of tense and person are common to FIS. and I. and are so familiar phenomena that they will be passed over here.
  As has been demonstrated by the examples cited above, the only difference between I. and FIS. is in many cases that of dependence vs. non-dependence on a governing sentence. If it is further borne in mind that it is not always easy to define the exact limits between I. and FIS., it might be tempting to reshuffle the terminology by saying that the indirect reproduction of speech and thought may be either (a) largely subjective or (b) largely objective, in view of the fact that in a

text like the one under consideration it is hardly possible to demonstrate that a change of the stylistic tone has occurred simultaneously with a transition from I. to FIS. However, this is a mere suggestion which may prove untenable in the light of a larger material.

The gradual transition from I. to FIS. may be illustrated by the following quotation:

It was not a love letter though it expressed so much love, but was written just as he would at any time have spoken to me... It told me that I would gain nothing by such a marriage, and lose nothing by rejecting it, for no new relation could enhance the tenderness in which he held me, and whatever my decision was, he was certain it would be right. But he had considered this step anew, since our late confidence, and had decided on taking it... (p. 610.)

The break begins at 'for no new relation ...', but only becomes quite clear at 'But he had considered ...'

In some cases the author's narration and FIS. coincide formally in such a way that only by considering a longer context does the reader realize that what at first appeared to him as R. is actually FIS.:

He is borne into Mr. Tulkinghorn's great room, and deposited on the Turkey rug before the fire. Mr. Tulkinghorn is not within at the present moment, but will be back directly. The occupant of the pew in the hall, having said thus much, stirs the fire, and leaves the triumvirate to warm themselves. (p. 376.)

The last part of the quotation below should presumably be taken as a case of FIS. because of the imperative:

Policeman at last finds it necessary to support the law, and seizes a vocalist; who is released upon the flight of the rest, on condition of his getting out of this then, come! and cutting it – a condition he immediately observes. (p. 144.)

The following example is also puzzling: it is difficult to decide whether the first sentences are to be interpreted as the author's information or as a kind of FIS. abruptly breaking into D.:

Sir Leicester receives the gout as a troublesome demon, but still a demon of the patrician order. All the Dedlocks, in the direct male line, through a course of time during and beyond which the memory of man goeth not to the contrary, have had the gout. It can be proved, sir. (p. 218.)

All the quotations given so far are instances of the potential coincidences between I. and FIS. To complete the picture it should be added that although these potentialities are frequently realized in *Bleak House*, there *are* certain differences. Thus, an imperative may be transferred to FIS. unchanged:

He didn't know, he said, really. It wasn't a bad profession; ...suppose he gave it one more chance! (p. 241.)

whereas in I. some paraphrase must be resorted to:

Tony again entreats that the subject may be no longer pursued, saying emphatically, 'William Guppy, drop it!' (p. 488f.)

where we find both the indirect and the direct version.

Both I. and FIS. have the drawback that as a consequence of the shifting of persons the third person is often ambiguous, so that it becomes necessary to add a name in parentheses. But on the whole FIS. has the advantage over I. of facilitating greater concision. It is true that explanatory sentences of the type 'he said' may occur in FIS.; but in that case they are always syntactically (and sometimes also typographically) parenthetical without any governing function:

She was greatly occupied during breakfast; for the morning's post brought a heavy correspondence relative to Borrioboola-Gha, which would occasion her (she said) to pass a busy day. (p. 58 f.)

But as a rule the advantage of FIS. is precisely that the writer avoids having to use the cumbrous and monotonous repetitions 'he said', 'she said', etc., by virtue of the condensed meaning peculiar to verbs in FIS., where 'he hoped' comes to stand for 'he said he hoped'. This is particularly advantageous in dialogues in FIS.:

Sir Leicester is apprehensive that my Lady, not being very well, will take cold at that open window. My Lady is obliged to him, but would rather sit there, for the air ... (p. 569.)

The writer may also gain concision when leaping from D. to FIS.:

'Be so good as to go on. Also ..., to take a seat, if you have no objection.'
    None at all. Mr. Bucket brings a chair... (p. 726.)

Generally speaking, FIS. resembles D. more than does I. Apart from the fact that in *Bleak House* this difference between FIS. and I. is not pronounced, the statement also requires other qualifications, and it should be remembered that it is not always feasible, starting from I. or FIS., to reconstruct the exact wording a statement would have had in D., because the writer may twist his material so as to obtain a heightened effect. Thus the following quotation:

Name, Jo. Nothing else that he knows on. Don't know that everybody has two names. Never heerd of sich a think. Don't know that Jo is short for a longer name. Thinks it long enough for *him*. *He* don't find no fault with it. Spell it? No. He can't spell it. No father, no mother, no friends. Never been to school. What's home? Knows a broom's a broom, and knows it's wicked to tell a lie. Don't recollect who told him about the broom, or about the lie, but knows both. Can't exactly say what'll be done to him arter he's dead if he tells a lie to the gentlemen here, but believes it'll be something wery bad to punish him, and serve him right – and so he'll tell the truth. (p. 148.)

is unrealistic in the sense that what appears as a monologue is really a kind of dialogue, the writer using a stylistic trick by which the general import of the questions put to Jo by his interlocutor is revealed to the reader through Jo's answers, a turn that makes for brevity while leaving the reader in no interpretative doubt. In a different way the writer may consciously remove FIS. from D., later giving the more exact wording:

This ballad, he informs Mrs. Bagnet, he considers to have been his most powerful ally in moving the heart of Mrs. Bucket when a maiden, and inducing her to approach the altar – Mr. Bucket's own words are, to come up to the scratch. (p. 675.)

Here the intention is to obtain a slightly humorous effect from the contrasting of the two wordings 'to approach the altar' and 'to come up to the scratch'. The quotation also shows that a statement in I. or FIS. may be 'coloured' not only by the character uttering it, but also by the author himself; in either case it is, of course, the author who does the colouring, but the stylistic effect is different.

On the whole the I. of *Bleak House* may be characterized as rather strongly coloured by D., a fact that may be taken as a symptom of Dickens's vivid and subjective style. One might compare this with other spheres in which his subjectivity is prominent, the writer interfering in an otherwise comparatively objective narration. This he may do by 'borrowing' from one of his characters, as in:

'...Is this fellow *never* coming!'
This fellow approaches as he speaks. (p. 447.)

'Serjeant, I told you the last time I saw you that I don't desire your company here.'
Serjeant replies... that he has received this letter. (p. 483.)

A slightly ironic note is produced by Dickens's using 'Serjeant' of the person to whom he otherwise always refers as 'Mr. George'. – And in the quotation below we hear the words of 'the active and intelligent' – or perhaps of the whole neighbourhood – suddenly forcing their way into the author's R.:

Then the active and intelligent, who has gone into the morning papers as such, comes with his pauper company to Mr. Krook's, and bears off the body of *our dear brother* here departed... (p. 151; my italics.)

Finally, the many personifications occurring in his descriptions may perhaps also be considered a symptom of Dickens's subjective style.[12]

Notes

1. 'Substitutionary Narration and Description', *English Studies* XX (1938), p. 97-107.
2. Concerning terminology see e.g. W. Günther, 'Probleme der Rededarstellung', *Die neueren Sprachen*, Beiheft Nr. 13 (1928), p. 85, and O. Jespersen, *The Philosophy of Grammar*, 1948, Ch. XXI; J. Brøndum-Nielsen has recently coined the term *Oratio Tecta* (in *Dækning – Oratio Tecta i dansk Litteratur før 1870*, Copenhagen 1953).
3. *Die 'Erlebte Rede' im englischen Roman.* Ihre Vorstufen und ihre Ausbildung im Werke Jane Austens, Zürich 1937, p. 84.
4. '*Ursprung und Bedeutung der sog. "Erlebten Rede"* ("Rede als Tatsache")', GRM 16 (1928), p. 464.
5. 'Die erlebte Rede im Englischen', *Anglia* 57 (1933), p. 236.
6. 'Zur Entstehung der sog. "erlebten Rede"', GRM 16 (1928), p. 331.
7. 'Zur "Erlebten Rede" bei Galsworthy', *Englische Studien* 64 (1929), p. 454.
8. *Op. cit.*, p. 54. An even worse instance of 'psychological' over-interpretation occurs on p. 74.
9. The edition referred to is The New Oxford Illustrated Dickens, 1951.
10. 'Die klangliche Form der erlebten Rede', *Die Neueren Sprachen,* 39 (1931), p. 180.
11. See *English Studies* 1951, p. 43 ff.
12. I am much indebted to Professor C. A. Bodelsen for several valuable suggestions.

JOHNSONESE IN *NORTHANGER ABBEY:*
A NOTE ON JANE AUSTEN'S STYLE

The extent to which Jane Austen's style contains Johnsonese features has been variously assessed. Most critics seem to be of opinion that the points of resemblance are very far from being negligible. This is true of statements made by Mary Lascelles,[1] C. S. Lewis,[2] Andrew H. Wright,[3] and B. C. Southam.[4] The last-mentioned of these critics observes that the six novels are characterized by an 18th-century style, while *Sanditon* is stylistically a new departure. The point has also been made that although Jane Austen is stylistically indebted to Dr Johnson, she is usually not a slavish imitator of him, like Fanny Burney.[5] On the other hand a recent survey of the history of English prose, Ian A. Gordon's *The Movement of English Prose*,[6] lists Jane Austen among those who write 'speech-based prose', a result the author could surely only have arrived at by concentrating mainly on Jane Austen's dialogue. I am in general agreement with the above-mentioned critics who stress the importance of the Johnsonese features in Jane Austen; at the same time I believe that certain aspects of Jane Austen's sentence-structure and word-order may call for a somewhat more detailed reassessment than the mere reference to 'rhythm', 'harmony', and 'cadence' that is often met with. The features to be dealt with below are present in all the six novels, but it is my impression that they are particularly prominent in *Northanger Abbey*, whose date of composition has not been settled with absolute certainty, but which I take to be an early work, in accordance with the view expressed by W. A. Craik.[7]

Jane Austen was an ardent admirer of Dr Johnson's writings and not least his *Rambler* essays; in fact there is a reference to one of them in Ch. 3 of *Northanger Abbey.* An examination of stylistic similarities between the two writers might therefore naturally consist in a comparison between *The Rambler* and *Northanger Abbey*. The salient feature of the prose of *The Rambler* is the author's predilection for rhetorical amplification. Dr Johnson is first and foremost a moralist who wishes to drive his points home as thoroughly as possible by the use of rhetorical emphasis. This is not true of Jane Austen to the same extent; her main interest may be said to be the

---

[1] *Jane Austen and Her Art*, O.U.P. 1965 (originally published 1939), Ch. III.
[2] 'A Note on Jane Austen', in *Jane Austen. A Collection of Critical Essays*, ed. Ian Watt, New Jersey 1963, p. 34.
[3] *Jane Austen's Novels. A Study in Structure*, London 1961, p. 173.
[4] *Jane Austen's Literary Manuscripts*, O.U.P. 1964, p. VI.
[5] See for instance Frank W. Bradbrook, *Jane Austen and Her Predecessors*, C.U.P. 1966, p. 94. But it should be emphasized that Fanny Burney's first novel, *Evelina* (1778), is far less in the Johnsonese manner than *Cecilia* (1782) and *Camilla* (1796), and that these two novels are Johnsonese not least on account of their Latinate vocabulary.
[6] Longmans 1966, p. 151.
[7] *Jane Austen: The Six Novels*, Methuen 1968, p. 4.

psychology of the characters she creates — but she is certainly not devoid of a moralizing strain, and she shares some of Dr Johnson's rhetorical patterns. The method by which Dr Johnson builds up his sentence-structure to put across his message has aptly been described by George Saintsbury as *tessellation*,[8] and the essential features of this style have been thoroughly analysed by W. K. Wimsatt.[9] In this paper I intend to concentrate on some points that have not, as far as I know, been subjected to detailed examination before. It is of course not my intention to assert that Jane Austen is a complete Johnsonian in respect of her stylistic similarities with Dr Johnson, but just to show that Johnsonese modes of expression are distinctly traceable in Jane Austen, as regards both form and content.

Let us proceed, then, to consider some of these similarities. It is hardly necessary to point out that some of the features to be dealt with are not confined to our two writers; but cumulatively, they may be taken to be typically Johnsonese or Augustan.

Amplification may assume various shapes in Dr Johnson. Sometimes we find a more general statement followed by specific illustrations:

He has totally divested himself of all human sensations: he has neither eye for beauty, nor ear for complaint; he neither rejoices at the good fortune of his nearest friend, nor mourns for any publick or private Calamity.

(*Rambler* 24, I, p. 157)[10]

We may compare this with the description of Catherine Morland which, it is true, does not show Johnson's pointed parallelism, but which does conform to the pattern: general statement plus illustrations:

At fifteen, appearances were mending: she began to curl her hair and long for balls; her complexion improved, her features were softened by plumpness and colour, her eyes gained more animation, and her figure more consequence.

(*NA* p. 14)

In Jane Austen we occasionally find a slightly different type of rhetoric: a general statement is capped by a dictum of epigrammatical conciseness:

In marriage, the man is supposed to provide for the support of the woman: the woman to make the home agreeable to the man; he is to purvey, and she is to smile.

(*NA* p. 77)

A writer who has a pronounced tendency towards repeating the same or almost the same idea is bound sometimes to use the characteristic semantic resumption that occurs both in Dr Johnson and in Jane Austen:

---

[8] *The Peace of the Augustans*, World's Classics 1948, p. 197.
[9] *The Prose Style of Samuel Johnson*, Yale Studies in English, vol. 94, 1941.
[10] Quotations are from *The Works of Samuel Johnson* I - XVI, New York 1903. Quotations from *Northanger Abbey* are from *The Novels of JANE AUSTEN. The Text based on Collation of the Early Editions by R. W. Chapman*, vol. V, Oxford 1948.

..the perpetual vicissitudes of life, and mutability of human affairs...
(Rambler 52, I, p. 334)

If indeed, by any strange mischance his father should have gained intelligence of what she had dared to *think* and *look for*, of her causeless *fancies* and injurious *examinations*...
(NA p. 231; italics mine)

But there are other ways of expatiating on a topic. One of the modes frequently resorted to by Johnson is that of listing a number of variations of the same basic idea, or parallel expressions suggesting slightly different aspects of the same idea : [11]

My resolution was now to ingratiate myself with men
    whose reputation was established,
    whose high stations enabled them to prefer me, and
    whose age exempted them from sudden changes of inclination.
(Rambler 27, I, p. 177)

The parallels are underlined by the use of anaphora. The same is true of the following quotation from Jane Austen :

It would be mortifying to the feelings of many ladies, could they be made to understand
    how little the heart of man is affected by what is costly or new in their attire;
    how little it is biassed by the texture of their muslin, and
    how unsusceptible of peculiar tenderness towards the spotted, the sprigged, the mull or the jackonet.
(NA p. 74)

Besides the comment already made on it, two points must be made in connexion with the last example :

(1) Jane Austen, like Dr Johnson, seems to have a very strong predilection for three-member structures, *oratio trimembris* (though, as will be clear from subsequent illustrations, not necessarily in the form of sentences). It is true that there are also many instances of *oratio bimembris*, and some of four or even five parallel members; but the figure three appears to have held a particular fascination for her.

(2) In many of the three-member structures there is in both writers a distinct tendency towards adhering to what in German is referred to as *das Gesetz der wachsenden Glieder*: the second member tends to be heavier than the first, and the third heavier than the second (as in the formula 'the truth, the whole truth, and nothing but the truth'), the stylistic effect being one of strong pregnancy. Here is a typical example from Johnson :

He was divested of his power,
    deprived of his acquisitions, and
    condemned to pass the rest of his life on his hereditary estate.
(Rambler 190, IV, p. 107)

The same tendency is apparent in the instance given below, and the effect

---

[11] Here, as well as in other later quotations where it is suitable for emphasizing parallel structure, I shall take the liberty of indicating the parallels typographically.

is here further heightened through the use of three imperatives followed by three rhetorical questions (the extract is taken from the scene in which Henry Tilney lectures Catherine) :

Consult your own understanding,
  your own sense of the probable,
   your own observation of what is passing around you —
Does our education prepare us for such atrocities ?
Do our laws connive at them ?
Could they be perpetrated without being known, in a country like this,
  where social and literary intercourse is on such a footing;
  where every man is surrounded by a neighbourhood of voluntary spies, and
  where roads and newspapers lay every thing open ?
              (*NA* p. 197)

The above example contains three parallel sentences. Here are a couple of typical three-member constructions in which the members are not sentences :

... and if she had given way to their entreaties, she should have been spared the distressing idea of
  a friend displeased,
  a brother angry, and
  a scheme of great happiness to both destroyed, perhaps through her means.
              (*NA* p. 103)

Catherine had no leisure for speech.
being at once blushing,
   tying her gown, and
   forming wise resolutions with the most violent dispatch.[12]
              (*NA* p. 165)

In my discussion of *oratio trimembris* I started out with examples showing formal and to a certain extent also semantic parallelism. It is important to note, however, that there is often a characteristic difference in the way the three-member construction is used by Dr Johnson and by Jane Austen. In the former's essays we generally find, besides the formal parallelism, at least a rough semantic conformity between the members. This is far from always being the case in Jane Austen, who seems to have got this formal mould into her system without feeling obliged to stick to a corresponding parallelism of content. Occasionally she uses it in such a way that the third and longest member peters out rather lamely instead of constituting a resounding climax :

The time of the two parties uniting in the Octagon Room being correctly adjusted, Catherine was then left to the luxury of a raised, restless, and frightened imagination over the pages of Udolpho.

---

[12] Incidentally, this example shows the occurrence of the very rare expanded participle, cf. Jespersen's *Modern English Grammar* IV 13.59. Another example occurs on p. 52 of *Northanger Abbey*.

lost from all worldly concerns of dressing and dinner,
incapable of soothing Mrs. Allen's fears on the delay of an expected dressmaker, and having only one minute in sixty to bestow even on the reflection of her own felicity, in being already engaged for the evening.

(NA p. 51)

An example like this would seem to contradict the categorical assertion made by W. A. Craik that 'such cadences as she has are the result of meaning not phrasing...'.[13]

In other passages Jane Austen exploits the three-member construction as a vehicle for her gentle satire, introducing a third member that is semantically and logically incongruous with the two preceding members:

Mrs. Allen was now quite happy — quite satisfied with Bath.
She had found some acquaintance,
had been so lucky too as to find in them the family of a most worthy old friend; and, as the completion of good fortune, had found these friends by no means so expensively dressed as herself.

(NA p. 36)

... a day never passes in which parties of ladies, however important their business, whether in quest of
pastry,
millinery, or even (as in the present case) of
young men,
are not detained on one side or other by carriages, horsemen, or carts.

(NA p. 44)

Thus the construction may accommodate a flippancy very characteristic of Jane Austen, though it is of course not confined to this construction; it recurs in a slightly different form below, again with the same surprise effect brought about by the unequal yokefellows, and in this case reinforced by alliteration:

... she meditated, by turns, on
broken promises and broken arches,
phaetons and false hangings,
Tilneys and trap-doors.

(NA p. 87)

As a final example we may consider the quotation that follows, in which it is the ridiculous conflict between faultless and the enumeration of exceptions that produces the satirical effect, since the reader naturally expects the exceptions to be trivial ones and not factors that actually invalidate the preceding statement:

"As far as I have had opportunity of judging, it appears to me that the usual style of letter-writing among women is faultless, except in three particulars."
"And what are they?"

---

13 *Op. cit.*, p. 29.

"A general deficiency of subject,
a total inattention to stops, and
a very frequent ignorance of grammar."

(*NA* p. 27)

In *Northanger Abbey* the particular butt of the author's satire is the contemporary Gothic and sentimental novel (and to a less extent contemporary social manners and the general foibles of humanity). In the last examples listed we may note one way in which the author gives expression to her satire: examples like these may be said to be Johnsonese with a difference. In many cases Jane Austen adopts Dr Johnson's syntactic moulds, but we sometimes find a clash between form and content that produces a certain satirical and ironical effect. A corresponding clash may be exemplified by the passages in which the author deliberately spoils the traditional fictional convention by intruding her own self into the narrative (for instance in the long digression on the novel in Ch. 5). It seems natural to assume that both types of clash are brought about intentionally, since Jane Austen is at all times extremely language-conscious, sometimes even at the metalinguistic level, as in the passage where Henry Tilney ridicules Catherine's use of the expression 'promised so faithfully': [14]

"Promised so faithfully ! — A faithful promise ! — That puzzles me. — I have heard of a faithful performance. But a faithful promise — the fidelity of promising ! ..."
(*NA* p. 196)

— and other similar examples might be adduced.

It seems reasonable to assume, then, that Jane Austen deliberately applies certain Johnsonese syntactic moulds to obtain the particular burlesque effect she is aiming at producing.

In an examination of stylistic similarities between the two writers there are one or two points relating to word-order that call for brief comment.

Dr Johnson favours certain types of word-order, sometimes to such an extent that they almost give the impression of being mannerisms. Thus, for the sake of emphasis and variation, he often places a dependent question or a *that*-clause before their main sentences :

Whether this sentiment be entirely just, I shall not examine...
(*Rambler* 29, I, p. 192)

That the maxim of Epictetus is founded on just observation will easily be granted...
(*Rambler* 17, I, p. 109)

We find a similar word-order in Jane Austen :

How proper Mr. Tilney might be as a dreamer or a lover, had not yet perhaps entered Mr. Allen's head, but that he was not objectionable as a common acquaintance for his young charge he was on inquiry satisfied...
(*NA* p. 30)

---

[14] Incidentally, this satirical outburst of Henry's is based merely on idiosyncratic antipathy, cf. OED s.v. *faithfully*.

A similar peculiarity shared by both writers is the emphatic position of prepositions at the head of a sentence, particularly the preposition *of* :

Of misfortune it never can be certainly known whether... it is an act of favour or of punishment;...

(*Rambler* 32, I, p. 210)

Of the way to the apartment she was now perfectly mistress;...

(*NA* p. 193)

Dr Johnson's predilection for abstract diction is well known. One of its manifestations, which may be defined by the formula *the x-ness of y* (as for instance in *Rambler 27:* 'the extent of his knowledge, the elegance of his diction, and the acuteness of his wit') is also a great favourite with Jane Austen, as in :

... the solitude of her situation, the darkness of her chamber, the antiquity of the building...

(*NA* p. 227)

and in numerous other passages.

Another mannerism of Dr Johnson's is his peculiar way of varying his adverbs, as in :

... calamities sometimes to be sought, and always endured...

(*Rambler* 178, IV, p. 42)

... he that is never idle will not often be vicious...

(*Rambler* 177, IV, p. 40)

a device the excessive use of which tends to irritate the reader. But though we find in Jane Austen examples like :

... for she was often inattentive, and occasionally stupid.

(*NA* p. 14)

His manner might sometimes surprize, but his meaning must always be just...

(*NA* p. 114)

she avoids overworking it.

Some points of similarity between the styles of Dr Johnson and Jane Austen have now been surveyed. But while they should not be overlooked, it would be onesided and therefore misleading to press the point too much, since the fact is that Jane Austen's is a mixed style, combining affinities with Johnsonese and features characteristic of the spoken language, the latter seen for instance in her expert rendering of dialogue and in her ability to characterize a speaker through his or her language. Thus, in Ch. 6 of *Northanger Abbey*, the gushing and insincere Isabella is made to reveal herself thoroughly — at first only to the attentive reader, later to the heroine as well — in her use of superlative expressions: 'My dearest creature', 'I have been waiting for you at least this age', 'these ten ages at least', 'I have an hundred things to say to you', 'I scold them all amazingly about it', 'I must confess there is something amazingly insipid about her', 'Every thing is so insipid', 'That is an amazing horrid book', 'They are very often amazingly impertinent', etc. Such character-drawing is often thrown in relief through the medium of *style indirect libre*, as in the following rendering of Isabella's speech :

It was ages since she had had a moment's conversation with her dearest Catherine; and, though she had such thousands of things to say to her, it appeared as if they were never to be together again...

(NA p. 67)

From a formal point of view, this is report, but the presence of some of Isabella's favourite superlative expressions quickly makes the reader realize that we have here a subtle rendering of Isabella's direct speech. However, as has been pointed out by Mary Lascelles,[15] Jane Austen may well have taken her cue for this device from Dr Johnson.

Jane Austen's style never runs the risk of descending into monotony in the way straight Johnsonese is bound to do at least occasionally. While her style contains Johnsonese features, these are combined, as the narrative situation requires it, with other, more vivid features, but the admixture of the latter is hardly such as to entitle us to term her style 'speech-based'.

---

[15] *Op. cit.*, p. 110.

LANGUAGE AND SOCIETY
IN L.P. HARTLEY'S »FACIAL JUSTICE«

Any author of a utopia is faced with the task of creating the illusion of an alien environment, sufficiently distant and different from the familiar here-and-now, and yet not an environment that is *too* different, if he is to carry his reader with him. Creating a convincing utopian world probably presents greater artistic difficulties than writing a novel the scene of which is laid in the writer's own world, or in the more or less well-known past, since by definition utopias are descriptions and interpretations of imaginary societies that necessitate extrapolation from known societies. Here the language problem obtrudes itself: for with contemporary English at one's disposal, how can one describe imaginary societies in such a way that they carry conviction?

Part of Huxley's solution, in *Brave New World*,[1] is to create his own technical vocabulary to convey the atmosphere of his future state; we learn, for instance, about *Predestinators* (p. 20), *hypnopaedia* (p. 31), *the Feelies* (p. 38), and *sexophonists* (p. 67), and to a certain extent Huxley adapts current English sayings and proverbs, so that they fit his utopia and its ideology. Thus *Lord* is consistently replaced by *Ford:* "'Oh, Ford!'" (p. 34), "his fordship" (p. 37), "Ford knew what" (p. 38), and "cleanliness is next to fordliness" (p. 92). In some cases the author endeavours to bring home the semantic changes that have overtaken current English words as a consequence of altered social conditions: thus *father* has become a comically smutty word (p. 122), and with this we may compare: "To say one was a mother – that was past a joke: it was obscenity." (p. 124). But on the whole it must be said that Huxley describes his future state in terms of current English.

To glance briefly at another well-known utopia: Orwell, in *1984,* can

---

1. Quotations are from the Penguin edition.

hardly be said to make any serious attempt at creating a language that is a true reflection of his Oceania. What he does is to postulate that the conditions and the ideology of the New State have produced and are producing radical changes in English as we know it. But the instances that occur often give the impression of being laboriously superimposed: "You were abolished, annihilated: *vaporized* was the usual word" (p. 19)[2]; ". . . to wear an improper impression on your face . . . was itself a punishable offence. There was even a word for it in Newspeak: *facecrime*, it was called." (p. 53). The explanatory additions are significant. In a couple of passages there is an ironical reference to the Continental fashion of indicating time by the 24-hour system, a system that has been officially adopted in Oceania; for instance: "The clock's hands said seven-twenty: it was nineteen-twenty really." (p. 112). Orwell's *doublethink* with its semantic consequences remains a postulate. He may have felt this himself since he added an appendix accounting for the principles of Newspeak; but this implies that his Newspeak creations have not become integrated in the language of the novel.

I have referred briefly to these two utopias as a point of departure for a discussion of Hartley's *Facial Justice* (Penguin 1960). Hartley's manner of handling the language problem appears to me to be somewhat different from the methods used by Huxley and Orwell, and in the following pages I shall try to show that to some extent Hartley really comes to grips with the problem of integrating language and society in his utopia.

Like so many other utopias, *Facial Justice* (1960) is not first and foremost a vision of an imaginary country projected into the future. True, the scene is supposed to be laid in England some time after the Third World War, but this is merely a device that gives the author scope for effecting his principal aim, that of satirizing social and moral tendencies in contemporary Britain, and indeed in the entire contemporary world. That this is so is brought out stylistically right from the opening of the novel:

> In the not very distant future, after the Third World War, Justice had made great strides. Legal Justice, Economic Justice, Social Justice, and many other forms of justice, of which we do not even know the names, had been attained; . . . (p. 9)

Now the past tense or the pluperfect is of course regularly employed to

2. Quotations are from the Penguin edition.

describe future states; but by joining it with a time indication like "in the not very distant future" and at the same time obtruding his own and his readers's egos ("of which we do not even know the names"), Hartley makes it clear that he does not attach any importance to upholding the fiction of a utopia laid in the future. These opening lines are characteristic in that they show the style mixture which Hartley employs repeatedly for the purpose of suggesting that the ostensibly future conditions he describes really apply to the contemporary scene. Let us consider some of the ways in which Hartley exploits his linguistic medium to convey his satire.

Hartley is at all times language-conscious to a high degree. One need only bear in mind the way the children in *A Perfect Woman* criticize their mother's linguistic snobbishness.[3] This stylistic acuteness is very pronounced in *Facial Justice,* and he exercises it by 'translating' normal contemporary English into the sort of English that one may imagine is used by English people after the Third World War, an English that reflects their social and moral situation. On the surface, the English of *Facial Justice* conveys the characteristics of post-Third-World-War England, while in reality the language criticizes social and moral facts and tendencies of the writer's own period. The medium of this criticism is a language that deviates in some respects from normal contemporary English. We shall consider this, but before we do so it may be useful to outline the salient features of Hartley's society.

The New State is a dictatorship. It is the unknown dictator's avowed aim to create a society whose inhabitants are all equal, who are treated as a collective mass, and who give up their identities as well as their property. As the dictator puts it near the end of the book, when she realizes that she has failed:

> In my play I tried to rob you of your identities: for who is not happier without one? (p. 201)

A little earlier the totalitarian point of view has been expressed that "the State knows what's best for you" (p. 198), and elsewhere we find the well-known idea that this kind of state is not really a dictatorship:

3. For instance, Isabel instructs her children: '"... go and get yourselves tidy for ... for luncheon," she added, for Alec's benefit. – "What's luncheon?" Janice demanded. "We always say lunch, when we don't say dinner." – Caught out, Isabel coloured deeply.' (Penguin p. 179).

> Did you realize that my provisions for you are the form your free-will takes? (p. 151)

Any kind of privacy is frowned upon:

> Private motoring was not allowed: it was considered dangerous, deciviliz-ing, individualistic, and ideologically unsound. (p. 41)

Thus the political regimentation is anti-individualistic and also anti-intel-lectual. An example of the means whereby this attitude is induced is a "regulation speed-limit of three miles an hour imposed on pedestrians" (p. 107). In the principal character's mind this physical restraint is converted into a mental restraint:

> Slow motion, slow motion was the rule, and Jael's thoughts, losing their urgency, began to catch the rhythm and slow down. Thinking at the same pace as the rest, she began to think what they did, she felt the tug, the attraction of a common thought ... instinct replacing intellect ... (p. 107)

We must not forget that a condition of this sort of transference taking place is that the citizens of the New State have become physically and morally weakened, and if the State considers that their weakness is not sufficient to make them anonymous units in a mass, quite drastic means are available:

> ... to inject the healthy with some form of not necessarily serious illness, so that the level of physical and mental well-being in the New State should be roughly regularized – no one too ill, no one too well? (p. 172)

The endeavours to level the population are, however, only partly success-ful. In *Brave New World* there are dissident voices, and in Hartley's novel we find a group of people rebelling against indoctrination. But even among the common people the levelling tendency produces social unease. The system itself contributes to this, for it is not logical: it entails a division of the citizens into Alphas, Betas, and Gammas. The Alphas are the élite, while the Betas and Gammas represent the majority. However, although Envy – "Bad E" (Equality is "Good E") – is frowned upon, it is apparent that relations between Betas and Gammas are strained; in one passage a Beta says:

> " .:. It isn't that we look down on the Gammas – you shouldn't look down or up, you should only look ahead, your own height – we just feel, if a Gamma comes along, that she's different. We don't despise them, but they embarrass us. We don't know what to say to them, any more than you know what to say to somebody who's ill – you have to choose your words, and put on a special voice ..." (p. 72)

This resembles the attitude adopted by many 'enlightened' people today towards Negroes or Jews.

Apart from the prescriptive element contained in the last quotation ("you shouldn't look down or up . . ."), the illustrations given so far are straightforward inasmuch as they do not deviate linguistically from normal contemporary English. But let us now turn to some cases in which Hartley twists his medium in order to convey the flavour of the new society.

One ideal of the New State has already been touched upon: depersonalization. This is given comical relief in the following speech:

> "I'm as fond of you as one human unit can or ought to be of another."
> (p. 63)

This reference to human beings as units occurs elsewhere in the novel, and it has its ironical counterpart in the treatment of plants as sensitive beings:

> "Imagine living in a time," said Joab, "when plants were so tormented! The most precious things we have, and yet they were treated far worse than human beings in concentration camps . . ." (p. 37)

Closely allied with the concept of people as depersonalised units is the tenet that no citizen should possess private property. The linguistic *reductio ad absurdum* of this principle is that strictly speaking a pronoun like *mine* should be ruled out, only practical considerations prevent this:

> "'Mine" is not a word you ought to use,' the Sister said. 'We only use it because we haven't found a substitute. We can say it's "yours", of course, but yours means everyone's. "In my charge", you ought to say, or "in my care" or "in my keeping", only it takes so much longer.' (p. 76)

This aptly illustrates the quandary that ideologically sound citizens find themselves in: it is impossible to change one's language overnight, or even in the course of a longish period, so that it conforms to the altered conditions of society:

> Mental habit dies hard; the survivors of the Third World War helped out their thoughts with pre-war images . . . the language was still, as ours is now, a storehouse of dead metaphors . . . (p. 101)

Just as the animosity against private possessions calls forth adverse comment on the word *mine,* so the principle of levelling gives rise to similar ridiculous philosophizing over *who* and *whom:*

> "Didn't you read that correspondence in the *Daily Leveller* – all about "who" and "whom", and the tyranny of the Objective Case: Lots of people thought that the cases should be standardized – it wasn't fair for a word to be governed by a verb, or even a preposition. Words can only be free if they're equal, and how can they be equal if they're governed by other words" (pp. 177–178)

Even if one accepts the principle of levelling, this must of course mean social levelling, and it is absurd to apply this principle to grammar. Apart from the specious verbal manipulation one senses the author's criticism of contemporary grammatical permissiveness.

Criticism of the inventory of language because it does not match social conditions is one outcome of linguistic conservatism. Another result of this mismatch between language and society is semantic confusion, which is sometimes deliberately introduced by the rulers as a means of regimenting the citizens. Obviously an expression like "Voluntary Compulsory" (p. 140) tends to bewilder people, and so do the two E's: "good E" = equality, and "bad E" = envy:

> Confusion between the good and bad E's was so frequent that some of the more devout and law-abiding members of the New State found it safer to abstain from abstract discussion. (p. 16)

The memorization of stock epithets in referring for instance to foreign countries is necessary for the citizens if they are to conform to linguistic-cum-ideological standards, only there is the difficulty that these epithets tend to change all the time:

> ... Denmark might be delightful, delicious, distinguished, dutiful or even duty-free (pp. 34–35)

and these changes are introduced deliberately:

> Many such verbal booby-traps had official sanction; it was said that they kept people mentally and harmlessly on the alert, and were valuable agents of civic instruction. (ibid.)

It is not difficult to think of contemporary parallels.

The few dissidents who have some measure of independent thinking left have nevertheless been indoctrinated, like the rest of the population, with the result that they are torn between their own common sense and the pressure exerted on them by official usage and ideology; in the following situation we find them getting into serious semantic and ideological trouble:

"We shan't get anywhere if we're not unanimous," the Chairman said.
"Unanimous? But that's just what we don't want to be – it's what we're
up against – thinking alike, talking alike, looking alike, being alike – we
want to spread dissension –"
"Perhaps," the Chairman said, "but don't spread it here." (p. 131)

In another situation an idiomatic relic of the old world is repressed just in
time by a speaker who remembers that it conflicts with one of the maxims
of the New State:

"Well, there's no accounting –" he began. He checked himself and
added, rather sternly: "But of course, there is no such thing as tastes.
There is only taste." (p. 41)

Thus, on the negative side, the ideology of the New State imposes awkward
linguistic tabus. On the other hand, the tension between contemporary
English and the usage of this imaginary nightmare state gives the author
scope for many ironical comments. He repeatedly employs unusual collocations to bring his criticisms home. Here are some examples.

On the very first page there is a reference to "the Equalization (Faces)
Centre". One has to know something about the New State before one can
interpret this. In fact it alludes to one of the basic concepts of the book,
viz. the fundamental symbolic rôle played by faces; but even when one has
realized this, one is struck by the incompatibility between this piece of legal
phraseology (cf., for instance, *the Shops (Sunday Trading Restriction) Act*)
and the words that have been used to fill this pattern. The incompatibility
emphasizes the absurd importance attaching to faces, and there are other
references to it:

... she must ... prepare, as an old woman does, for being disregarded,
for not counting, for being devalued, not worth her face-value. (p. 60)

And again:

" ... it was all this face-saving business, as it's called, that started me
off." (p. 104)

That Hartley's criticism is quite obviously directed against conditions in
contemporary society is seen from his description of the way children are
treated:

... among the many institutions that the New State took on from the Old,
was the segregation of children. (p. 29)

The employment here of a word that today has primarily racial overtones suggests a parallel between the use of kindergartens and the isolation of Negroes. Later in the same passage there occurs another striking expression:

> There was another argument for segregation. Most of the children were so inured to communal life and being in an age-group that they did not take kindly to solitary confinement with their parents. (p. 30)

One is hardly in doubt about the author's view of kindergartens; on p. 27 we are told that Family Children (i.e. children brought up by their parents) are looked upon with contempt.

Hartley is quite adept at modifying his language in such a way as to shed light on conditions in the New State. This is true not only of the social system, as in the examples given above, but also of physical conditions which, it is suggested, form a parallel to the ideological system. Here are a couple of illustrations:

> ... the weakest went – not to the wall, for there were no walls – but out of the struggle for survival. (p. 29)

> Round the next bend the Square came into sight, square in name but oval in shape, because of the Dictator's aversion to angles and straight lines. (p. 50)

Thus the narrator corrects himself when using traditional expressions that are at variance with actual conditions. This juxtaposition of the physical and the abstract levels occurs repeatedly; in another passage he deviates from established usage by employing in its literal sense a figurative and proverbial idiom:

> In the New State it never rained but it poured, and poured for days, turning the crumbling earthy surface into a swamp. (p. 206)

Cumulatively such deviations from normal English usage tend to strengthen the illusion of an alien world that is not, however, so different from contemporary Britain that we cannot accept the illusion.

There are other stylistic features that as it were straddle the two worlds: contemporary England and the New State. No doubt the author's intention in using them with such great frequency is to impress upon the reader that these features represent tendencies that are very prominent – too prominent – in his own world.

For instance the novel abounds in slogans, catch-phrases, and advertising jargon. For all the talk of equalization and levelling the social system of the New State is really a Fascist Dictatorship: the pure Alpha class is a *corps d'élite,* "a chosen and choice body with whom we should never dream of comparing ourselves" (p. 170). In theory the rest of the population should be "level in littleness and equal in insignificance" (ibid.), but this is a mere fiction:

> All three grades had catch-phrases of their own which they used among themselves to distinguish them from the others. Jael had learnt some of them in preparation for her Betahood: "It was all beautiful and beta," for instance, as a term of praise. Gammas would say: "How gloriously gamma!" The Failed Alphas were more chary of using their language. Overheard by lower grades, such expressions as "How absolutely alpha" sometimes produced raised eyebrows and shrugged shoulders. (pp. 18–19)

In other words, the New State is at least as classbound as the Old. The above quotation represents the equivalent of U and non-U distinctions, and the meaningless class-indicating catch-phrases are often characterized by alliteration: "Beta is best" (p. 13), "Excellence belongs to the Elect" (p. 15), "Alpha is anti-social" (p. 11). There are also many slogans which are not specifically associated with any one class, but which represent aspects of the ideology of the New State: "luck is a leveller" (p. 12), "daylight is dangerous" (p. 23), "the me doesn't matter" (p. 17), "Height means fever" (p. 72), and "the Ego's Exit" (p. 75). The excessive and automatic use of such slogans is akin to brainwashing, and consistency is of course not to be expected: on p. 31 we are told that any form of hurry was discouraged; nevertheless one of the Beta slogans is "Busy-Beta (a play on busy bee, of course)" (p. 48).

The principal butt of Hartley's satire is probably the Communist countries; one important element in the technique of brainwashing consists in placing the deviant person in a position of psychological disadvantage right from the outset, and for this reason the Dictator invariably addresses the citizens as "Patients and Delinquents" (or simply as "Ps and Ds", p. 31); but the author certainly also lashes out against the American way of life: "Worry is Waste of Time" (p. 48; cf. "keep smiling"), "Careers for the Courageous" (p. 137; this is a coinage made by the dissidents); and "make the New State safe for mediocrity" (p. 176). The last example is of course double-pronged: partly it alludes to Woodrow Wilson's dictum "The world must be made safe for democracy", partly it reflects the levelling of the New State.

Punning, as will already have appeared, is a prominent feature of the novel. It often takes the form of extrapolation from current English idiom, the sayings being adjusted to the conditions of the New State. Thus we find:

"And my dear, you can't think how he's changed for the beta! You hadn't heard that one? Well, it's fairly new. A bit obvious perhaps, but then it's beta to be obvious." (p. 68)

And again:

"Can you Beta it, as they say. Or can you Beta me to it!" (p. 75)

The ritual dance imposed as a penalty on those citizens who put themselves in the wrong by offending against the rigid linguistic conventions is the explanation of the following passage:

... smacks, blows, scuffles were the order of the dance ... (p. 30)

The title of the novel is also in the nature of a pun: it alludes to the faces characteristic of the various groups of citizens, and at the same time it strongly suggests the notion of superficiality. This key-concept we may compare with the motto of the book: "The spirit that dwelleth in us lusteth to envy", and with the two epigraphs. For Part One it is: "Every valley shall be exalted . . .", from Handel's *Messiah,* and this is in its turn from Isaiah XL 3; the continuation: ". . . and every mountain and hill shall be made low . . ." is not given, but obtrudes itself after a reading of the book. The second part of the quotation tallies well with a statement made by one of the characters on p. 148: ". . . It is easier to lower a standard than to raise one." For Part Two the epigraph is a quotation from *Troilus and Cressida* (1.3. 109–110):

Take but degree away, untune that string,
And, hark, what discord follows!

This leaves us in no doubt about Hartley's attitude: he is anti-egalitarian, against depersonalization, for the rights of the individual, for the intellect. No doubt some readers would describe the book as the product of a conservative, if not reactionary, mind; but at least one reader would prefer to consider it a warning, the *reductio ad absurdum* of certain present-day tendencies. However, the main emphasis of this article has been laid not on the message as such, but rather on the relationship between medium and message. As for this relationship, one may form the opinion that the author often tries to put across his message in too crude a manner, and that some of his puns fall rather flat. Authorial intrusion detracts somewhat from the artistic merits of the novel. But what is most interesting about *Facial Justice* is the stylistic handling of the theme; realizing to the full the important part played by language in the moulding of our moral and social lives, Hartley has set himself the task of extrapolating from contemporary English to the sort of English that may be imagined to be current in the New State; this is his ostensible endeavour, while his real aim is to criticize contemporary language and society. The experiment may not be wholly successful, nor may all its details be quite convincing (though some of the inconsistencies are deliberately introduced to suggest that the ideology of the New State is muddled); but I hope I have succeeded in showing that his pinpointing of the uses and misuses of language is thought-provoking: it applies very much to the contemporary scene.

III
VOCABULARY

REVIEW

A Supplement to the Oxford English Dictionary. Edited by R. W. BURCH-FIELD. Oxford: The Clarendon Press. Volume III. O — Scz: xvii + 1579 pp. 1982. Price £ 55.

This volume is bound to have almost universal appeal: it will interest the lay-man owing to the wealth of information that it sheds on recent historical, cultural, social, and technical events and advances; and it will spellbind the specialist whose task it is to explore English language and literature, as well as the user who suffers from *onomatomania* ('a morbid preoccupation with words').

To consider, first, some items that will interest the layman and the specialist alike: there are entries like *Ostpolitik, Paisleyism, Poujadism, Powellism,* and *Reaganism* that encapsulate recent movements. Students of Nazi Germany will note with interest that the phrase *heads will roll* was coined by Hitler (as reported in 1930 in the *Daily Herald*; cf. *roll, v.*^{2}, 11.g), while the statement commonly attributed to Goering: 'When I hear anyone talk of Culture, I reach for my revolver' occurs in the 1933 play *Schlageter* by H. Johst (cf. *reach, v.*^{1}, 12.c.). It is surprising to note the rapidity with which the proper name *Quisling* underwent commonization; the first quotation (from *The Times*, April 15, 1940) speaks of 'possible "Quislings" inside the country' [i.e., Sweden], and the name almost immediately spawned a number of derivations: *Quisling-hearted, quis-lingism, quislingite,* and the back-formation *to quisle* (labelled 'jocular'). The abundant documentation following entries like *proto-* and *radio-* is eloquent testimony to advances in science and technology, while such first-elements of compounds as *pseudo-, psycho-,* and *quasi-* point, among other things, to phil-osophical and psychological developments. Dickensians will note with amusement that the adjective *Pickwickian* has been adopted by the medical profession in *the Pickwickian syndrome,* 'occurring in some obese adults (rarely in obese children) characterized by somnolence, respiratory abnormalities, and bulimia', in allusion to the fat boy in *Pickwick Papers*; the form is also employed as a noun denoting 'a person with the Pickwickian syndrome'.

And now for more technical matters. There appear to be three fundamental areas that call for comment: (1) coverage, (2) the chronological information provided, and (3) definitions and stylistic labels.

COVERAGE. The first point that may be noted here is that occasionally a special sense of a word has been deleted since the quotation on which it was based has turned out to be a misreading. This is true of *rabble, sb.*[1], 2.e. ('rabblement, confusion'), in connexion with which we are informed that 'The word printed "rabble" in the 1766 ed. of *Swift's Lett.* is "babble" in the author's MS'.

In a few cases the definitions given in the Dictionary were not supported by quotations. This has now been remedied, so that for instance the adjective *promise-breaking* (s.v. *promise, sb.,* 5.) is illustrated by a quotation from Dickens.

One's first impression as one leafs through the volume is that coverage is as full as can reasonably be expected. We cannot check the Bibliography till volume IV has been published, but among the most frequently occurring names of sources may be noted Jane Austen, Charlotte Brontë, Aldous Huxley, Joyce, Kipling, Shaw, Mark Twain, and P. G. Wodehouse, not to mention the Baltimore *Sun* and Queen Victoria; and incidentally, several non-English grammarians have also been drawn on. Such varied sources suggest that no stylistic stratum has been neglected.

For some time I have been interested in compounds of the type *rinse-out,* which are nominalizations of phrasal verbs; when I checked my material against the Supplement, I found that some of my examples were missing, while on the other hand some compounds were listed that had escaped my attention. It is perhaps a bit strange that for instance *rinse-out* should have been left out since it is in A. P. Cowie & R. Mackin's *Oxford Dictionary of Current Idiomatic English,* Vol. 1: Verbs with Prepositions & Particles (1975), a book that the Supplement occasionally uses as a source. But this area of word-formation is extremely fertile, and there are bound to be omissions. Besides, the use of the hyphen is not fully regularized, so that an example like 'The prospect of a glorious *potter about* was too much for Amanda' (*potter, sb.*[3], 1955) may be said to be syntactically ambiguous.

Fullness of coverage is certainly suggested by series like *Oxford, Oxfordian, Oxfordish,* and *Oxfordy*; *preg, preggers, preggo,* and *preggy*; but there is one type of entry whose *raison d'être* may perhaps be queried. This type may be exemplified by a form like *orl,* representing 'a "phonetic" spelling of a vulgar pronunciation of ALL'. Similar examples are *orter, oughta, ornery, parm* (for 'pardon me'), *partickler, prolly* (representing a colloquial pronunciation of 'probably'), *reg'lar,* and *refayned, refeened.* Once it has become editorial policy to give separate entries to such forms, there seems to be no end to them. Perhaps a distinction might have been made between those that have acquired a certain independent status — forms like *ornery, refayned*, and *tuppence* — and the rest of them. As it is, consistency is difficult to achieve: *reg'lar, a.* and *adv.*, is given a separate entry, but under *regular, a., adv.*, and *sb.* 5., we find the example 'you shall go reg'lars in the profits'. If *pint* (= 'point') is given independent status, why not *pison* (for 'poison')? The spelling *pison* actually occurs in a quotation s.v. *poison, sb. (a.)*, 2.b. Volume II has no separate entry for *niver*.

If this treatment of forms that deviate from standard orthography errs on the side of inclusiveness, I should wish to add that from my (necessarily limited) knowledge of the volume there are few sins of omission. Let me comment on one or two. In *Great Expectations*, ch. 17, Dickens uses the idiom *to go partners*. If one turns to the main body of the Dictionary (s.v. *go, v.*, 35.c), one is informed of the existence of phrases like *go shares, go mates*, and *go partners*, and one is referred to the nouns involved. Under *partner* there is, however, no example of the idiom, and the Supplement is also silent on this point. So one is left in the lurch if one wants to ascertain whether Dickens was the first to use this idiom. The same is true of the idiom 'to give somebody the price of ...', which occurs in *Bleak House*, ch. 11, but which is unrecorded in the main body of the Dictionary as well as in the Supplement.

What is the lexicographer to do with idioms containing more than one noun? There seems to be no established practice. The volume under review, s.v. *pistol, sb.*, 1.d., lists the idiom *to hold a pistol to (at) (a person's) head*, = 'to threaten him', the first example given being from 1917. Volume II of the Supplement, s.v. *head, sb.*, 62., has *to put a pistol to somebody's head*, = 'to coerce him', the first occurrence of which is from 1841. There ought to have been a cross-reference here.

Occasionally one misses a piece of morphological information that is provided by other dictionaries. The Supplement lists the verb *to output*, but has no comment on its preterit; this can be formed on the analogy of *to put*, but according to *Webster's New Collegiate Dictionary* (1974) and the *Concise Oxford Dictionary* (sixth edition, 1976) the form *outputted* is also current; parallel cases that come to mind are Mr Wegg who (in *Our Mutual Friend*) declined and *falled* the Roman Empire, and a verbal expression, formed on the noun *wheeler-dealer*, the preterit of which is *wheeled and dealed*. It is a pity that there seems to have been no co-operation between the compilers of the Supplement and those of the *COD*.

CHRONOLOGICAL INFORMATION. One of the obvious aims of a dictionary on historial principles is to provide detailed and exact chronological information on word-histories. This aim can never be fully realized because there is not time for compilers and their informants to read everything. But it is possible to come very close to the ideal even on the basis of selective reading when it is as extensive as is the case here. Though the dates given of the first appearances of words should not be taken as gospel truth, they are in most cases probably not far out. The present volume of the Supplement, like the others, contains a number of antedatings. Thus, for the word *scientist*, which used to be dated to 1840, a quotation from 1834 has now been found. It is impossible for one person to assess the total number of words that have been antedated. I may, however, suggest the extent of this chronological revision by giving the following figures. At the end of 1982 I had a list of 120 words (from O to Scz) which were said by the OED to have made their first appearance in Dickens's writings. Out of these, 11 — or just under 10 per cent — could be antedated on the evidence of the Supplement, the extremes being by 71 years and by three years; philologists who work with neologisms need not despair if 90 per cent of their findings are valid. Sometimes the dates given by the Supplement are open to correction. Thus the first occurrence of *reception* in the sense of 'an ovation granted a popular actor on taking the stage' (5.c.) is dated to 1847, but there is an example of this sense of the word in *Nicholas Nickleby* (1838), ch. 29. The Supplement compilers do not appear to have consulted *A Chronological English Dictionary* (Heidelberg 1970); if they had, they might have noted that this dictionary dates *poltergeist* to 1838 as against the Supplement date of 1848.

DEFINITIONS AND STYLISTIC LABELS. In not a few cases definitions have been changed owing to changes of cultural and social background. Thus we are told that *rape, sb.*[2], can in modern usage also refer to a sexual assault upon a man (3.a.). Sense 3 of *pantomime, sb.*, has been given a lengthy addition to its definition: '... The entertainment ... is now based on the dramatization of a fairy tale or nursery story, and includes songs and topical jokes, buffoonery and slapstick, and standard characters ...'. *Peasant, sb.*, has also been given a new definition, accompanied by the following note:

Circumstances have changed considerably since the publication of the Dictionary and although modern sociologists agree that a 'peasant' works the land, the more wealthy peasants may also be land-owners, rentiers, hirers of labour, etc., and in these capacities share interests with completely different social groups. Hence in the analysis of many rural societies divisions within the class frequently have to be made.

One realizes how much thought must have gone into the formulation of such a note. This is one of the cases in which the user is given an explicit semantic-cum-sociological definition. Obviously, it was impossible to do so everywhere: but throughout the volume the reader is given examples that are presented in such a way as to enable him to draw his own conclusions. Occasionally we have a glimpse of the dictionary-maker's battle with intractable material; thus the following note is appended to *pay-off*, 4.: 'It proved unrealistic to attempt to separate the examples that follow into clearly distinct sections. Many of them stand contextually at the border of at least two senses or embrace more than one sense'. This is certainly an approach that is preferable to one that imposes distinctions which may prove not to be valid.

Much helpful information on the status of words is provided by labels like *obsolete, rare, colloquial,* and the like. It is obvious that such labels are extremely difficult to apply since they may involve an element of prophecy. In this connexion it is worth noting the cautious definition of *nonce-word* given on p. xxx of the 'General Explanations' in the Dictionary: 'Words apparently employed only *for the nonce,* are, when inserted in the Dictionary, marked *nonce-wd*. Such assessments, made at a given time, may subsequently prove invalid, and there is therefore nothing surprising about the revised labelling that occurs again and again in the Supplement. In the Dictionary the noun *pollutant* is labelled *rare*; the Supplement deletes this label and adds twentieth-century examples. In the Dictionary, sense 2. of the noun *paper* ('written documents collectively') is labelled *obs.* (there are just two fourteenth-century examples); the Supplement deletes *obs.* and adds recent examples. The adverb *oldly* has been promoted from *obs.* to *rare*. The verb *panic* began its life as a transitive verb and was considered a nonce-word in the Dictionary; this label is no longer applicable, and besides, the verb has developed an important intransitive function since the beginning of the present century. The somewhat controversial noun *overview* is still regarded as obsolete in the sense of 'inspection, supervision'; but it has recently acquired a new sense, roughly 'a comprehensive review of facts or ideas'. There appears to be a tendency for many words which until recently were considered rare or obsolete to be given a new lease of life; when the fourth volume of the Supplement comes out, it will be interesting to see if the recently recycled interrogative adverb *whither* (as in *Whither Democracy?*) has managed to keep alive.

The basic Editorial approach is clearly descriptive: it is the aim of the Supplement to record linguistic facts, not to praise or condemn usage. But this principle is not adhered to everywhere. Occasionally one comes across Editorial comments on acceptability. Of the verb *to prioritize* (recorded since 1973) it is coyly remarked that it is a word 'that at present sits uneasily in the language'; and there is a defence of the use of the plural of *protagonist* to denote the leading characters in a story, etc., a use that had been branded as absurd by Fowler. The label 'catachrestically' is sparingly used; could and should it not have been employed to characterize the adverb *predominately*? Under *non-word* in volume II of the Supplement there is a quotation that refers to 'the non-word *predominately*'. The user who looks up the word in the Supplement will learn that it is no longer rare, and will implicitly be given to understand that it has full currency. And should not a form like *picker-upper* have been labelled 'colloquial'?

Regular consultation over a six-month period has brought to light the merits and demerits that have been discussed above, but a definitive assessment can only be made after a much longer period. Books should, however, be reviewed not too long after their appearance, and I am pretty sure that my final verdict will not differ from my provisional one: this is a volume that is as good as it is humanly possible to make it. There is every reason to expect that the fourth and last volume of the Supplement will be up to this excellent standard; may we not have to wait too many years for its publication!

PHRASAL VERB INTO NOUN

SUMMARY. — The type of word that is a nominalization of verb stem + particle (*cutback, pickup*, etc.) is widespread and very productive in contemporary English. The article points out some historical causes that have facilitated the growth of this type of noun. It begins to appear in late Middle English, but it is not till the 18th and 19th centuries that it grows popular; in the present century new formations have been so numerous that they are not fully recorded even in the largest dictionaries. These nouns are characterized by great semantic diversification; for instance, a *pickup* means, among other things, 'the tone-arm of a record player', 'a truck', 'power of acceleration', and 'a casual acquaintance'. The existence of one noun may bring about a more or less fanciful antonym; thus *buildup* has recently produced *builddown*. Some recent formations are not nominalizations: there is no phrasal verb corresponding to *brownout*. Many members of the type are colloquial, others are technical.

Otto Jespersen once wrote an article in which he emphasized the importance of monosyllabism in Modern English.[1] If one studies the nominalization of phrasal verbs, one may be tempted to add that disyllabism, too, is far from being negligible, since most of the members of this class of noun consist of two syllables. This is because there is a strong tendency for monosyllabic verbs to enter into combination with monosyllabic particles (particularly *out* and *up*) and for such combinations to be nominalized. Thus, from the phrasal verb *to cut back* we get *a cut-back*, and similar disyllabic nouns are *comedown, kickoff, lockout, pickup*, and many more. This is the dominant type; it has been calculated that 'the twenty [monosyllabic] verbs *back, blow, break, bring, call, come, fall, get, give, go, hold, lay, let, make, put, run, set, take, turn* and *work* have entered into 155 combinations with over 600 distinct meanings or uses'[2]. That calculation was made as early as 1920, and today we should no doubt have to add considerably to this figure. Less frequently, one or both of the components consist of more than one syllable, so that we get examples like *limber-up, poke-around*, or *potter-about*. In contemporary English this type of noun has numerous exponents, and it is highly productive; new members of the type are being created all the time. At the outset it may be reasonable to ask why the type has grown so prolific, and if we try to answer that question, we shall have to glance briefly at two aspects of the development of the English language.

(1) In Old English there were virtually no phrasal verbs corresponding to the modern type. Compound verbs consisted of prefix plus verb: *forbærnan* equals *burn up, tōteran tear up*. This type is still represented to a limited extent today, as in *forgive, understand*, and *withhold*, but most of its members began to fall into disuse in Middle English, so that the old type of compound was largely ousted by the postpositive combination: *āgiefan* was replaced by *give up*. This example of the verb-particle combination is attested from the mid-12th century; but the spread of the type was not at first spectacular, perhaps owing to the adoption in Middle

---

[1] *Linguistica*, Copenhagen 1933, pp. 384–408.
[2] Albert C. Baugh/Thomas Cable, *A History of the English Language*, third edition, 1978, p. 338, reporting the findings of A. G. Kennedy, *The Modern English Verb-Adverb Combination*, Stanford University, 1920.

(272)

English of many French compounds like *admit, confess,* and *reject* which were formally and semantically similar to the Old English type of compound. However, by the 15th century the verb-particle combination exemplified by *give up* had become the dominant type.[3]

(2) There is another historical fact that it is important to bear in mind if we are to account for the rise and growth of the phrasal-verb nominalizations, namely the phenomenon of conversion (also termed zero derivation or functional shift). This is a derivational process whereby a word belonging in one word-class is made to do duty in another word-class without any alteration of its form. It is a process that gathered momentum in Middle English when distinctive endings were largely lost. For instance, nouns might be converted into verbs, and verbs into nouns. In Old English there was a noun *dōm*, and its corresponding verb was *dēman*. After the loss of endings in late Middle English it became possible to treat the noun *doom* as either a noun or a verb: 'the day of Doom', 'he was doomed to failure' (the verb dates from *c.* 1450), and it became possible to give the original verb *deem* a similar double function. We still have the verb *deem*, and besides there existed in early modern English a noun *deem* that appears first in Shakespeare, but which is now obsolete. The process of conversion was then extended from simplex words to verb-particle combinations, so that by the 15th century the way was prepared for the creation of this type of noun: some phrasal verbs were in existence, many more were to be created, and it had become a common process to convert verbs into nouns.

Let me briefly define my inventory. It comprises deverbal nouns that consist of the stem of a verb plus a particle denoting movement. On the one hand this definition excludes words like *diehard, knowhow, say-so,* and *stay-at-home* since their non-initial elements do not fit the description, and on the other hand it rules out words like *dugout* and *leftover*, in which the first element is a past participle (but these types are of course somewhat similar to the type I shall discuss). In speaking of the verb-particle type of noun I should add that there are a few of the members of the type that seem to occur only — or practically only — in an adjectival function: a *bring-together* volume[4] (i.e. a composite work) and a *come-hither* look are cases in point. I shall, however, consider such words as belonging to my inventory since they may be regarded as potential nouns. — I should also add that these nouns are normally fore-stressed.

The verb-particle nouns are not uniformly spelt: sometimes the two elements are written solid, sometimes they are hyphened, and sometimes they are written as two words. This circumstance may occasionally throw doubt on their membership. How, for instance, should we analyse examples like 'Have a quick *bat around* and

---

[3] Cf. Barbara Strang, *A History of English*, London 1970, p. 275f.
[4] *The Listener* 9:12.1976, p. 748.

see what's in the shops'[5] or [the dinghy] was now 'turning over and over in a slow *sink down* to the far-away sea-bed'[6]. Does the latter example contain a description of 'a slow sink / down to the sea-bed' or of 'a sink-down to the sea-bed'? It is hard to tell. It may be added that a few of these nouns have double plurals. For instance, according to the *OED* Supplement, vol. I, the plural of *break-away* is either *break-aways* or *breaks-away*, the latter being a form that suggests that the amalgamation of the two components is less than complete. This is, however, exceptional; most of these nouns are undoubtedly true compounds.

I said a moment ago that this type of noun consists of the stem of a verb plus a particle. The term 'stem' is non-committal; but in fact it has been suggested that the origin of the type may be found in imperative phrases.[7] This seems not unlikely; at least it makes sense if we think of words denoting persons, like *showoff, standby,* and *tearaway,* and perhaps in other cases as well: the synomym of *apron,* a *pinafore* (i.e. 'pin before, pin on the dress in front') might well be imagined to have arisen out of a command.

Let me briefly sketch the history of the growth of these deverbal nouns by giving you some statistics taken from Uno Lindelöf's paper.[8] The first instance occurs in Langland's *Piers Plowman* (1377), where we read of 'Robert *renne-aboute*'[9], i.e. 'a runabout', a person who runs from place to place. From the 15th century we may note a word that is still current, *a lean-to* 'a shed', while the graphic term *a sit-up* (1483) 'a surprise' is now obsolete. There are 25 examples dating from the 16th century, 27 from the 17th. Shakespeare makes his contribution to the type when he has Falstaff use the derogatory term *a sneakup* 'a sneak'[10], and elsewhere the same character refers to 'her assistant or *go-between*'[11]. In the 18th century there are 34 examples, and when we come to the 19th century, the type begins to grow very popular. The first half of the century sees 75 new formations, the second half 181. It is hardly possible to give precise figures for the 20th century, but a thousand would not be a wild guess.[12] The point is that it is difficult to keep track of recent neologisms, which proliferate more and more as the century progresses. It takes time for the dictionaries to cope with them. Still, a lot of interesting information can be culled from the *Oxford English Dictionary* and its supplementary volumes I—III, from the *Barnhart Dictionary of New English 1963–1972* as well as from

---

[5] A. P. Cowie/R. Mackin, *The Oxford Dictionary of Current Idiomatic English*, Vol. 1: Verbs with Prepositions & Particles, 1975, p. 11.

[6] Dick Francis, *Slay-Ride*, London 1973, p. 12.

[7] Uno Lindelöf, 'English Verb-Adverb Groups Converted into Nouns', *Societas Scientiarum Fennica. Commentationes Humanarum Litterarum.* IX.5, 1938, p. 35.

[8] Uno Lindelöf, op. cit.

[9] B VI 150.

[10] *I Henry IV*, 3.3.99, 1596.

[11] *The Merry Wives of Windsor*, 2.2.273, 1598.

[12] Fritz Preuss, in 'Substantivische Neologismen aus Verb und Adverb', *Lebende Sprachen* 7, 1962, pp. 1-3, records that he has collected over 650 neologisms.

Cowie & Mackin's *Oxford Dictionary of Current Idiomatic English,* Vol. 1: Verbs with Prepositions & Particles.

Statistical information can, however, do no more than convey a rough idea of the tempo at which these verb-particle nouns have proliferated, since many of them undergo great semantic diversification, and there is not agreement on how many separate senses of a given word we should operate with. I shall try to illustrate this by taking a look at a phrasal verb and some of its nominalizations.

The *OED* and its Supplement list 18 different uses of the phrasal verb *to pick up*. I am not going to go through them all, and I shall leave out technicalities, but I shall comment on a number of them, giving examples from the *OED*.

The basic meaning of *pick up* is 'take (up)' or by implication 'receive'. There is an example dating from 1687 in which it is synonymous with capturing (a vessel), and from 1871 dates the first example in which it means 'arrest (a person)': 'They are picked up for taking horses or sheep...' This produces the noun *a pickup* 'an arrest', which has been current since 1908. *Pick up* could also — euphemistically — mean 'rob', 'steal', or 'swindle', and in 1770, according to one source, highwaymen were interested in 'intelligence of who is worth picking up'. The corresponding noun, meaning 'theft', only crops up in 1938: 'He had been persuaded to try his hand at "the pickup" (stealing from unattended motor cars)'. The verb can also have human beings as its object. In 1698 Jeremy Collier published his *Short View of the Immorality and Profaneness of the English Stage*, in which we learn that nothing is more common than to see 'Women debauch'd, and Wenches Pick'd up...', i.e. for immoral purposes. By 1871 the process had been nominalized, for from that year dates a definition of *a pickup* as 'a street-walker, of the less disreputable sort'. It may be added that the person involved need not nowadays be a professional; 'The pickup lacked grace and she made it clear she was bored'. The noun also denotes the act of establishing such a (casual) relationship. Besides, *a pickup* may be a quite innocent phenomenon: it may mean 'a free ride in a car' (since 1938), or a stop made to collect passengers or goods, or again, the people or things that are collected. Further, it may denote a train that picks up passengers, as in this — the first — example from 1877: 'The last train at night...is called the Pick up.' More recently — in the 1930s — *pickup* has come to be used of a small truck or van that carries light loads. While we are on the subject of vehicles, it may be added that the phrasal verb is used about a car gaining speed: 'He noted how quickly his car picked up', and the corresponding nominalization is seen in 'This car has a good pickup'.

We move from vehicles to health. *To pick up* in the sense of 'recovering, improving' is attested as early as 1741 (in Richardson's *Pamela*), and the corresponding noun crops up in 1916: 'his recovery...his pickup'. This use of the noun denotes a process and its subsequent result, and the medicine that may start the process of recovery is also termed a *pickup* (1881—), being synonymous with a *pick-me-up*, i.e. a tonic to relieve depression.

To pick up, as I began by saying, may by implication mean 'receive', 'detect', and the like, by means of an appropriate instrument. This use of the verb has been on record since 1888, and the corresponding noun, meaning 'reception', was first used in 1925: '"Pick-up" of unwanted [radio] stations'. I promised not to discuss technicalities, but this is what I would call a popularized technicality, and so is the use of *pick-up* when it means 'the tone-arm of a record-player'. There are other technical uses of the noun: it occurs in special senses in cricket, printing, music, nuclear physics, and engineering, but these I shall leave out of account. It should be clear from the examples given that phrasal verbs have a tendency to develop many sense-differentiations, and that several of them will in due course be nominalized. But there are other causes underlying the proliferation of these nouns. Let me comment on three such causes.

(a) Some of the verb-particle combinations were originally only adjectives, but have subsequently been converted into nouns. Thus a *tumble-down* house (1818) may later be referred to simply as a *tumble-down* (1866), and similarly *button-up* shoes becomes *button-ups, clip-on lenses, clip-ons*.

(b) Sometimes the existence of one noun brings about the creation of its antonym. The noun *feedback* is attested since 1920, and this probably gave rise to *feedforward*, which is defined in the *Barnhart Dictionary* as 'the control of a feedback process by anticipating any defects in the process before it is carried out'. Let me illustrate the definition with an example from 1968: 'Consider another and a peculiarly interesting example of feedforward: what you have it in mind to say *before* you have begun to put it into any sort of words. This feedforward can be very definite. It can unhesitatingly reject any and all of your efforts to say it. "No," you note, "That isn't it at all."' A similar pair is *flashback* and *flashforward*. The former is well known as a technique in films and has prompted the creation of *flashforward*, 'a motion-picture or literary technique, in which a scene of a future event is given ahead of its occurrence in a chronological sequence' (Barnhart). A further antonymous coinage, dating from the autumn of 1983 (as far as I know), is *builddown*, based on *buildup*; this odd term is employed to refer to negotiations held between the superpowers for the purpose of reducing their nuclear arsenals.

(c) The noun *blackout*, attested since 1913, is presumably behind the form *dimout*, as in 'a "dimout" of Christmas lighting'[13], i.e. a reduction of lighting; there are phrasal verbs corresponding to both. Parallel formations are *brownout, greyout,* and *whiteout*. A *brownout* means 'loss of electric power that causes dimming of an area's lighting'; a *greyout* is a less severe form of blackout; and a *whiteout* denotes an atmospheric condition, especially in polar regions, marked by dense snow-cloud and a total obscuration of physical features: 'Sudden storms bring gale-force winds, and visibility frequently drops to zero during a "whiteout"'[14]. The striking point

[13] *Time* 3.12.1973, p. 42.
[14] *Time* 5.1.1976, p. 56.

about the last three words is that they are *not* nominalizations of phrasal verbs, which are non-existent in these cases. It seems, then, that the existence of the compound pattern and the fact that *black* in *blackout* is ambiguous (either verb or adjective) have supported the coinage of these anomalous forms.

In this connection it may be instructive to consider the type *sit-in*, which may be defined as 'a form of civil disobedience in which demonstrators occupy seats in a public place and refuse to move as a protest'[15]. There are numerous similar forms, for instance *die-in, love-in, pray-in, ride-in, swim-in,* and *teach-in,* and they all share the semantic feature of denoting an organized protest against something institutional. These forms arose in American English in the sixties and were originally connected with the civil-rights movement. A *die-in* is a group protest against the construction of nuclear energy plants, a *love-in* is a gathering, often by hippies, to celebrate love or to express their mutual love, a *pray-in* is a protest gathering characterized by prayers and sermons, a *ride-in* takes place — or rather, used to take place — in segregated buses, a *swim-in* in segregated swimming-pools, and a *teach-in* is a long meeting or session held by university teachers and students for the purpose of expressing dissenting or critical views on an important political or social issue. But while they all have this semantic element of protest in common, they are none of them — except for *sit-in* — derived from phrasal verbs. The same is obviously true of the word *tree-in*, which means 'climbing a tree to prevent its being felled'[16], and of *sick-out*, 'the organized absence of employees from their jobs'. Besides, it should be noted that in some coinages of this type the protest element is absent: a *sail-in* simply means an annual sailboat regatta, a *design-in* is a convention of designers, and a meeting of psychiatrists has been referred to as a *shrink-in*[17]. All these examples show how popular is the morphological type consisting of a monosyllable (not necessarily a verb[18]) followed by *in*. And if we widen the perspective, considering not just the *-in* forms, but all such nouns, there is some evidence to suggest that a number of these nouns may appear simultaneously with or actually earlier than the corresponding phrasal verbs: according to the *OED* both *to dim out* and *a dimout* were first used in 1942; the first example of *a crackdown* is from 1935, while the phrasal verb *to crack down (on)* is from 1940. The first instance of *countdown* is dated to 1953, while *to count down* is not attested till five years later, in 1958. It is of course possible that the dictionary has provided insufficient chronological data on these words. But if that is not the case, it may perhaps be assumed that the proliferation and firm entrenchment of this type of noun occasionally enable exponents of it to come into existence *without*

[15] *Collins Dictionary of the English Language.* 1980.
[16] *Time* 8.4.1974, p. 28.
[17] K. B. Harder, 'Coinages of the Type of "Sit-In"', *American Speech* 43, 1968, p. 62f.
[18] Cf. Cowie/Mackin, op. cit., p. xxxiv: 'There are several nominalized forms...which are 'anomalous' in the sense that there are no corresponding verb + particle expressions from which they can be derived.'

the support of a phrasal verb; if so, it becomes easier to account for those words in which the first element is not a verb.

In most cases, however, the phrasal verb precedes the noun in time, sometimes by many centuries. An extreme case is *to give up*, which was first employed in the sense of 'surrendering' in 1154, while the first example of the nominalization *give-up* dates from 1895. At the other extreme we may note that in a given context a writer first introduces a phrasal verb, subsequently proceeding to nominalize it: 'The city...would...start laying off those who had been most recently hired...the layoffs lasted only a month'[19]. An example like this may perhaps be said to epitomize the creation of the majority of these nouns.

My previous discussion of the word *pick-up* may serve as a point of departure for an analysis of some of the semantic and stylistic characteristics of these nouns.

It will have been noted that *pick-up* can denote both the act of picking up — in various senses —, the thing that picks up, and the person or thing that is picked up. In his very detailed book on English word-formation[20] Hans Marchand in fact sets up two semantic types: the dominant impersonal one (represented by *blackout*) and the type that denotes persons and which has fewer members (represented by *showoff*). This division into two types is hardly expedient, in my view, since many words belong to both types. That is true of a *dropout*, a word that is probably best known as a term denoting a person who drops out (of school, etc.), but which also means 'a drop-kick' (in Rugby football) besides having a couple of non-personal, technical uses in photography and tape-recording. On the other hand, a *comeback* is probably best known as referring to a situation in which somebody successfully returns to a former position: 'He staged a comeback'; but the word is also used of a person who has returned. A *ripoff* can mean either 'a swindle' or 'a thief' (both since 1970). It is true that there are a few nouns which only denote persons: a *go-between*, a *layabout* 'a lazy person', a *butt-in* (meaning 'an intruder', also called a *buttinsky*); but it may well be imagined that even these may acquire non-personal uses in course of time. For a prominent characteristic of these formations is their semantic versatility: *stirabout* was first (1682) used about a porridge made by stirring oatmeal in boiling water; later (1870) the word came to be used about 'a bustling person', and subsequently (1905) it acquired the sense of 'a bustle, a state of confusion'.

The fact remains, however, that the impersonal senses dominate; and they differ widely. Take a recent newcomer like a *hangup*, which means a psychological problem or a cause of annoyance, thus a fairly abstract sense. More often, what is denoted is an act, a process, or an event corresponding to what is expressed in the verbal phrase, as exemplified by a *walkout*, a *fade-away*, and a *get-together*. Besides,

[19] *Time* 25.6.1984, p. 41.
[20] *The Categories and Types of Present-Day English Word-Formation*, second edition, München 1969. p. 382.

these nouns may denote substances and physical objects of various kinds: *makeup* may be synonymous with 'cosmetics'; a *mock-up* is a model, a *paste-on* a slip added to a manuscript, and a *pull-over* an article of clothing.

Stylistically, these verb + particle nouns are generally colloquial, and they often fit well into the transitive sentence pattern that is so characteristic of contemporary English. A statement like 'he shouted' is less idiomatic than 'he gave a shout', where we have a general verb, in this case *give* (others are *do, have,* and *take*) followed by an object. The reason why the transitive pattern is preferred is that it lends greater end-weight to the sentence than does the intransitive pattern, and the verb + particle noun is accommodated in this transitive pattern in examples like 'She gave it a brisk look-over', 'Have a good look-round', 'He made a mess-up of the job', 'He took down a standard textbook and had a quick thumb-through', 'She gave me the brush-off', etc.

From colloquialisms we move insensibly towards slangy and vulgar expressions. A *carve-up* may be employed as a graphic term denoting the distribution of an estate, or to be less technical, the sharing of an inheritance (where the money involved is regarded as booty). A *booze-up* is a party where a lot of drinking goes on. There are numerous words of our type conveying the notion of 'failure' or 'mistake', and they are not all of them equally acceptable in polite society: *balls-up, bog-up, botch-up, cock-up, foulup, fuckup, mess-up, muck-up, screwup.* This last batch of examples may remind us of the many other cases of synonymity (or near-synonymity) between two or more terms. Both *crackup* and *breakdown* may mean 'collapse'. A *flyby* and a *flypast* both denote a procession of aircraft or — in space travel — 'a flight which does not land on a planet but passes close enough to obtain pictures and other information'. If we want to convey the idea of a hearty meal, we have available both a *dig-in,* a *fill-out,* a *tuck-in,* and a *tuck-out,* and the food can be bought either at a *take-away* or at a *take-out.* A student who interrupts his studies may be variously referred to as a *dropout,* a *stopout,* or a *walkout.* Is there any difference? Well, I have noted a comment made by a member of an organization called the Carnegie Commission apropos of the word *stopout*: 'Our Commission coined this word, which has now become popular, to convey a constructive aspect to the earlier denigrating term of dropout.'[21] This observation was made in 1973, and we cannot be sure whether the sense-differentiation has become generally accepted; but the examples of synonyms I have given suggest how popular and productive is the type.

As we have seen, there may be internal synonymity between representatives of the verb-particle type of noun; but there is of course also synonymity between members of this colloquial stratum and members of the neutral or formal strata of the vocabulary, and this facilitates stylistic variation. A *blow-up* is an explosion. A bribe may be termed a *payoff*; the orderly withdrawal of troops is a *pullback*;

[21] *The Times Higher Education Supplement* 19.10.1973, p. 11.

evasive answers may be called *putoffs*; and a recluse or a hermit may be referred to as a *shut-in*. This kind of variation is particularly favoured in American English (which has, incidentally, contributed a very substantial number of verb-particle nouns). Let me illustrate this point by giving a couple of examples from *Time* Magazine: 'A few Argentines even compare the faceoff with the IMF to their confrontation with the British over the Falkland Islands.'[22] 'Berger's latest book is either a grossly awkward takeoff on the excesses of Women's Lib or a blundering satire about the way men treat women.'[23] Here *takeoff* almost equals *satire*; but if we read of '"speak-outs" and conferences'[24], it is difficult to decide whether or not there is a sense-differentiation. If an ultra-colloquial term appears in a traditionally solemn context, it produces a shock effect, and may incidentally be in rather poor taste. Here are examples from recent novels; 'I felt they were unconsciously celebrating the late Mr Johnson with a two-minute shut-up'[25]. — 'The day before, there had been a sob-in, as some of the younger set called a funeral service'[26].

No matter which aspects of modern life we want to describe, these nouns are available; but there are some semantic fields in which they are particularly numerous. One such field is sports and games. There are not a few verb-particle nouns that describe technicalities: in baseball (e.g. *fadeaway*), cricket (e.g. *breakback*), golf (e.g. *tee-off*), hockey (e.g. *bully-off*), and tennis (e.g. *putaway*). These are for insiders, while others have general currency. Before any game begins, there will be a *warmup* or a *limber-up*, perhaps in the form of a few *pressups* or *pushups* (the latter term being mainly American English). If it is a football match, there may be some *kick-about* before it begins, to loosen up the muscles of the players. There may also be some *kick-in*, i.e. practising goalshooting. The *kick-off* marks the start of the game. If the ball is kicked out of play, there will be a *throw-in*.

Descriptions of modern warfare are sprinkled with these nouns, especially in American English. There may be a *callup* of citizens for military service, and a *callout* of reserves. If détente is working, there may be a *drawdown* or a *thinout* of forces; if not, there may be a *stepup* in military activity, possibly leading to a *faceoff*, i.e. a confrontation. Unfortunately there may also be the risk of a nuclear explosion, followed by *fallout*, radioactive dust. It goes without saying that many of these terms also occur in non-military contexts.

I turn briefly to another relevant field, that of commerce. A key term here is *turnover*: the volume of business that is done in a particular period. Another central word is *takeover*: gaining control over a business company by buying most of the

[22] *Time* 25.6.1984, p. 39.
[23] *Time* 14.5.1973, p. 66.
[24] *Time* 13.10.1975, p. 45.
[25] Bernice Rubens, *Sunday Best*, London 1971, p. 41.
[26] Peter DeVries, *Into Your Tent I'll Creep*, London 1972, p. 67.

shares. Prices go up and down, and a *markup* is a price increase, the opposite being a *markdown* or a *rollback*. If somebody gives something in part payment when he buys an article, we speak of a *tradein*. Instead of the formal term *repurchase* one finds dealers in oil referring to *buybacks*. If it is necessary to raise a loan, it may be of the rollover type, *rollover* meaning the kind of loan for which interest rates are adjusted at fixed intervals. If by an illegal arrangement somebody receives a secret payment that is made in return for a business favour, we speak of a *kickback*.

It is a remarkable fact that verb-particle nouns, being basically colloquial, should have extensive technical uses. Sometimes there is a glaring discrepancy between the deceptive simplicity of such forms and the lengthy explanations that are required to make it clear what is meant. I have come across two names of tree diseases, *dieback* and *stopback*, and shall give the dictionary definitions of them. *Dieback*, according to the Supplement to the *OED*, is 'The progressive dying of a shrub or tree shoot from the tip backwards, caused by disease or unfavourable conditions, esp. a disease of fruit trees'. And *stopback* is defined as follows in *Webster's Third New International Dictionary* (1961): 'a condition in peach and pear nursery stock caused by the attack of the tarnished plant bug...and characterized by the death of the tender terminal bud of the principal shoot and the forcing of the development of lateral shoots'. These two words represent the extreme of encapsulation, *multum in parvo*. They are like shorthand signs, summing up the gist of the matter in just two syllables each. But of course they only make sense to insiders. Paradoxically, in spite of being colloquial in form they are only known to specialists; and as far as I know, there exist no formal, learned synonyms.

These are, however, extreme cases. If we turn to modern means of transportation like cars, planes, and space-ships and consider some of the examples of verb-particle nouns that are employed to describe them, we shall see that on the whole much briefer and simpler paraphrases are needed to explain these terms. It is true that if we are to make sense of the expression *toe-in*, used about motor cars, we need to be told that this word means 'a slight forward convergence given to the wheels to improve steering and equalize tyre wear'. This explanation is not nearly so lengthy as those given for the two diseases I have just mentioned, and there is even less discrepancy between the form *tune-up* and the explanation of this phenomenon as 'adjustments made to an engine to improve its performance', while a term like engine *start-up* is self-explanatory. The *takeoff* of an aircraft is the beginning of its flight, and the *blast-off* or *lift-off* of a space vehicle are synonyms of *takeoff*. The minutes and seconds immediately before the launching of a space vehicle will be taken up by the *countdown*, and when the vehicle lands in the sea, the phenomenon is referred to by the suggestive term a *splashdown*.

Though the verb-particle noun is undoubtedly in a dominant position today, it does have a weak competitor in the nominal compound that consists of particle plus verbal stem. The 19th century saw the creation of *downpour* (1811), and nouns like *outcome, upkeep,* and *uptake* became current in the 19th century; according to

Jespersen they are of Scottish origin.[27] If we consider *putin* and *input*, we have an atypical situation. *Putin* is not much used today; where it occurs, it means 'one's turn to speak'. *Input* is another Scottish form, dating from the mid-18th century, which led a languishing existence until the end of the 19th century, when it began to be revived, and as is well known, the 20th century has seen an enormous extension of its use, not least in computer terminology. Another exception to the general tendency is the noun *upswing*, as in 'an upswing in technological progress'. This must be a fairly recent word; it is not in the *OED*, though it *is* listed in *Webster* (1961).

Normally, when representatives of the two types exist side by side, they are semantically quite distinct. Thus we speak of an *outbreak* (1602) of disease or of hostilities, while a *breakout* (1820) is typically used about people escaping from a prison. An *outlet* (1250) may give vent to one's feelings, while a *letout* (1836) means a loophole, an excuse: 'There is no easy letout'. *Uplift* (1845) may refer to moral improvement, while the modern form a *lift-up* has a physical sense, as in 'He gave me a lift-up'. There is, however, less semantic difference between an *offprint* (1885) 'an extra printing of an article' and a *printoff* (modern) 'a print from a negative film'. And if we compare a *turndown* (1902) and a *downturn* (1926), there appears to be little to choose between them: we may speak of 'a turndown in the economy' and of 'a downturn in industrial production'. According to Cowie & Mackin *downturn* is the more usual form; this shows that the older type has not been completely ousted.

I have tried to give an account — on the whole neutral and factual, I hope — of major aspects of the rise, spread, and present-day use of the verb-particle noun, which must be said to have become very important in modern English word-formation. It may be added that this type of noun is popular not only in the English-speaking countries; some of its representatives have been adopted by other languages. Thus, among English loanwords in modern German and Danish we find *comeback, drive-in, feedback, knockout, lockout, love-in, makeup, pullover,* and *sit-in.* Both in German and in Danish these words are stressed on the last syllable.

Perhaps a few critical comments are now in order. The spread of the type has not gone unheeded. These nouns are largely derived from phrasal verbs, the proliferation of which has been criticized among others by A. P. Herbert[28] and Sir Ernest Gowers. The latter recognizes that the use of phrasal verbs as nouns has proved 'an invaluable method of enriching our vocabulary vigorously from native material instead of relying on foreign borrowing', but he adds that this useful resource is now being abused[29]. There is some justice in this criticism if we think of

[27] *A Modern English Grammar,* vol. 6, 1942, p. 161.
[28] *What a Word!,* London 1935, pp. 151ff.
[29] *A Dictionary of Modern English Usage,* by H. F. Fowler, second edition revised by Sir Ernest Gowers, Oxford 1965, p. 451.

examples like *check up, close out, lose out, match up, miss out,* and *win out*; and some of these have produced nouns whose raison d'être is less than convincing: 'One might wish for a better match-up between the ideal and the real'[30]; 'A background in contract close-out'. The latter example, in which *close-out* means 'completion', is commented on as follows by Kenneth Hudson: 'A crude and unnecessary piece of business jargon. ... The 'completion' or 'signing' of a contract is reckoned to suggest an over-respectable and slow-moving company, whereas 'close-out' is appropriate to the dynamic, shirt-sleeved brigade.'[31] It can hardly be denied that there are certain areas in which the coinage of these verb-particle nouns tends to run riot; fortunately, at the same time it seems probable that some of these more faddish coinages will turn out to be shortlived.

But there are some of these neologisms that one would miss if they turned out to be ephemeral. One such is *inchback*. It is not — or not yet — in the dictionaries. When it appears in a suitable context, as in a 'plan for an inchback: a series of reductions'[32], it is wonderfully expressive. At the same time it may conveniently be used to illustrate the fate of some English words over a period of a thousand years. The noun *inch* (OE *ynce*) was borrowed from Latin *uncia* in Anglo-Saxon times. In 1599 it was first converted into a verb; *to inch* is 'to move by small degrees'. It then combined with particles to form phrasal verbs, so that one could *inch forward* or *inch back*; and finally — probably quite recently — it was nominalized. Thus we have moved from a noun to a verb to a new noun through the process of conversion, and no doubt the future will see many similar developments.

[30] *Time* 27.1.1975, p. 2.
[31] *The Dictionary of Diseased English*, New York 1977, p. 36.
[32] *Time* 6.1.1975, p. 38.

IV
LINGUISTIC
INTERFERENCE

THOMAS LODGE'S *SENECA*

Thomas Lodge is perhaps best known as the author of *Rosalynde*. But like many Elizabethans, he was a versatile writer, and he is also among the diligent translators of the age. Some time ago the present writer published a thesis on Lodge's *Seneca*[1], some findings of which will be discussed below in the light of later investigations.

I. Lodge's Use of his Sources

Tracing the sources of a typical Elizabethan like Lodge is a task that requires considerable patience. In my thesis I established that in preparing his Senecan translation of 1614, *The Workes both Morrall and Natural of Lucius Annæus Seneca,* Lodge drew on several aids: Arthur Golding's translation of 1578, *The woorke of the excellent Philosopher Lucius Annæus Seneca concerning Benefyting,* Justus Lipsius's Senecan edition of 1605, whose commentary he frequently incorporated in his rendering, Pincianus's *Castigationes in omnia Senecae scripta* (1536), and perhaps several learned treatises on the antiquities[2]. Besides, I suspected that he at least occasionally consulted another Latin edition which I was unable to identify. During a recent visit to the British Museum I had an opportunity to inspect E.A. Tenney's *Thomas Lodge*[3], which may provide the clue to the solution of this problem. According to Tenney[4] an entry in the Stationers' Register as early as April 15, 1600 can be taken to refer to Lodge's projected Senecan translation. This entry contains the passage '...a booke to be translated out of French and Latyn...' – if correct, a highly surprising statement, since it would mean that the translator did not content himself with using the several aids mentioned above, but drew on a French translation as well. In fact, however, this turned out to be the case, and an examination even shows that Lodge employed *two* French translations.

In the period before Lodge published his rendering of Seneca there had appeared three French translations:

(1) *Les SEPT LIVRES de Seneque, traitant des bienfaits. Auec la vie dudit Seneque. Le tout traduit de Latin en François, par Sauueur Accaurrat,* Paris 1561.

(2) *LES ŒVVRES MORALES ET MESLEES DE SENECQUE. Traduites de Latin en François, & nouuellement mises en lumiere par SIMON GOVLAR[R]T SENLISIEN,* I-III, Paris, 1595 (later editions 1598, 1604, 1606).

(3) *LES ŒVVRES DE L. ANNÆVS SENECA, mises en françois par Mathiev de Chalvet,* Paris, 1604 (later editions 1609, 1616, 1618, 1624, 1628, 1634, 1638).

The first of these renderings only comprises the *De beneficiis,* and there are no indications that Lodge knew or used it. But a comparison between his text and Goulart's and Chalvet's translations reveals obvious similarities. Undoubtedly Lodge borrowed from both, but curiously enough he drew on Chalvet in preparing the treatise placed first in the *Workes,* viz. *Of Benefits,* while for one of the last works, *The naturall Questions,* he utilized Goulart; in view of the dates of publication of the two French translations one might have expected the reverse to be the case. I have not examined the intervening works, and the present article does not pretend to be exhaustive – in any case that would probably be a hopeless task – but from a fair number of test samples I shall list below some specimens that show the nature of Lodge's indebtedness.

First let us consider the translation of the *De beneficiis*[5]. Several of Lodge's marginal notes turn out to be almost word-for-word renderings of Chalvet's notes, for instance:

Goulart	Chalvet	Lodge
1[r] *Des grandes & diuerses fautes que les hommes cõmettent a faire, receuoir, & reconoistre plaisir les vns des autres.*	1[r] L'indiscretiõ des hommes à donner ou receuoir plaisir, rend l'ingratitude si frequente.	1 *Mens indiscretion in giuing & receiuing benefits maketh ingratitude so frequent.*
21[v] *Quelles sõt les principales sources de l'ingratitude.*	17[v] Trois principales causes de l'ingratitude, l'opinion desoy, la conuoitise, l'enuie.	34 *Three principall causes of ingratitude, selfe-opinion, couetousnesse, and enuie.*
[Nothing]	4[r] autre subtilité de Chrysippe.	6 Chrisipppus *triuiall subtiltie.*

Besides demonstrating Lodge's dependence on Chalvet, a comparison between these notes also sheds light on Chalvet's occasional borrowings from Goulart, though Chalvet does not normally borrow verbatim from his predecessor. But Lodge's indebtedness to Chalvet is perhaps brought out in a more convincing manner if we compare some parallel passages from the text:

Lipsius I. 2 In priore versu vtrumque reprehendas. nam nec in vulgus effundenda sunt; & nullius rei, minime beneficiorum, honesta largitio est.

Goulart 4[r] Il y a deux choses à reprendre au premier vers. Car il ne faut pas estre ainsi au commandement de tout vn peuple, & n'y a pas honneur de semer ainsi les choses (moins encor les bienfaits) à poignees:...

Chalvet 2[v] Tu peux iustement reprendre les deux poincts de ce premier vers, par ce qu'il ne les faut point prodiguer indifferemment à chacun. En outre il n'est pas honneste d'vser de largesse & prodigalité d'aucune chose, & moins encor des bienfaicts.

Lodge 3 In the former Verse thou maiest iustly reprehend both these two clauses; for neither must our benefits bee profusedly lauished on euery man, neither can the prodigalitie and largesse of any thing bee honest: especially that of benefits.

Lipsius IV.39 deserentem vis maior excusat.	Goulart 57^r Qui ne se trouue à l'assignatiõ il peut proposer ses excuses & defences, receuables, quand elles sont legitimes.
Chalvet 49^r Car s'il y a quelqu'vn qui soit empesché par force & par vne legitime cause, il est excusé par exoine.	Lodge 90 For if there be any one that is hindered by force, or by a lawfull cause he is excused by essoyne.

If taken together, the similarity between Lodge and Chalvet and the difference between Lodge and Goulart leave no doubt as to which of the French translations Lodge drew on in these and in several other passages of *Of Benefits*. Note especially the peculiar technical term *essoyne* which I wrongly supposed had been suggested to Lodge by his legal past[6].

If we proceed to examine the *Naturales quaestiones,* we observe a close similarity in many passages between Goulart and Lodge. Here again there are sometimes indications that Chalvet borrowed suggestions from Goulart, but he generally embroiders them, so that his version differs much more from Lodge's than does that of Goulart. This can only mean that for reasons best known to himself Lodge had by this time given up using Chalvet, turning instead to Goulart. Let us consider a few extracts[7]:

Lipsius IV. 13 Iubes me cum luxuriâ litigare	Goulart 106 Ainsi; tu veux que ie plaide contre la dissolution
Chalvet 479^r Tu me veux mettre en querelle auec la prodigalité	Lodge 843 Thou willest me to pleade against dissolution
Lipsius III.20 Aut furit, aut patitur grauitate soporem.	Goulart 75 Il deuient furieux, ou tombe en lethargie.
Chalvet 465^r Il deuient furieux, ou tout soudainement/Vn sommeil estourdy le presse griefuement	Lodge 818 Growes furious, or els fals to Lethargie

Marginal notes, *Nat. quaest.* II.2:

Goulart 27 *Des elemẽs ou corps simples, l'vn desquels est l'air.*	Chalvet 445^r Discours general des elemẽs ou corps simples & premierement de l'air.	Lodge 778 *Of the Elements or simple body, whereof one is the aire.*

One becomes even more convinced of Lodge's indebtedness to Goulart in *The naturall Questions* when one notices that Chalvet leaves out a good many of Goulart's marginal notes, while several of these notes occur in Lodge.

An analysis of these parallel passages gives rise to another observation. In the first quotation listed above Lodge goes on to refer to *dissolution* as *she, her,* and these pronouns may well have been suggested by the French *la, elle;* in other words: his personification of abstracts need not always be exclusively due to Latin influence[8]. Similarly, there may be French influence behind some of Lodge's subjunctives[9]; consider the following instance:

Nat. quaest. I.4

Goulart 9 L'image ou representation qui se fait à cause du miroir, ne paroit iamais sinon que le miroir *soit* opposé en telle sorte...

Lodge 764 The image and representation which is made by reason of the mirror, neuer appeareth except the mirror *be* opposed in such sort...

In view of the haphazard and hurried manner in which Lodge frequently used other helps[10], it would not be surprising to find him handling Goulart with a similar carelessness. There are indeed several instances of mistranslation caused by slovenliness and hurry, of which I shall give here a rather comical one. It is highly puzzling to note that Lodge renders the place-name *Patrae* by the form *Patrassa;* but a glance at Goulart's text explains the crux:

Nat. quaest. VI.25 Cum laborauit Ægium, tam propinquas illi Patras de motu nihil audisse?

Goulart 149 Ægium fut rudement agitee, & *Patra sa* voisine n'en omit rien.

Lodge 877 Ægium was violently tossed, and *Patrassa* that was neare vnto it, heard nothing of it.

(Chalvet 497[r]: *Patræ*).

The translator here committed a kind of semantic dittography.

It should not, however, be inferred from the above that Lodge's use of the French translation is stamped by injudiciousness throughout. On the contrary it is clear that he must constantly have consulted other aids, for when Goulart skips a passage, as sometimes happens, it nevertheless appears in Lodge. This is for instance true of the somewhat unsavoury account of Hostius in the *Nat. quaest.* I.16, which Goulart's squeamishness (or piety) forbids him to refer to in more explicit terms than 'ses vilenies prodigieuses, trop execrables pour estre representees aux yeux du lecteur' (p. 21), while Lodge includes all details, relying on Lipsius and perhaps on Chalvet as well. Another mark of his critical and independent attitude is the fact that many of his marginal notes containing moral reflections and precepts are his own contribution. Consider his fervent apostrophe to the reader *à propos* of the Hostius story:

Modest eies blush & Christian ears abhorre these relations: shamelesse; reade it with shame, for such like actions, O can there be such? breede confusion for euer. (p. 774)

This outburst has no counterpart in the French versions.

One of the principal motives underlying Lodge's wish to present English readers with a rendering of Seneca was the latter's moral message, generally interpreted by the translator in terms of Christianity. And the best way of accounting for the copious use he made of his various aids is to assume a genuine urge on his part to clarify and elucidate his edifying text as much as possible. The procedure he adopted must have been laborious in the extreme, and it is

(316-317)

understandable that he did not everywhere acquit himself equally well; it is not that he was lacking in diligence, but unfortunately his diligence was not matched by a corresponding degree of meticulousness. It gives food for thought, however, that he did not content himself with consulting a single translation, but drew selectively on a Latin commentary and three previous renderings. Plagiarism is not an apposite term to apply to his working method, for the Elizabethans did not share the modern attitude where borrowing was concerned: 'Not only were Englishmen from 1500 to 1625 without any feeling analogous to the modern attitude towards plagiarism; they even lacked the word until the very end of that period'[11].

It would be a mistake to believe that the list of Lodge's helps referred to above is exhaustive. Perhaps the most useful lesson to be drawn from a study like the present is to realize that there are practically no limits to the omnivorousness of Elizabethan translators; and unfortunately modern source investigation is rendered difficult by the fact that there was no moral obligation for translators and writers to state their sources. As has been shown by Alice Walker[12], Lodge composed some of his prose pamphlets by dovetailing a medly of extracts translated from various sources. By a combination of patience and luck it is possible to trace some of these sources, but there will always remain cruxes. To take a single instance from the *Workes:* where did Lodge borrow his definition of *Casma?*

Casma is when much vapour is inflamed in a watry cloud, or one that is very thin.

(marginal note p. 772)

This note was hardly of his own composition, for Lodge was not a scholar; he does not appear to have used contemporary dictionaries, and the French translations have no notes on this passage.

In this connexion I want to draw attention to a point dealt with by Alice Walker in the article mentioned above. She states that among the works Lodge borrowed from when composing *Wits Miserie, and the Worlds Madnesse* (1596) was Robert Holkot's *In Librum Sapientiæ Prælectiones,* to which she attributes an anecdote from the *De beneficiis* (IV.37). On checking the sources I found that Lodge's rendering (pp. 16-17 of the 1596 edition) differs considerably from Holkot's version (p. 37 in the 1586 edition), which in its turn differs from the Senecan text, so that Lodge can hardly have based his anecdote in *Wits Miserie* on either Seneca or Holkot since he normally follows his source closely. In my view, then, one is forced to assume the existence of an unknown intermediate work, a possibility Alice Walker had foreseen, but rejected. When seen in isolation the problem may appear a trivial one, but it is of great theoretical importance: it shows the difficulty of determining a source relationship.

In my thesis I expressed some surprise at the slovenly character of Lodge's *Seneca.* Since then I have come to realize the significance of a number of facts which may enable us to reconstruct the unfavourable circumstances in which the translator tackled his self-imposed task. The work may have been in progress, or at least projected, before the turn of the century since the entry in the Stationers'

Register dates from 1600. The fact that Lodge used Chalvet first (Golding only translated the *De beneficiis*) is further corroborated by the sequence in the *Workes* which corresponds exactly with that found in most pre-Lipsian Latin editions and thus also with Chalvet's, while it deviates from the Lipsian arrangement (and also from Goulart's sequence). Lipsius placed the *De beneficiis* last among the philosophical works: '*Hos libros inter Philosophiæ vltimos pono...*' (argumentum). Lodge translated Lipsius's argument, forgetting that it did not make sense as he had adopted Chalvet's sequence which placed the *De beneficiis* first. The Lipsian edition was published in 1605, but though the influence from the commentary is manifest throughout Lodge's *Seneca*, the fact that its sequence is not the Lipsian, but Chalvet's makes one suspect that Lodge did not discover the Lipsian edition till several years later. On the title-page of the *Workes* the year of publication is given as 1614, but on two inner title-pages (p. 161 and p. 495) the date is 1613. This discrepancy may suggest that the translation was intended to appear in 1613, but that it was delayed, and that it was forgotten to alter the dates of the two separate title-pages. From Lodge's Latin preface (sig. b2ᵛ) we know that his brother died in 1612, by which time he had completed about half the translation. His brother's death threw him into abject misery, rendering him unfit for work for a year. When he resumed his work in 1613 on 'dimidium Senecæ alterum quod imperfectum reliquera*m*', the printer had grown impatient and would grant him no respite for revision. If one assumes that Lodge only discovered the Lipsian edition shortly before his MS was going to press and nevertheless did his utmost to revise it along the lines of the Lipsian commentary and text, one should view the translator in a not too unfavourable light, for then one almost begins to wonder that the errors and inconsistencies are not more numerous; Lodge's wish to incorporate last-minute corrections testifies to a conscientiousness of no mean order.

In this connexion I want to make a few comments on the list of errata, *Faults escaped in the Printing,* of whose existence I had no suspicion till recently, since they are not included in the copy of the Royal Library of Copenhagen which I used[13]. These corrections cover approximately the first half of the translation (pp. 4-578) and may shed further light on the strain under which Lodge worked. There are some corrections of regular misprints, for instance *care* for *case,* probable misreadings of the MS, as when *expalliate* is corrected into *expatiate, preserued* into *preferred* (*f* misread for the long *s*), and also some genuine revisions. Some of these may testify to his having re-checked his sources; thus *admission* (p. 240) is changed into *admonition,* perhaps because Lodge had consulted the Lipsian note on the passage: '... *Alij tamen libri,* admonitio' (p. 465, Epist. 49). These corrections may be taken to show that Lodge worked on the first half of his MS (though not the Senecan biography) till the last minute; probably he did not have time to enter the corrections before the printing but had to hand over the *Faults escaped* to the printer. If this reconstruction is correct, it is another proof of his conscientiousness.

II. Lodge's Life of Lucius Annaeus Seneca

In my thesis the only part of the *Workes* subjected to analysis was the translation of the *De beneficiis.* To supplement the picture of Lodge the translator I shall now go on to examine some points in his *Life of Lucius Annæus Seneca, described by Iustus Lipsius,* a subject that merits attention for several reasons.

In the first place it is obvious that as far as most of the *Life* is concerned Lodge was left to his own devices, there being no previous translations of Lipsius's *Vita* available. A comparison between the *Life* and *Of Benefits* leaves the general impression that in the former there occurs a somewhat higher proportion of errors due to carelessness than in the latter. This suggests that when devoid of aids, Lodge achieved poorer results than when there were cribs available. The fact that the list of *Faults escaped* does not cover the *Life* might mean that Lodge did not decide to include it in the *Workes* till the last minute, and that he was thus even more pressed for time when translating this section, but this is mere guesswork. Nor does it seem very probable that the inferior quality of the *Life* is due to beginner's difficulties, seeing that one of the treatises translated last, the *Naturales quaestiones,* is of no higher standard than *Of Benefits,* the first work. And besides, Lodge was an old hand at translating by this time; his *Josephus* had appeared as early as 1602. It appears to me, then, that the lack of aids for translating the *Vita* is the main reason for the poor quality of the *Life.*

Let us consider some instances of Lodge's slovenly and uncritical treatment of the Lipsian text. Some chapter-references are wrong, for example Lipsius xiiij: *Epist.CVIII* > Lodge c3^r: Epist. 113[14], and where – quite exceptionally – Lipsius gives a wrong reference[15], Lodge uncritically adopts it: Lipsius xiij: *Cons. ad Helu. cap. XVI* (should be *XVII*). On the whole Lodge renders everything in Lipsius indiscriminately, a procedure which may lead to curious results. Thus, in Ch. VIII of the *Vita* Lipsius has a comment on the preceding Tacitean account, rendered by Lodge as follows:

Lipsius xv Quid fæminæ hæc fuerit, & quo marito, in Notis meis ibi disces	Lodge c4^r What woman this was, and what husband she had thou shalt learne by my notes

- *my notes* being of course the Lipsian notes, which were left untranslated by Lodge.

It is a similar inability to put himself in his readers' shoes that makes him transfer a philological doubt entertained by Lipsius:

Lipsius xxiij *Aduersus præsentem formidinem mollitus.* Non rescribo temere: tamen ambigat aliquis, an non *mollitam,* & ad vxorem referatur. Sequentia videntur inducere, cum rogat temperaret, dolori, & quæ iungit.	Lodge d4^v-d5^r Being hardned against present feare, I write it not againe rashly, yet some man may doubt, should it not be *Molitam* that she was mollified, hauing relation to his wife? That which followeth seemeth to inferre the same, when hee requireth her to temper her sorrow; and that which he annexeth:...

This seems oddly out of place, for presumably there were many readers of the translation who had no Latin.

In the passage where Lipsius extols Seneca's austerity (in the matter of always having *cold* baths) which was only relaxed when he was at death's door, the sense is completely spoilt by Lodge's rendering:

Lipsius xxiij *Stagnum calidæ aquæ.* & tunc primum calidâ vsus, cum non vltra vsurus.	Lodge d5ʳ A Bath of hot water: he meaneth some Bathing-tub, and then first vsed he *colde* water when he should vse it no more.

Obviously it is not the translator's ignorance that causes such blunders; it is his hurry and inattention. There is no better proof that this is so than a comparison of the following two extracts:

Lipsius xxiij Nam vapore, & acrimoniâ caloris, *exanimatum* ostendit.	Lodge d5ʳ for hee sheweth that by the vapour and acrimonie of the heate, he was *strangled.*
Lipsius xxiij sed verba *examinata* non huc eunt.	Lodge d5ʳ But *dead* wordes passe not farre.

The second passage occurs a few lines after the first. We all know how this kind of mistake creeps in: a second *exanimata* suggests itself to the hurried reader because he has just come upon the word; it is the kind of blunder that a thorough revision would have removed.

As a final instance I may mention that Lipsius's heading of *Cap. X:* 'Libri, qui *non* exstant' is rendered by Lodge: 'Those bookes of his that *are* extant' – the more surprising as the works listed in Chapter X are unambiguously referred to as either missing, supposititious, or fragmentary. This error was not even corrected in the 1620 edition of the *Workes.*

A similar lack of revision and correlation is apparent in many of the Senecan quotations occurring in the *Life.* In the *Vita* Lipsius cites a number of passages from Seneca's writings on account of their biographical value. It is interesting to note that after translating them in the *Life,* Lodge retranslates these extracts in his text without comparing them with his first translation, and in these circumstances it is natural that the two versions should differ. Now the question is: are there any significant differences in quality between them? Before I try to answer that question, it is necessary to emphasize that the material on which any conclusions can be drawn is scanty: there occur a total of 17 passages translated twice, and one extract has been rendered three times because it appears twice in the *Vita;* moreover, some of these quotations are very brief. Nevertheless some differences seem important enough to call for comment.

The general impression of carelessness conveyed by the *Life* is corroborated by an examination of Lodge's handling of these passages. But it should be stressed that if they are on the whole less correct and more awkward than the corresponding passages in the text, the reason may well be that a brief extract, studied in isolation, makes heavier demands on a translator than if it is read in its natural context where, besides, there are previous translations and a commentary to rely on. And that Lodge did not in the first translation examine the context seems probable from his renderings of the following passage:

De clem. II.2 Diutius me *momari* hîc patere, non vt blandiar auribus tuis: nec enim mihi mos est.

d2ʳ Suffer me to *stay* here a little longer with thee, not to flatter thine eares, for this is not my custome.

605 Suffer me to *insist* a little longer on[e] this point, not to the intent to tickle or flatter thine eares, for it is not my custome.

Though to *stay on a topic* was current Elizabethan usage, there is no evidence for the absolute use of the verb in this sense, and even if it is considered a Latinism (which does not appear very probable), the first translation is at least ambiguous; it was only by consulting the context that Lodge could have realized that *morari* is here used in a transferred sense. – Slavishness is apparent in several passages. In the quotation given below would not a perusal of his draft translation have made Lodge revise it along the lines of the second version? In the latter the deficiency has been remedied by the addition of a single word:

Epist. 108 Cum coeperat voluptates nostras traducere, laudare castum corpus, sobriam mensam, puram mentem, non tantum ab illicitis voluptatibus, sed etiam superuacuis: ...

d2ʳ When he beganne to traduce our pleasures, to praise a chaste bodie, a sober table, a pure minde; not onely from vnlawfull pleasures, but also from superfluous ...

444 When he began to traduce our pleasures, to praise a chaste bodie, a sober table, a pure mind, not onely *exempted* from vnlawful pleasures, but also superfluous ...

Considering the almost complete identity of the two versions an alternative explanation presents itself, viz. that here Lodge *did* consult his first translation, but that it was too late for him to alter it.

On the whole there is clearly a greater striving for clarity and intelligibility in the text than in the *Life.* Thus the *prodigium* of the *Nat. quaest.* I. 1 is first rendered simply by *prodigie* (c3ʳ) and is then expanded into *Meteor, and prodigie* (758). And though the first translation of *caussam dicere* is passable, it is less precise and idiomatic than the second rendering:

De ira III.36... apud me caussam dico

d2ᵛ [I] examine my selfe

577 [I] pleade before my selfe

It should be added that there is an additional way of accounting for some of the discrepancies between the two versions. In the *Vita* Lipsius does not always give his quotations in exactly the same wording as in the text. A comparison shows that in the *Vita* he appears to have relaxed his customary meticulousness with the result that there occur both omissions and transposed word-order and the substitution of synonymous terms. Sometimes he adapts his quotations to fit in with his own account, sometimes one has a suspicion that he quotes from memory. True, these discrepancies do not as a rule affect the passages seriously:

there is not much to choose between for instance *Vita* p. xx *ciuilem vitam* and Epist. 108 p. 634 *ciuitatis vitam,* or between *Vita* p. xvij *in familiâ meâ* and Epist. 50 p. 467 *in domo meâ.* But that these textual variations may have their share in causing different versions in Lodge is obvious from a passage like the following:

Vita xiiij *Adolescentia* eius in *Tiberij principatum incidit,* vt ipse fatetur: idque eo tempore, quo *aliena sacra mouebantur.*	c3ʳ his youth hapned in the beginning of *Tiberius* gouernment, as he himselfe confesseth, and about that time, when forraine sacrifices were remoued and abolished.
Epist. 108 In Tiberij Cæsaris principatum iuuentæ tempus inciderat: alienigenarum sacra mouebantur...	445 It was in my yonger dayes, at such time as *Tiberius* was Emperour, when as the Religions of strangers were banished out of Rome...

Though the two versions of the extracts translated twice do not differ radically, then, it is nevertheless unmistakable that in point of quality the second version is the better, being on the whole more correct and idiomatic.

The Lipsian *Vita* contains a number of poetical quotations from Juvenal, Martial, Statius, and the Senecan tragedies of *Medea* and *Octauia.* For the translation of some of these quotations Lodge might theoretically have drawn on previous Englishings, for instance John Studley's *Medea* and T. Nuce's *Octauia,* but a comparison does not reveal any indebtedness.

On the other hand there can be no doubt that in translating the Tacitean extract included in the *Vita* Lodge borrowed numerous suggestions from an earlier rendering. Then the question arises: why should he have gone to the trouble of consulting another version in this instance while he apparently did no such thing where the poetical extracts were concerned? Probably the answer is that the Tacitean extract, the well-known account of Seneca's death, was fairly long (*Annales* XV, 60-65, three folio pages in Lodge), for the translation of which it was really worth his while to use a crib in order to save time (the time factor would be especially important if we assume that the *Life* was almost a stop-press affair). This procedure of Lodge's also substantiates the theory that in translating the *Vita* he felt sorely in need of aids, that he resorted to them where he could do so with advantage, and indirectly it suggests the importance of these aids for the quality of the Senecan translation.

The year 1598 had seen the publication of Richard Grenewey's translation of Tacitus, *The Annales of Cornelius Tacitus, The Description of Germanie*[16], which was used by Lodge. First let us establish his dependence on Grenewey by quoting a number of parallel passages that are so strikingly similar as to rule out coincidence:

Tacitus – Lipsius xxj Poppææ & Tigellino coram, quod erat sæuienti Principi intimum consiliorum

Grenewey 241-242 In presence of *Poppæa* and *Tigellinus,* who was of the cruell Princes inward counsell	Lodge d3ᵛ in the presence of *Poppea* and *Tigellinus,* which were inward Counsailors to this mercilesse Prince

Tacitus – Lipsius xxj – xxij ... rogitans: Vbi præcepta sapientiæ? vbi tot per annos meditata ratio aduersum imminentia?

Grenewey 242 Asking where were the precepts of wisedome? where the resolution so many years premeditated against imminent dangers?

Lodge d3ᵛ asking them, where are the precepts of wisedome? where that premeditated resolution, which you haue studied for so many yeares against imminent dangers?

Tacitus – Lipsius xxij deinde oblatâ mitiore spe, blandimentis vitæ euictam: cui addidit paucos postea annos laudabili in maritum memoriâ ...

Grenewey 242 then a milder hope offered, that she was ouercome with the sweetnes of life, vnto which she added a few yeeres after, with a laudable memory towards her husband ...

Lodge d4ʳ but when more apparant hopes were offered, that then she was ouercome with the sweetnesse of life, whereunto shee added a fewe yeares after, with a laudable memorie towards her husband.

There are many such correspondences and near-correspondences, though admittedly some of them are of slight demonstrative value since in certain passages the translators may well be imagined to have used the same translation simply because it was the most natural and obvious rendering.

As far as one can judge from such a comparatively brief extract, both translations may be characterized as mediocre. Grenewey's translation was indeed severely censured by Thomas Gordon in 1728:

... Greenway is still worse than Savill; he had none of his learning, he had all his faults and more; the former has at least performed like a schoolmaster, the latter like a schoolboy.'[17]

Gordon's is mainly a stylistic evaluation; still, it would hardly be fair to subscribe to these terms, though the *Annales,* like Lodge's extract, are marred by misunderstandings and erroneous translations. More interesting from our point of view are the instances, not of actual mistranslation, but of a too strict dependence on the Latin. A comparison between the two translations shows that though Lodge does not necessarily follow Grenewey verbatim throughout a latinized period, he repeatedly takes over his predecessor's sentence structure, in its turn transferred from the Latin; this is further evidence of the eclecticism so characteristic of Lodge the translator[18]. By way of illustration let us consider the specimens below:

Tacitus – Lipsius xxij Sæuis*que* cruciatibus defessus, ne dolore suo animum vxoris infringeret, atque ipse visendo eius tormenta, ad impatientiam delaberetur, suadet in aliud cubiculum abscederet.

Grenewey 242 & being wearied with cruell torments, least he should discourage his wife with his griefe, and himselfe descend to impaciencie, by seeing the torment she indured, perswadeth her to go into another chamber.

Lodge d4ʳ And being wearied with cruell torments, lest by his paine he should weaken his wiues courage, and he by beholding her torments should fall into some impatience, he perswaded her to step aside into another chamber.

This period is not inordinately long, from an English point of view; the Latinization consists in the imitation of the sequence of the members and particularly in the position of the concessive clause[19]. A passage like the above – and there are others of a similar character even in the short extract – testifies to Lodge's stylistic impressionability, while it is not possible to decide with absolute certainty that here he was influenced by Grenewey rather than by Tacitus himself. However, that he did in fact sometimes model his style on Grenewey appears from his use of an idiom which he never, to my knowledge, employs in his Senecan translation, but which is a favourite with Grenewey, viz. the omission of a pronominal subject where the Latin has no pronoun:

Tacitus – Lipsius xxj Simul lacrymas eorum, modo sermone, modo intentior in modum coërcentis, ad firmatatem reuocat ...

Grenewey 242 Withall, hindereth their teares, now with speech, now more earnestly as it were rebuking them, and calling them backe to constancie ...

Lodge d3ᵛ And therewithall recalleth their teares, and calleth them to constancie by speeches, now by expostulations, after a more intended manner ...

Compare also

Tacitus – Lipsius xxij Exin balneo illatus

Lodge d4ʳ Then put into the Bath

Grenewey 243 Then put into the bath

where the Tacitean concision is imitated by both translators.

The impression left on the reader after a perusal of Lodge's rendering of Tacitus on the whole tallies with one's impression of Lodge the translator of Seneca: he is diligent, but not meticulous enough. And with his peculiar inconsistency he sometimes departs from his crib and even descends to sheer nonsense, as when he rejects Grenewey's *the comforts of life* (p. 242), rendering *vitæ delinimenta,* in favour of his own *proportions and images of life*[20] (apparently a confusion with *lineamenta*). In fairness it should be added that where Grenewey goes wrong, Lodge not infrequently amends his predecessor's version. In other words, to characterize Lodge's Senecan translation and the rendering of the Tacitean extract as well one can hardly find a more apposite word than unevenness.

In what light, then, should one view Lodge the translator after this supplementary examination? One may admire his amazing diligence and acknowledge the fact that he evidently *wished* to be thoroughly conscientious: this is reflected not least in the impressive array of aids he consulted – and there are still undetected sources. But even if one makes allowance for the particularly unfavourable circumstances under which he worked, one is bound to admit that the quality of his translation is mediocre because he is never able to keep up a fair standard of scholarship for a long time together. However, begging the reader's forgiveness for the triteness of the quotation – but the cap fits – a generous critic might say by way of conclusion:

Ut desint vires, tamen est laudanda voluntas[21].

174

1. *Thomas Lodge's Translation of Seneca's* DE BENEFICIIS *Compared with Arthur Golding's Version. A Textual Analysis with Special Reference to Latinisms* (Copenhagen, 1960); referred to below as *KS*. In the Scandinavian countries we have preserved the mediaeval custom of defending a thesis orally, and some of the points here elaborated were suggested by the comments of one of the *ex officio* critics, Professor Dr. Eric Jacobsen, who kindly placed his MS notes at my disposal.
2. Cf. *KS,* Ch. I.
3. Cornell Studies in English, vol. 26 (1935).
4. *Op. cit.* pp. 180 ff. Cf. Arber's *Transcript,* III. 159.
5. Quotations are from Goulart's 1595 edition, Chalvet's 1609 edition, and Lodge's 1614 edition. Latin quotations are from the Lipsian edition of 1605 – though for obvious reasons the French translators cannot have used this text. I have been unable to establish whether Lodge used any other Latin edition besides the Lipsian.
6. Cf. *KS* p. 71.
7. The Goulart quotations are here from the 1606 edition.
8. Cf. *KS* pp. 86 ff.
9. Cf. *KS* pp. 75 ff.
10. Cf. *KS* p. 49.
11. H. O. White, *Plagiarism and Imitation During the English Renaissance,* Harvard Studies in English, vol. 12 (1935), p. 202.
12. 'The Reading of an Elizabethan: Sources of Thomas Lodge's Prose Pamphlets', *RES,* 8 (1932), 264-81.
13. I have seen three copies of the 1614 edition of the *Workes,* all different, so to be on the safe side it would seem as necessary to give exact descriptions of printed books from the Renaissance as of MSS.
14. For his similar trouble with the Roman numerals in the *De beneficiis* see *KS* p. 37.
15. This might be evidence that in preparing the *Vita* Lipsius used a different edition with slightly varying chapter-divisions; cf. below on his textual variations.
16. Published together with Henry Savile's translation of the *Histories* and *Agricola,* which had appeared already in 1591; there were later editions of Savile-Grenewey in 1604, 1612, 1622, and 1640. Quotations are from the 1612 edition.
17. Introduction to Gordon's own translation, p. 1.
18. Cf. *KS* passim.
19. Cf. *KS* pp. 101 ff.
20. Where Lipsius has occasion to repeat this phrase later in his account (xxiij), Lodge renders it *the portraiture of life* (d5[r]).
21. After I had finished the above, my attention was drawn to an article by Harold H. Davis, 'An Unknown and Early Translation of Seneca's *De beneficiis',* Huntington Library Quarterly, 24 (1961), 137-144, which describes yet another Senecan translation, *The Line of Liberalitie Dulie Directinge the Wel Bestowing of Benefites and Reprehending the Comonlie Used Vice of Ingratitude,* London, 1569 (*STC* 12939). This translation, which was done by one Nicholas Haward, only comprises the first three books of Seneca's treatise and does not acknowledge its source. The specimens quoted by Davis do not suggest that Lodge was dependent on Haward – in places, the latter's is a very free rendering. However, I have had no opportunity to inspect *The Line of Liberalitie* myself, and it is theoretically possible that a thorough comparison of Haward and Lodge might lead to interesting results.

NICHOLAS HAWARD'S
TRANSLATION OF SENECA

A RECENT ARTICLE by Harold H. Davis[1] established that *The Line of Liberalitie*, published by Nicholas Haward in 1569 (*STC* 12939), has as its source the first three books of Seneca's *De beneficiis*. It is thus the earliest known English rendering of that work. However, in Renaissance terms "translation" may mean almost anything from exact and faithful rendering of the original to heavy indebtedness to earlier translations combined with capricious paraphrase, abounding in addition and omission. It is the purpose of this study to show that *The Line of Liberalitie* belongs mainly in the latter category, since it turns out to draw copiously on an earlier French translation and indirectly on a still earlier Italian translation of Seneca. Moreover, since Haward is far from consistent in his borrowing, it seems natural to add a brief account of the way in which his independent style asserts itself.

Standard works of reference have dealt with Haward's book unsuspectingly, as if it were an independent effort. Here, for example, is the verdict of *The British Bibliographer*:[2]

The volume is divided into three books; the first contains fifteen chapters, upon the nature, extent and pleasure of applying benefits; the second thirty-five chapters, of secrecy and promptness in the application, without being solicited, and of gratitude in the receiver, and the third book,

[1] "An Unknown and Early Translation of Seneca's *De beneficiis*," *Huntington Library Quarterly*, XXIV (1961), 137-144.

[2] Ed. Samuel E. Brydges and Joseph H. Haslewood, II (London, 1810), 156.

thirty three chapters of ingratitude or forgetfulness, and benefits received from inferiors. The whole is interspersed with apposite relations from history, and forms an amusing and instructive collection.

It is perhaps not strange that Haward's source should have gone undetected until very recently, for he seems to have taken every trouble to remove possible clues. As was pointed out by Davis, he omits to state his source in "The Epistle Dedicatorie," and furthermore, whenever the name of Liberalis (to whom Seneca dedicated his work) occurs in the text, Haward leaves it out, though it is rendered in the earlier translations. These are deliberate omissions, and they are mentioned here simply to account for the fact that *The Line of Liberalitie* was taken to be an original achievement; for it should be borne in mind that Haward was writing in an age which did not recognize the term plagiarism in the modern sense of the word.[3] And over and above this, Haward's book in several respects bears the stamp of a genuine Elizabethan work, a point that will be discussed later.

The French translation that Haward used was *Les* SEPT LIVRES *de Seneque, traitant des bienfaits. Avec la vie dudit Seneque. Le tout traduit de Latin en François, par Sauveur Accaurrat* ... (Paris, 1561). The first thing that strikes one when one compares Accaurrat and Haward is that in numerous cases the marginal notes in the two renderings are practically identical. Here are a couple of typical correspondences:

SA 2[r] Vraye description de celuy, qui ne fait plaisir, qu'à force, & par importunité.

NH 3[r] The true description of him that dothe no pleasour but by importunat request.

SA 8[v] La loy de vie, c'est à dire, la maniere de vivre, & converser les uns avec les autres.

NH 12[r] The law of lyfe is to showe the waye how to live & to be conversante among others.

There is an obvious indebtedness here, though, as will be seen, Haward does not always retain Accaurrat's word-classes. Altogether

[3]Cf. Harold O. White, *Plagiarism and Imitation during the English Renaissance*, Harvard Studies in English, XII (Cambridge, Mass., 1935), 202.

144 of Accaurrat's notes are rendered more or less precisely by Haward, while he disregards 89 of the Frenchman's notes and adds 13 of his own composition (or perhaps from an unknown source). The degree of his indebtedness in respect of the marginal notes tallies fairly well with his indebtedness to Accaurrat as far as the text itself is concerned; for though he borrows copiously, he does not do so consistently, but reserves the right to embark on one of his own expansions whenever he feels like it.

Let us now proceed to consider a couple of passages that show how closely Haward might at times follow Accaurrat:[4]

II.10 Lacerat animum, & premit frequens meritorum commemoratio.

SA 31ᵛ Au demeurant, il n'y a rien, qui plus fasche & tourmente l'esprit de la personne, que de ramentevoir souvent le bien, qu'on luy a fait.

NH 48ʳ There is nothynge that more vexeth or troubleth the mynde of anye man then the often repetyng and reciting the plesours whiche have bene done to him.

We may note here two instances of parallel phraseology not found in the Latin text. In several passages the French translation shows a mild degree of expansion, which is often copied by Haward, as in

I.i . . . quam multi indigni luce sunt? et tamen dies oritur.

SA 4ʳ Ne voyons nous pas, combien il y en a par le monde, qui sont indignes de veoir la lumiere du soleil? Et toutesfois le jour leve sur eux, aussi bien que sur les autres.

NH 5ᵛ See we not how many there are in the world unworthy to behold the brightnes of the Sonne, and yet he casteth his beames aswell uppon them, as upon the good menne.

It is obvious from numerous such similarities that Haward is dependent on Accaurrat. This having been established, it is time to introduce the third translator, the Italian Benedetto Varchi, whose rendering, *Seneca De benifizii tradotto in volgar Fiorentino*, was published at Florence in 1554. A comparison between all three translations gives the interesting result that in many passages they are so

---

[4]Throughout this paper the Latin text is quoted from *Opera L. Annaei Senecae . . . per Des. Erasmum Roterod. & Matthaeum Fortunatum . . . emendata* (Basel, 1529); this is presumably not the text used by Accaurrat, but I have been unable to establish which edition he employed.

similar that some sort of dependence must be assumed. Compare, for example, typical passages like the following:

I.i . . . occupationes simulavit. . . .

Varchi 2 . . . non finge d'haver mille faccende?

SA 2ʳ⁻ᵛ . . . ne feignist avoir mille empeschements, mille occupations?

NH 3ʳ . . . or feigned to have a thousande lettes and a thousande businesses otherwayes?

II.14 Tum initia beneficiorum suorum spectare, tum etiam exitus decet, et ea dare quae non tantum accipere, sed etiam accepisse delectet.

Varchi 31 La ragione porta, che noi consideriamo si il principio de' benifizii nostri, & si ancora la fine, & dare quegli, i quali giovino non solamente quando si pigliano, ma ancora dopo.

SA 35ʳ La raison veult que soigneusement nous prenions garde tant aux commencements qu'aux fins des bienfaits, & de donner choses, dont on prenne plaisir, non seulement quand on les recoit, mais aussi puis apres.

NH 53ᵛ For Reason would that we shold take as good regard to thend as to the beginnings of suche plesours as we are to doo: and that wee should geve such thinges wherby a man may take plesour not onely when he receiveth them, but afterwarde also.

On the strength of such juxtapositions as the above—many more of which might be quoted—one might be tempted to suspect that Varchi's translation was drawn on *independently* both by Accaurrat and Haward, were it not for two facts: in the first place Varchi and Haward only conform where there is also conformity with Accaurrat; and in the second place, where Accaurrat deviates from Varchi, he is often followed by Haward, as in

I.2 Ego illud dedi, ut darem.

Varchi 4 . . . perche i benifizii si danno per dare, non per riceverne il cambio.

SA 5ʳ Je ne donne cela pour autre intention, sinon que j'avois delibere le donner: & non, pour en recevoir la pareille.

NH 7ᵛ That whych I gave, I dyd it as fully resolved and determined before hand to geve it, and to that end that I might accompt it geven, without looking to receive anye the lyke againe.

Even if Accaurrat and Haward are not quite similar here, it can hardly be doubted that Accaurrat's expansion was taken up and developed by Haward.

The upshot of this comparison of the three translations is, then, that to a certain extent both the French and the English rendering strut in borrowed plumes: for many of Varchi's excellent wordings are taken over directly by Accaurrat and indirectly by Haward, which implies that some of the praise accorded to the latter by Davis (p. 139) is really due to Varchi (and, in a lesser degree, to Accaurrat). This is not to deprive Haward's translation of *any* independent merit; for there are passages in which Accaurrat goes slightly wrong, but is not uncritically followed by Haward. And since it seems unlikely—as pointed out above—that Haward used the Italian translation, we are led to the assumption that when he found Accaurrat infelicitous, he abandoned his crib to consult the Latin original and his own stylistic instinct. It is difficult to prove conclusively that he did in fact consult the Latin text; but a glance at the passage given below renders this likely: Accaurrat's *au contraire* is clearly borrowed from Varchi, but Haward must have realized that where Accaurrat has placed it, it is not quite logical, introducing as it does a member of the same import as the preceding member. And though in other respects Haward may have been influenced by Accaurrat in this passage, he disregarded the latter's *au contraire*, a fact suggesting that he had an independent look at the source:

I.6 Animus est, qui parva extollit, sordida illustrat, magna & in precio habita dehonestat.

Varchi 10 L'animo è quello, che accresce le cose picciole, & illustra le scure: & per lo contrario scema le grandi, & rende vili le pregiate . . . .

SA 11ᵛ Le cueur seul & bonne volonté est celle, qui agrandist, & eleve les choses basses, & de petite consequence: & au contraire, qui illustre & esclarcist les sordides, & abbaisse les grandes, & celles qui des autres sont en grand pris & estime.

NH 17ʳ It is the minde that extolleth and commendeth thynges of small valour, and of no regard, and disgraceth & quyte debaseth other some thinges of estimacion and great price.

It is well known that Renaissance translators tended to fuse text and commentary.[5] Similarly, we have here the case of an English translator producing in places a blend of the Latin original, the French translation he had at his elbow, and, unwittingly, Varchi's translation.[6]

The points mentioned so far do not, however, constitute an exhaustive description of Haward's translation. As suggested above, *The Line of Liberalitie* does not draw consistently on Accaurrat; in many passages the translator demonstrates his independence, the result of which is a stylistic deviation from the original manifesting itself in copious expansion and paraphrase, in a repeated attempt to heighten the effect, and at times in a characteristic endeavor to edit and interpret the text for moral purposes.

As mentioned above, Accaurrat's translation reveals a mild expansionist tendency; compared with the French translation, Haward is at times extremely verbose (incidentally, the passage quoted by Davis [p. 141] does not show the full extent of Haward's verbosity, since it inadvertently leaves out a substantial portion of his rendering). In several passages it looks as if Accaurrat's mild expansion has given a fillip to Haward's wordiness, thus in

II.5 Nihil æque amarum, quam diu pendere. Aequiore quidam animo ferunt praecidi spem suam, quam trahi.

SA 27^r Il n'y a rien plus amer, que d'estre long temps suspens, & n'avoir à la fin despesche de ce qu'on pretend. Aucuns disent, qu'ils aimeroient mieux, que l'esperance, qu'ils ont à une chose, fust du tout rompue, que de la faire longuement trainer. (43 words)

NH 40^v There is nothing that breedeth so great gryef or is suche a corosif to a man, as to be long foded fourth with wanne hope, and in fine faile of

---

[5]E. g., see Eric Jacobsen, *Translation a Traditional Craft* (Copenhagen, 1958), p. 130, and Knud Soerensen, *Thomas Lodge's Translation of Seneca's* DE BENEFICIIS *Compared with Arthur Golding's Version* (Copenhagen, 1960), pp. 35 ff.

[6]Accaurrat does not content himself with borrowing copiously from Varchi's translation. He also avails himself of several points made by Varchi in the latter's preface and incorporates them in his own preface after making the necessary alterations. Here is an example:

Varchi sig. A. iiii^r "credo non dimeno di potere affermare senza sospetto alcuno di dovere essere tenuto, o arrogante, o presuntuoso, che la lingua di questa traduzzione sia piu pura Fiorentina, che non è Romana quella di SENECA."

SA sig. e ij^v "J'oseray asseurement dire & affermer sans arrogance, que le langage de ceste mienne traduction ne sera trouvé de ceux de bonne volonté & jugement estre moins bon François, que celuy de Seneque est bon Latin."

his purpose also. For few there are but had rather be abbridged of their hoping with a flat denyall at ones, then to be lingred forth with fayer promises, and finde no deedes when all is done. (67 words)

But in other passages Haward's rendering is so free and expanded that it amounts to paraphrase. Thus, in the quotation given below there is at least no stylistic dependence on Accaurrat, who is rather brief here; as for the substance of the anecdote, it may have been provided either by the Latin original or by the French translation:

I.8 Socrati cum multa multi pro suis quisque facultatibus offerrent: Aeschines pauper auditor, Nihil, inquit, dignum te, quod dare tibi possim, invenio, & hoc modo pauperem me esse sentio.

SA 13ʳ Comme plusieurs, chacun selon ses facultez & puissances, offrissent à Socrates plusieurs presens, Æschines son pauvre auditeur luy dist: Je ne puis trouver chose (ô Socrates) pour te faire present, qui soit digne de toy, me resentant par ce moyen fort pauvre. . . .

NH 19ᵛ-20ʳ Socrates that worthie and famous Philosopher being accustomed to reede publiquely and geve preceptes of good governement, had repayring to his sayde Lectour a great and populouse audience. Among whom there were both ryche and poore. It fortuned that his scollers with a common concent on a time concluded among themselves that eche of them after their habilitie in token of their goodwills towardes their sayde maister, shoulde present him with litle or much, whych they did. Eschines one of the companye in welth farre unequall to the residew as he that had utterlye nothynge, and yet in good wil to gratifye his maister not inferiour to anye the best, when he sawe everye one of hys companions to geve unto Socrates their mayster presentes of great Price, came with a mery chere also to Socrates, and sayde. Syr in all thys woorlde have I nothyng that I may present thee withall. Whereby I acknowledge easely my great povertie.

This is a good example of Haward's chatty manner: gratuitous additions of specific details, explanatory matter, and doubling of synonyms loom large.[7] But there are other noteworthy features representing Haward's urge toward expansion. Thus we occasionally find

[7]A corresponding wordiness is met with in the "Epistle Dedicatorie": "what shall I recompt your rare sobryetie, greate lenytie, passyng familiaritie, commendable policie, gentle gravitie, pregnant wisedome, deepe discrecion, large liberalitie . . . ," etc. (sig. iiiᵛ). Incidentally, there is quite a lot of alliteration here, a feature not very predominant in the translation.

a loaded word expanded into a neutral term followed by a negative term:

II.21 Vivam cum obscoeno?

SA 44^r Vivray-je avec ce villain?

NH 68^v . . . shall I content myself to lyve with him, and frame my lyfe after hys filthie condicions?

In a similar way, the Latin "non amare" is rendered "hate and not love" (NH, 92^r). But perhaps the most striking feature is Haward's endeavor to go one better than Seneca and Accaurrat. A single representative example may suffice to show how he goes about heightening the effect of the original:

II.11 Quousque dices, Ego te servavi, ego te eripui morti? istud si meo arbitrio memini, vita est, si tuo mors est.

SA 31^v Jusques à quand me reprocheras-tu, Je tay gardé, je t'ay delivré de mort? Si de mon vouloir il m'est souvenue du bien que tu m'as fait, cela m'est vie: si par ton moyen, ce m'est une mort.

NH 48^v How long wilt thou continew thus castinge in my tethe, I am he that hath saved thy lyfe? I did deliver thee from banishment? if this had bene acknowledged by me without thy telling, it had bene asmuche woorth as double my lyfe, but sith that by thee it is thus notified, it seemeth woorse to me then death.

One might have thought that "life" and "death" were in themselves sufficiently strong expressions.

Sometimes Haward's independent attitude toward the original takes another course: he repeatedly intersperses his translation with racy and proverbial expressions, which of course deviate stylistically from the Latin, but which make the text very Elizabethan—probably one of the reasons why its source remained undetected for so long. Here is a specimen of his colloquialism:

III.3 Deinde irrumpit in animum aliorum admiratio, & ad ea impetus factus est, uti mortalibus mos est, ex magnis maiora cupiendi, protinus excidit, quicquid ante apud nos beneficium vocabatur.

SA 60^{r-v} Puis l'admiration des autres choses saisit nostre cueur, ausquelles nostre desir s'addonne & aspire, comme est la façon de faire des hommes, de couvoiter apres les grandes choses celles, qu'ils voyent estre encor plus excellentes: de sorte que aussi tost ce, qui de nous estoit appellé bienfait, s'escoule de nostre memoire.

NH 93ᵛ But so sone as we begin to take a smatche of other greter plesours, and that we feele any lyfe (as they say) in it, that it is coming & maye be got, (as the guise of men is nowadayes after they have obtained great thynges to hunt still after greatter,) then farewell that we before had in so great price, & after the other with might & mayne.

Very amusing is the anachronistic employment of "alebenche" below:

III.26 Excipiebatur ebriorum sermo.

SA 79ᵛ La parolle des yvrongnes . . . estoit recevë pour veritable.

NH 119ʳ There was presented what talke men had of him as they sat on their alebenche.

and at II.5, where the subject debated is the arrogance of courtiers, Haward introduces a gratuitous, but charming comparison: "Lyke glorious Pecockes boasting onely in their tayle" (41ʳ). In this connection, attention may also be called to the use of "Syr" in the quotation given above, the anecdote about Socrates (I.8).

Proverbs occur repeatedly, and their presence is often explicitly indicated by Haward, as in the following example:

II.34 . . . parcissimum tamen hominem vocamus pusilli animi & contracti, cum infinitum intersit, inter modum & angustias.

SA 56ʳ Toutesfois nous appellons le par trop chiche & espargnant, homme de petit cueur, pource qu'il y a grande difference entre mediocrité & chicheté par trop estricte.

NH 87ʳ . . . and yet wee call a Misar, him that hungar drops out of his nose (as we say) one that is so neere himself that he is not woorthie to beare the name of man, him call we a niggard also. Thus wee see and can discerne a great diversitie to be betwene meesure and extremitie. . . .

Normally the proverbial element is Haward's own contribution; but in one passage we detect Accaurrat's influence: one of his locutions is copied by Haward and generates two additional synonymous expressions in the English rendering:

II.4 Hæc itaque curæ habebis, si grate æstimari quæ præstabis voles, ut beneficia tua illibata & integra ad eos, quibus promissa sunt, perveniant sine ulla, quod aiunt, deductione.

SA 26ᵛ Si donc tu as vouloir, que le bien & plaisir, que tu fais, soit prisé, & receu avec gré, tu prendras soigneuse garde, à ce que tes bienfaits parviennent, non de main en main (comme lon dit) mais sains & entiers, à ceux, à qui ils sont promis.

NH 40ʳ . . . wherfore if thou wouldest doo a plesour and wouldst have it accompted of as a frindly plesour, then in any wise see it be not suche that shall come from hande to hande be tost from post to pillar, and passe the pickes (as the proverbe is) but that it comme wholly from thy self and that immediately, to them to whom thou woldst show suche plesour.

Though Haward did not want to acknowledge his source, one has the impression that he endeavored to do his best to bring home to the reader the moral message conveyed by Seneca; for many of his expansions are to be considered not as the mere outcome of his proneness to verbosity, but as attempts at exegesis. This applies to a passage like the following, which first renders Seneca's thought and then goes on to paraphrase it:

II.7 Fabius Verucosus beneficium ab homine duro aspere datum, panem lapidosum vocabat, quem esurienti accipere necessarium sit, esse acerbum. SA 28ᵛ Fabius Verucosus appelloit le bienfait, qui estoit donné rigoreusement, par homme cruel & maupiteux, un pain pierreux: lequel il fault de necessité, que l'homme affamé recoie, & auquel il semble estre bon, pour aigre & difficile qu'il soit.

NH 43ᵛ Fabius verucosus was wont to lyken and compare, the benefit whiche any hard natured man with paine dyd, to gravely or greety bread. Which notwith standyng he ys very hard pinched with hungar, feedeth wel on, & semeth to find savour & swetnes therin, though it be [e]ver so painfull in chewing. But what doth not necessity? As none wold fede on suche bread that might chose, and could get other, so none would accept such rough benefits & unplesaunt plesours, that might well spare them, & doo wellenough without.

This may be compared with a passage in which both translators try to make it clear to the reader what *pietas* stands for; obviously Haward is indebted to Accaurrat, but in his customary manner he has added slightly to the Frenchman's exegesis:

III.36 . . . pietas . . . .

SA 90ʳ L'amour & obeïssance, qu'on doit tant à Dieu, qu'a ses pere & mere, & l'affection, que les parents portent à leurs enfants. . . .

NH 127ᵛ Pietie which is properly the dewtie which eche man is most streightly bounden to owe of dutie to God first, and next to his parentes children kinsfolkes and contrey native . . . .

Haward's moral fervor affects his rendering in an indirect way as well. Mention was made above of his tendency to use racy expressions; but in one respect he is extremely squeamish: rather than having to translate passages dealing with any kind of sexual aberration, he leaves out such passages altogether. This is true of I.9.3-4, a lament on the decay of morals, containing details that he apparently considered too spicy. Again, at I.14.4 Seneca introduces a comparison, in the course of which he has occasion to use the word *meretrix*, which is rendered by Accaurrat, but omitted by Haward. References to adultery (III.16) and harlotry (III.28.4) are likewise passed over in silence. There are numerous other omissions, some of them quite brief and probably made inadvertently, while in other cases one has a suspicion that passages were left out because Haward thought them too technical; this applies to the mythological and etymological passage at I.3.6 and to the legal passage at III.7.5-7. These omissions are further evidence of Haward's independence of his original.

The Line of Liberalitie is the earliest known translation of the *De beneficiis*. Later renderings were done by Arthur Golding in 1578 (*The Woorke of the Excellent Philosopher Lucius Annaeus Seneca concerning Benefyting*) and by Thomas Lodge in 1614 (*The Workes of Lucius Annaeus Seneca, Both Morrall and Naturall*). Golding does not appear to have been dependent on any earlier translations, whether English, French, or Italian. On the other hand, Lodge drew on numerous aids: in chronological order, Pincianus' *Castigationes in omnia Senecae scripta* (1536), Golding's translation, Simon Goulart's translation of 1595, *Les oeuvres morales et meslees de Senecque*, Mathieu de Chalvet's translation of 1604, *Les oeuvres de L. Annaeus Seneca*, and Justus Lipsius' 1605 edition of Seneca, besides possibly other helps.[8] Since Lodge was so heavily indebted to his

[8]Soerensen, *Thomas Lodge's Translation*; id., "Thomas Lodge's *Seneca*," *Archiv für das Studium der neueren Sprachen und Literaturen*, CIC (1962), 313-324.

predecessors, he might be imagined to have borrowed from Haward as well; however, a comparison shows that this is not the case, probably because he did not know of Haward's translation.

Though there is thus no connection between Haward and Lodge, it is striking how similar their renderings are. Both borrow copiously, both show an urge toward expansion, and both display a subjective attitude toward the text, which they slant and edit in such a way as to elicit more clearly from it its moral message as they see it. Accaurrat's rendering shares some of these features, though in a milder degree. On the other hand, Varchi and Golding represent a different school of translators, who see it as their first aim to be as faithful as possible to the original and who consequently eschew expansion and extravagant language.

LATIN ORATIO OBLIQUA AND ENGLISH
FREE INDIRECT SPEECH

About twenty years ago a number of philologists were given the opportunity of reading a preprint, 'Latin Influence on European Syntax', written by Franz Blatt for the Second International Congress of Classical Studies[1]). This was an impressive and wide-ranging survey which inspired several people to pursue the theme within their special fields. The present article is yet another offshoot of Franz Blatt's seminal paper, although it deals with a syntactico-stylistic phenomenon for which Latin antecedents have not so far been considered a possibility.

The term *free indirect speech* is by now well on the way to becoming the established expression in English[2]); it corresponds to French *style indirect libre* and German *erlebte Rede* and refers to a mode of reporting halfway between direct and indirect speech. Let us consider a contemporary English example:

Maitland turned here to the other statements. Cook hadn't very much to say for herself, except that Wednesday was always her day. Wednesday and Sunday, and on one she went to the matinee at the Odeon, and on the other she went to chapel. And there'd never been nothing in her kitchen that could upset a fly. (Sara Woods, *Past Praying For* (London 1968), p. 70).

---

[1]) Later published in *Acta Congressus Madvigiani,* Vol. V (Copenhagen 1957), pp. 33–69; see also the same author's summing-up paper, *Influence latine sur la syntaxe européenne, ibid.,* pp. 223–235.

[2]) For instance it is used in a recently published important work, R. QUIRK/S. GREENBAUM/G. LEECH/J. SVARTVIK, *A Grammar of Contemporary English* (London 1972).

This is supposed to be the author's report of a statement given by a witness; but it is clear that it is not an objective report, for as such one would expect it to comply with generally acceptable grammatical rules which do not, for instance, permit double negation. The presence of this feature suggests the original direct speech. As in indirect speech, we find shifting of pronouns and tenses (*I go* becomes *she went*), but free indirect speech differs from indirect speech in that it contains no governing *verbum declarandi* or *sentiendi* (*she said that ...*, etc.). Free indirect speech has other characteristics, but those just mentioned are the principal ones.

It is generally taken for granted that the first English writer who used free indirect speech extensively and with a deliberate stylistic purpose was Jane Austen[3]). This is true, but sporadic instances—or at least forerunners—of the modern phenomenon occur as early as the fifteenth century, and possibly earlier[4]). But what is the origin of free indirect speech? There are probably more answers than one to this question. One factor is an indigenous stylistic spontaneity which might result in the formal coalescence of different narrative modes, especially in extended passages; compare the following example from Thomas Nashe's 'The Unfortunate Traveller' (1594).

Here he held his peace and wept. I glad of any opportunitie of a full poynt to part from him, tolde him I tooke his counsaile in worth; what lay in mee to requite in love should not bee lacking. Some business that concerned me highly cald mee away very hastely, but another time I hop'd we should meete. (Quoted from *Shorter Elizabethan Novels* (Everyman 1953), p. 337).

From the context it is obvious that the latter part of this quotation is an instance of free indirect speech.—Another factor, the one which will be our concern here, is the rendering of Latin *oratio obliqua* in early

---

[3]) WILLI BÜHLER, *Die „erlebte Rede" im englischen Roman. Ihre Vorstufen und ihre Ausbildung im Werke Jane Austens* (Zürich 1937); ALBRECHT NEUBERT, *Die Stilformen der „erlebten Rede" im neueren englischen Roman* (Halle (Saale) 1957); NORMAN PAGE, *The Language of Jane Austen* (Oxford 1972).

[4]) FRITZ KARPF, *Die erlebte Rede im älteren Englischen und in volkstümlicher Redeweise* (Die neueren Sprachen 36 (1928), pp. 571–581); id., *Die erlebte Rede im Englischen* (Anglia 57 (1933), pp. 225–276).

modern English. In the following pages we shall examine some translations from the sixteenth, seventeenth, and eighteenth centuries.

First of all it should be noted that only in special circumstances does *oratio obliqua* produce free indirect speech in English. In short passages where the Latin *verbum declarandi* or *sentiendi* is in evidence, the translation will as a rule have normal indirect speech. Let us first consider John Brende's translation of Quintus Curtius[5]:

Parmenio non alium locum proelio aptiorem esse censebat. (Liber III, pp. 40–41)	Parmenio was of opinion that this place was moste metest to abide Darius in, and geue him battaille ... (Fol. 21v)

And even in some passages where the governing verb is implied in the Latin, Brende reveals a predilection for making the context explicit; for instance:

Illi caduceatorem in turrim, & situ & opere multum editam perductum, quanta esset altitudo, intueri iubent, ac nunciare Alexandro, non eadem ipsum & incolas æstimatione munimenta metiri: se scire inexpugnabiles esse: ad ultimum pro fide morituros. (Liber III, p. 27)	They brought the herauld into an highe towre which was strong both by nature and workmanship, willing him to consider the thing, & to declare vnto Alexander y^t he wayed not sufficiently the strengthe of the place, for thei said they knewe it to be impringable, & if the worst should falle, yet were thei redy to dye in there truth & allegeance. (Fol. 12v)

It is presumably to preclude ambiguity that Brende has here intercalated the words *for thei said* ..., rendering *se scire* ... However, Brende's translation is not wholly without traces of free indirect speech. It is particularly in long passages that he feels tempted to dispense with the

---

[5] *THE HISTORIE OF QUINTUS Curcius, conteyning the Actes of the greate Alexander translated out of Latine into Englishe* (London 1553). Latin quotations are from *QVINTI CVRTII DE Rebus gestis Alexandri Magni* ... (Lvgdvni 1545), possibly the text used by BRENDE.

repetition of a governing verb—on the analogy of his original. Consider the following specimen:

Ingens solicitudo, & pene iam luctus, in castris erat. Flentes querebantur, in tanto impetu cursuque rerum, omnis ætatis ac memoriæ clarissimum regem non in acie saltem, non ab hoste deiectum, sed abluentem aqua corpus ereptum esse & extinctum: (1) instare Darium, uictorem, antequam uidisset hostem. Sibi easdem terras, quas uictores peragrassent, repetendas: (2) omnia aut ipsos, aut hostes populatos: per uastas solitudines, etiam si nemo insequi uelit, euntes, fame atq; inopia debellari posse. (3) Quem signum daturum fugientibus? quem ausurum Alexandro succedere?
(Liber III, p. 36)

Then there was a great desolacion and heuines in the campe, they wepte, lamented, and bewayled, that such a kyng, so noble a Capitaine as had not bene sene in any age, should thus be taken from them in the chief of his enterprise and brunte of all his busines, and that after suche a manner, not in battaile slayne by his enemies, but thus cast away bathing in a ryuer. (1) It greued them that Darius now beyng at hand should obtein the victory by suche a chaunce, without seing of his enemy, & that they should be enforced to retourne back agayne as men vanquysshed by those Countreis, through the whiche they had passed before as victorers. (2) In whiche countreis all thynges beyng destroyed by themselues or by their enemies, it was of necessitie for them to dye for hunger, though no man should persue them. (3) It became a question amonges them selues who should be their Capitayne in their flyeng away—or what he were that durste succede Alexander?
(Fol. 18r–v)

At the beginning of the quotation, *Flentes querebantur,* etc. is rendered as a traditional indirect speech construction, and at (1) we note an explanatory insertion which serves to make it clear that the following is what the soldiers said or felt. At (2) we find a passage of free indirect speech; but at (3) we come across another explanatory interpolation that shifts the translation back into indirect speech. Brende is not consistent, and it is unlikely that he uses free indirect speech as a deliberate stylistic device. Rather, he lapses into it at (2) so as to avoid too cumbrous a formulation.

One difficulty inherent in any discussion of free indirect speech is the fact that at times it may be impossible to decide with absolute certainty whether we have to do with free indirect speech or with the author's own account. A case in point is the following passage from Arthur Golding's translation of Caesar's Gallic War[6]):

... Considius equo admisso ad eum accurrit, dicit, montem, quem a Labieno occupari voluerit, ab hostibus teneri: id se a Gallicis armis atque insignibus cognovisse.
(I 22)

Considius came ronning to him vppon the spurre, and made report vnto him, that the hill which he would that Labienus shoulde haue taken, was possessed by his ennemies: the whiche he perceiued by the armes & antesignes of the Galles.
(Fol. 16v–17r)

As far as the Latin text is concerned, we are not in doubt: the last eight words, being an accusative with infinitive construction, are clearly marked as Considius's statement, reported by Caesar. But what about the corresponding English passage? Considered in isolation, the words after the colon are ambiguous: *he perceiued* could refer to what Caesar himself saw, since there is no explicit indication to the contrary. But on balance it is most reasonable to see in this passage a case of free indirect speech, brought about by fairly close translation and by the pressure of the context. The governing verbal phrase *made report vnto him, that ...* may be taken to apply to the ambiguous words, the more so as the colon suggests a connexion between the middle and the last part of the quotation. Although the passage is not very long, the conclusion that can be drawn from this and other examples is that period-length is of importance: the longer the period, the greater the scope for free indirect speech. In the following quotation we shall see what may happen to a fairly long passage of Latin *oratio obliqua*:

Haec cum animadvertisset, convocato consilio omniumque ordinum ad id consilium adhibitis centurionibus vehementer eos incusavit: primum quod,

When cesar understood theis thyngs he called a counsel, and assembling thither the Capteines of all the bandes, rebuked theym very sharplye. Fyrst in that they tooke vpon them

---

   [6]) *The eyght bookes of Caius Iulius Cæsar ... translated out of latin into English by* ARTHUR GOLDINGE G. (London 1565). As he explains in the *Epistle Dedicatory*, GOLDING had originally been commissioned to finish a translation that BRENDE had begun; but he decided to begin all over again so as to ensure a uniform style throughout.—Latin quotations are from *Bellum Gallicum*, ed. B. DINTER (Lipsiae 1890).

aut quam in partem aut quo consilio ducerentur, sibi quaerendum aut cogitandum putarent. (1) Ariovistum se consule cupidissime populi Romani amicitiam appetisse: (2) cur hunc tam temere quisquam ab officio discessurum iudicaret? (3) Sibi quidem persuaderi, cognitis suis postulatis atque aequitate condicionum perspecta eum neque suam neque populi Romani gratiam repudiaturum.
(I 40)

to be inquisitiue or carefull, whether or for what purpose they should be led. (1) As for Ariouistus, he had (in the tyme that he was Consul) sewed most earnestly for yᵉ frendship of the people of Rome: (2) and why than should any men misedeme, that he wold so rashly go back from hys duty? (3) He beleued verily, that if he ones knew hys demaundes, and vnderstoode perfectly howe reesonable offers he woulde make hym, he wold not reiect, either hys good wyll, or the good wyll of the people of Rome.
(Fol. 30v–31r)

Several points may be noted here: the dexterous manner in which Golding switches over into free indirect speech at (1); the form of the following rhetorical question (2) which, since it might actually be identical with a question in direct speech, makes for extra vividness; and the passage beginning at (3): *He beleued verily ...*, where we have an instance of condensation typical of free indirect speech: a verb expressing opinion takes on the function of a verb of saying, this verb being qualified by an adverb that is characteristic of direct speech[7]). Taken together, these features produce a passage that strikes the modern reader as being stylistically apt.

There is no standard rendering of Latin *oratio obliqua* in early English translations from the classics. Free indirect speech competes with indirect speech and with clauses introduced by conjunctions to render Latin accusative with infinitive constructions. These two solutions are illustrated

---

[7]) This use of *believe* (= 'say that one believes') has some affinity with what philosophers refer to as a performative utterance. For instance, the words *I promise such and such* are at the same time a statement and an act, and *promise* is a performative verb. If it is correct that such verbs normally only occur in the simple present, a verb like *believe* in the quotation given is not, however, a true performative. One could very well imagine an instance of free indirect speech like the following: *He was wondering whether this was the best solution,* meaning 'He said he was wondering ...'. See J. L. AUSTIN, *How to Do Things with Words* (Oxford 1962); ALFRED SCHOPF, *Untersuchungen zur Wechselbeziehung zwischen Grammatik und Lexik im Englischen* (Berlin 1969); MAX BLACK, *The Labyrinth of Language* (Pelican 1972).

below, where Golding uses indirect speech, Clement Edmundes[8]) a clause construction with the weighty conjunction *forasmuch as:*

Petierunt, uti sibi concilium totius Galliae in diem certam indicere idque Caesaris voiuntate facere liceret: sese habere quasdam res, quas ex communi consensu ab eo petere vellent. (I 30)

They made request that it might be lawfull for them to sommon a Parlament of Gallia at a certain day, and that it would please Cesar to ratify it with his consent; for they said they had certaine matters, which they wold sew vnto him for by a common assent.

(Golding fol. 22r–v)

And required further, that with his good leaue they might call a generall assembly at a day prefixed, of all the States of Gallia, forasmuch as they had matters of great importance to be handled, which they desired (with a common consent) to preferre to his consideration.

(Edmundes pp. 30–31)

A further possibility of rendering *oratio obliqua* is direct speech; this may be exemplified in the following extract from Edmundes's translation:

Tum demum Liscus oratione Caesaris adductus, quod antea tacuerat, proponit: (1) Esse non nullos, quorum auctoritas apud plebem plurimum valeat, qui privatim plus possint quam ipsi magistratus. (2) Hos seditiosa atque improba oratione multitudinem deterrere, ne frumentum conferant, quod debeant: praestare, si iam principatum Galliae obtinere non possint, Gallorum quam Romanorum imperia perferre; neque dubitare [debeant], quin, si Helvetios superaverint Romani, una cum reliqua Gallia Aeduis libertatem sint erepturi. (3) Ab eisdem nostra consilia, quaeque in castris gerantur, hostibus enuntiari: (4) hos a se coërceri non posse.

(I 17)

At length, Liscus, mooued vvith Cæsars speech, discouered (which before hee had kept secret) (1) that there were some of great authority amongst the Commons, and could doe more being private persons, then they could do being Magistrates. (2) These, by sedicious and bad speeches, did defer the people from bringing Corne: shewing it better for them, sith they could not attaine to the Empire of Gallia, to vndergoe the soueraigntie of the Galles, then the Romaines: for, they vvere not to doubt, but if the Romaines vanquished the Heluetians, they vvould bereaue the Heduans of their libertie, with the rest of all Gallia. (3) By these men are our deliberations and counsells, or vvhatsoeuer else is done in the Campe, made knowne to the Enemy: (4) neither vvere they able to keepe them in obedience; . . .

(p. 13)

---

8) CLEMENT EDMUNDES, *Observations vpon Cæsars Comentaries* (London 1609).

This is stylistically uneven. At (1) we have indirect speech, at (2) there is a transition to free indirect speech, which at (3) switches over abruptly into direct speech, to return to free indirect speech at (4). We note, then, that although free indirect speech occurs as one possible rendering of *oratio obliqua*, it is irregularly employed.

It is obvious that throughout the early modern English period the compactness of Latin presented a problem to translators. A writer like Livy, who tends to employ a very terse style in which the governing verb of saying is often implied, is treated with much the same degree of inconsistency from the sixteenth century to the eighteenth. This inconsistency is understandable if we bear in mind that a fully developed standard English had not yet been attained (though no doubt foreign models contributed somewhat to regularization), and that for this very reason it was difficult for translators to decide just how closely they could follow their Latin originals if they wanted to produce intelligible and at the same time vivid and acceptable English. Different translators' handling of *oratio obliqua* strikes the contemporary reader as more or less elegant.

Among the elegant translators must be reckoned Philemon Holland, whose 'Romane Historie Written by T. Livius of Padua' appeared in 1600. It is true that Holland takes liberties with his text. In the passage cited below, the Latin infinitival constructions are variously rendered[9]):

(1) Cum clamor impetusque multitudinis vix sustineri posset, ex superiore parte ædium per fenestras in nouam viam versas (habitabat enim rex ad Iouis Statoris) populum Tanaquil alloquitur, iubet bono animo esse: (2) sopitum fuisse regem subito ictu, (3) ferrum haud alte in corpus descendisse: (4) iam ad se redisse: inspectum vulnus absterso cruore,

(1) In this while the noice and violence of the people was so great that it could not well be suffered. "Then *Tanaquil* from the "upper loft of the house, out at a window "that opened into the new street (for the "king kept his court hard by the temple of "*Iupiter Stator*) spake unto the people, will-"ing them to be of good cheare. (2) The "king indeed (quoth she) was amased and "swowned at the suddaine stroke, (3) how-

[9]) According to H. B. LATHROP's *Translations from the Classics into English from Caxton to Chapman 1477–1620* (Univ. of Wisconsin Studies in Language and Literature, No. 35 (1933), p. 238), HOLLAND relied mainly on the edition of Livy printed at Paris in 1573. This is the edition quoted from here and later.

omnia salubria esse. confidere prope-
diem ipsum eos visuros.
(I 41)

"beit it went nothing deepe: (4) for now is
"he come againe to himselfe, his wound
"cleansed from bloud, and searched: all
"signes of life, and no danger of death: and
"I trust in God within a while you shall see
"himselfe againe . . .
(pp. 29–30)

Let us consider Holland's procedure. The passage opens with the author's report (1). The moment Tanaquil is introduced, the translator begins to use quotation marks (commonly—but not consistently—employed from *c.* 1600 to *c.* 1800 to mark *either* indirect, free indirect, *or* direct speech; perhaps this suggests that during these centuries the three narrative modes were not felt to be as distinct as they are today). At (2) we note a special kind of free indirect speech in which an *inquit* is added parenthetically by the translator. The pivotal point is the ambiguous sentence (3): at first sight one is inclined to consider it free indirect speech, but it is a formulation that Tanaquil might well have used in direct speech. Thus it functions as a transition to (4), which is unmistakably direct speech. Though it does not respect the grammar of the original, the passage as a whole reads smoothly and vividly; and the most interesting thing from our particular point of view is that the Latin text appears to have triggered off a type of formulation (3) which has turned out to be extremely fertile in later English.

It is not rare for Holland to convert *oratio obliqua* into direct speech, but it should be added that he also frequently combines indirect and free indirect speech as in the quotation that follows, where he employs the question *And why?* as a convenient point of transition between the two modes:

isque primus & petisse ambitiose regnum, & orationem dicitur habuisse
ad conciliandos plebis animos compo-
sitam. Cum se non rem nouam petere:
quippe qui non primus, quod quisdam
indignari mirariue posset, sed tertius
Romæ peregrinus regnum affectet . . .
(I 35)

Hee himselfe (as men say) was the first, that
both ambitiously sought for the crowne, and
also to win the hearts of the commons,
divised and framed an eloquent Oration.
Saying, it was no "new and strange thing
"that he stood for: And why? hee was not
"the first (that any man should be offended,
"or make any wonder) but the third alien

"that in Rome affected and aspired to the
"kingdome . . . .
(p. 26)

If Philemon Holland's translation of Livy is generally praised today,
this was not invariably the case in the seventeenth and eighteenth
centuries. It is a platitude that, since language changes, every age needs
its own translation of important classics. This is what Edmund Bohun
says in his preface to 'The Roman History written in Latine by Titus
Livius' (1686):

Though that [i. e. the translation of Livy] was perform'd by a Learned Man, and
very conversant in Labours of that kind, yet without any reflections on his worthy
pains, we may have leave to say, that our English Language is much refined within
the last fourscore years (for his Work is Dedicated to Queen Elizabeth.) And we
have been very unhappy if we have not express'd the Authors sense more briefly
and somewhat more significantly, and agreeable to the Gusto of modern English
Readers . . .

The same point is made, but rather more self-assertively, by the anonymous translator of 'The Roman History by Titus Livius' (1744):

It is a lamentable misfortune, that we have not a good translation of so excellent an
historian in the English language. And as no abler hand has hitherto undertaken
this work, we have attempted to exhibit it to our countrymen in their own language.

Let us take a brief look at the characteristics of these two translations. In
both there is a marked tendency to resort to explicit subordination in the
rendering of *oratio obliqua*; a typical example is afforded by the
extracts cited below, where we note the repeated use of the conjunction
that in both versions:

Sextus filius eius, qui minimus ex tribus erat, transfugit ex composito Gabios, patris in
se sæuitiam intolerabilem conquerens. Iam ab alienis in suos vertisse superbiam: &
librorum quoque eum frequentiæ tædere, vt quam in curia solitudinem fecerit, domo
quoque faciat, ne quam stirpem, ne quem hæredem regni relinquat, se quidem inter
tela ad [sic] gladios patris elapsum, nihil vsquam sibi tutum, nisi apud hostes L.
Tarquinij credidisse. (I 53)

... his Son *Sextus,* who was the youngest of three, fled away, by compact, to *Gabii,* complaining of his Fathers intolerable cruelty to him; telling them, that, *Now he had turned all his pride, from Strangers, upon his own Family; that he was now grown weary, even of his own Children, and resolved to cause the same solitude in his own House, as he had made in the Court, lest he should leave any off-spring behind him, or any one to Inherit his Kingdom: that he, indeed had escaped his Fathers Darts and Swords, but, thought himself safe in no place, unless it were among the Enemies of* Lucius Tarquinius.
(1686, p. 29)

... Sextus, the youngest of his three sons, according to concert, fled to Gabii, complaining of the inhuman cruelty of his father, and pretending, "That he had turned his "tyranny from others against his own family, "and was uneasy that his children were so "numerous, intending to make the same "havock in his own house which he had "made in the senate, that so he might leave "behind him no issue, nor heir to his king-"dom. That for his own part, as he had "escaped from amidst the swords of his "father, and other instruments of death, he "was persuaded he could find no safety but "among the enemies of L. Tarquin.
(1744, p. 97)

Where the 1744 version has quotation marks to indicate indirect speech, Bohun employs the equivalent typographical device of italics.—As will be seen, both translators have here chosen indirect speech; but exceptions to explicit subordination are by no means rare, for these two translations do not present a uniform picture: in a number of passages they exhibit the mixture of narrative modes found in earlier translations. The following quotation may serve as an illustration of this:

Turnus Herdonius ab Aricia ferociter in Absentem Tarquinium erat inuectus. Haud mirum esse, Superbo ei inditum Romæ cognomen (iam enim ita clam quidam mussitantes, vulgo tamen eum appellabant) an quicquam superbius esse quam ludificari sic omne nomen Latinum? principibus longe ab domo excitis, ipsum, qui concilium indixerit non adesse. tentari profecto patientiam, vt si iugum acceperint, obnoxios premat: cui enim non apparere, affectare eum imperium in Latinos? (I 50)

Turnus Herdonius, who came from *Aricia,* inveighed very severely against *Tarquinius* who was then absent; (1) saying, *It was no wonder, that the* Romans *called him* Tarquinius Superbus, (i. e. *Tarquinius* the Proud) (for so, they, now, though privately,

... Turnus Herdonius, a native of Aricia, had bitterly inveighed against Tarquin for his absence, (1) saying, "It was no wonder "he had the sirname of Proud given him at "Rome: for he was commonly called by this "name, though secretly and by whispers. "(2) Can there be a greater instance of

yet generally called him) *for* (2) *can any thing be a greater sign of pride, than thus to slight the whole Nobility of the* Latins: *For him, who appointed this Assembly of so many Nobles, that are come so far from home, not to be here himself:* (3) *that he did it to try their patience, and to find out, how much he could impose on them if they would submit to his yoke;* (4) *For who did not plainly see, that he affected Dominion over the* Latins; ...*
(1686, p. 28)

"pride, than thus to trifle with the Latine "nation; to summon a number of princes "to come hither from distant places, and not attend the meeting, which he himself (3) "had appointed? It was plain he tried their "patience, that if they should once submit "to the yoke, he might oppress them, when "they had put it out of their power to help "themselves. (4) For who could miss to "observe, that he aspired to a despotic power "over the Latines?
(1744, p. 92)

In Bohun's translation we note first the subordinating participle *saying* (1), followed by an unitalicized parenthesis corresponding to Livy's interpolation in the indicative; next there is a leap into the present tense, i. e. direct speech, which is continued until we come to (3), introducing a stretch of indirect speech; and finally at (4) the translator switches over into free indirect speech.—The 1744 version is characterized by a similar inconsistency: (1) marks the beginning of indirect speech; at (2) we move into direct speech, but the pluperfect at (3) makes it clear that the translator has now given up this mode in favour of free indirect speech, which is adhered to for the remainder of the passage. Besides we may note the free indirect question at (4), which in its turn governs a clause of indirect speech.—The conclusion is warranted, then, that if the two translators had stylistic consistency in mind, there was no cause for them to refer to their predecessor in disparaging terms. Free indirect speech occurs in both these translations, but not so frequently as in Philemon Holland's version.

The last examples have taken us up almost to the time when free indirect speech begins to be widely used in indigenous English literature. It is difficult to assess the precise degree to which English is indebted to Latin for this construction. But let us state some facts bearing on the problem. Free indirect speech occurs sporadically in non-translational literature dating from the early modern English period, but in that period the difference between the various narrative modes was probably felt to be less absolute than today (compare the use of quotation marks and italics illustrated above). As we have seen, free indirect speech also appears as one rendering of Latin *oratio obliqua,* particularly in longish passages where the translator may have lost sight of the governing verb or may have found that a repetition of it would be too heavy. It is probably true to say that where it occurs in early English translations, free indirect speech is often a more or less mechanical phenomenon, a 'stencil translation'[10]) that becomes stylistically apt only by accident, as it were, having not yet acquired its modern overtones: for it is *a syntactic variant* alternating with indirect and to some extent direct speech. It remains to consider the rôle played by translations from the classics. Writing on Elizabethan prose translation in general, James Winny states that

It is impossible to estimate how much the development of sixteenth-century prose was encouraged by the business of translation, which, beside introducing new words and ideas, itself helped to mould the prose style of the widely read translators. The stimulus to English writing from this source may be greater than we now suspect. (*Elizabethan Prose Translation* (Cambridge 1960), p. xx).

It should be borne in mind that translations of *Latin* writers loomed large in the sixteenth century and later, and it seems tempting to assume that influence from this source merged with the native English tendency so as to produce what was in due course to become an important stylistic innovation.

---

[10]) S. K. WORKMAN, *Fifteenth Century Translation as an Influence on English Prose* (Princeton Studies in English 18 (1940), p. 8).

COGNATE, BUT SUI GENERIS:
DIFFICULTIES CONFRONTING ADVANCED
DANISH STUDENTS OF ENGLISH

It is often said that it is easy for Danes — and indeed for Scandinavians in general — to learn English. This is both true and false, depending on what we mean by 'learning English'. It is true that it is easy for Danes to acquire an elementary knowledge of English; but where the difficulties begin to crop up is in the intermediate and advanced stages of acquisition. These facts thus run counter to the German saying 'Aller Anfang ist schwer', and the reason why this should be so is suggested by the title of my paper: although English and Danish are cognate languages and therefore share many similarities, they *are* separate linguistic structures, and as far as advanced students are concerned, their task is precisely to ascertain where the two languages are homologous and where they differ.

I am firmly convinced of the reality of linguistic interference or transfer. Insisting on this is not flogging a dead horse, for there are in fact people who are fond of minimising the importance of interference. In modern studies of language learning it is customary to operate with the terms L1 (the student's native language) and L2 (the target language). Somewhere in between these we find the student's interlanguage, a restricted and deviant version that changes all the time the more it approaches the target language. It is, however, a painful process for the foreign-language student to switch off his native language and indeed his specific cultural background. Ideally, the aim of the advanced-level foreign-language learner must be to shed his native ethnocentric habits and beliefs (in the wide sense of the term) and to acquire a new set of such beliefs. When these two sets of beliefs come to clash (as they are bound to do), the factor of interference must be tackled, and it *can* be tackled by the teacher who has a thorough knowledge of both the languages and cultures involved: in many cases at least it is possible to predict which areas are troublespots.

Let me try for a moment to enter into the minds of our Danish students of English. If the beginner feels that he can easily cope with the task, it is partly because the teacher at the elementary level tends to over-emphasize the similarities between the two languages. If the advanced student feels that he is up against a lot of difficulties, it is because he has now become the victim of a rude awakening: he has to face the fact that though there are similarities and parallelisms between the two languages, there are certainly also tricky dissimilarities and incongruities. Part of the blame for this state of things must, in my view, be laid at the door of teachers at the two levels who have neglected to correlate their efforts: in order to get his pupils started, the teacher at the elementary level tends to give undue emphasis to similarities, and this really means postponing some difficulties which then make themselves all the more strongly felt at a later stage.

Predicting the areas that are likely to cause trouble presupposes a contrastive analysis—what Otto Jespersen termed squinting grammar. But in spite of this not very flattering term the approach is useful and indeed indispensable, and it can be applied both to grammar and to other areas, to make students realize the causes of error.

I shall begin with the situation where the student's L1 contains one item, the target language two. In some of these cases there seems to be a psychological mechanism at work which prompts students to prefer the item that is most dissimilar to their native language. This may be illustrated by a phonological example. English has both /v/ and /w/ as distinct phonemes, Standard Danish only /v/. But even students who have long ago passed the elementary stage have an almost ineradicable tendency to substitute /w/ for /v/ because they believe it sounds more English.

Let me add here in parenthesis that there is a problem in connexion with the pronunciation of French loanwords in English. It is advisable for Danish—and other—students of English who have been taught French to unlearn the correct pronunciation, since the English tend to use pronunciations like ['kuːdeiˈtaː] (*coup d'état*) and [ʃəˈtə ubriːɑ̃] (*Chateaubriand*).

Another example which illustrates the deficiency of the student's interlanguage appears from the following brief dialogue, which is typical; the point may seem elementary, but many advanced students have difficulty in selecting the correct initiator to an answer:

'What do you think of this article?' — '*Yes*, it's very interesting.'

Here the student's interlanguage obviously equates Danish *ja* with English *yes* also in those cases where *well* is an obligatory initiator, namely in response to a *wh-* question. The correct sub-systems have one item in Danish, but two items in English: one for *yes-no* questions, another for *wh-* questions.

There is a crucial area within verbal syntax that presents problems. In many, perhaps most, cases the native speaker of English has to choose between two forms: the simple tense ('the sun *rises* in the east') and the progressive or expanded tense ('the sun *is rising* now'), depending on meaning and situation. The native speaker of Danish has only one grammatical form available, corresponding formally to the English simple tense, but semantically to both English tenses. How is this fact of English grammar conveyed to the student? We may, I think, distinguish three typical stages in the learning process. At the elementary stage, the teacher will concentrate on the simple tenses, which are formally parallel with Danish, postponing the introduction of the expanded tenses. At the next stage, however, they have to be introduced, and perhaps they are overlearned; anyway, the result is in many cases that students at the intermediate and advanced levels tend to overuse these verbal forms, to employ them in situations where they are not appropriate, possibly on the argument that since the expanded forms have no grammatical equivalents in Danish (they do of course have semantic equivalents, expressed periphrastically) and since ambitious students wish to sound as English as possible, they had better make frequent use of the expanded forms. The third and final stage is only reached—if ever—if the teacher succeeds in inculcating in his students the characteristic semantic and pragmatic differences between the forms.

The examples given so far are characterized by the student's native language having one item or form as against two in the target language. Let me comment briefly on the opposite situation, in which L1 has two classes, the target language one. A case in point would be gender: Danish has two genders (the common gender and neuter), but English nouns are not distinguished in this way. Obviously this state of things causes no problem for the Danish student of English. On the other hand the English student of Danish has considerable trouble over gender assignment (and it may be added that the many English nouns that have been introduced bodily into Danish as loanwords in recent decades show quite a lot of gender vacillation).

Next we may consider cases where there are two classes or possibilities in both languages. Both Danish and English nouns may behave as countables or uncountables, sometimes both (which involves reclassification, as in 'you won't get much chair for 10 pounds'). But on the whole there is conformity between the two languages; on the whole: for the trouble is that some English nouns are uncountables (at least primarily): nouns like *advice*, *information*, and *travel*, while the corresponding Danish nouns are countables. And occasionally we find the opposite distribution: English has *a toy* (and pl. *toys*), but the corresponding Danish word (*legetøj*) is an uncountable noun.

In some cases the two languages have the same patterns, but pattern (a) and pattern (b) do not have the same privilege of occurrence in the two languages. If we consider the competition between anaphoric and cataphoric pronouns in English and in Danish, it is important to note that in English, anaphora (or back-reference) and cataphora (forward reference) are equally acceptable:

(a) When *Smith* came home, *he* had a beer

(b) When *he* came home, *Smith* had a beer

where there is co-reference between the name and the pronoun. Both formulations are equally acceptable, and in fact some modern British writers seem to prefer cataphora.[1] As for Danish, it must be said that the anaphoric construction is preferred probably in 19 cases out of 20, so that cataphora is only marginally possible and is decidedly the marked pattern. The same holds for possessive pronouns in a corresponding function, so that in English we find '*Her* naval supremacy saved *England*' alternating with, and perhaps even preferred to, '*England's* naval supremacy saved *her*', while in Danish a cataphoric possessive pronoun would be a very rare occurrence indeed. So Danish students must be advised to exploit the opportunity of using cataphora when expressing themselves in English and to resist the temptation of uncritically transplanting cataphoric constructions when translating from English.

We note a similar kind of lopsided distribution between the two languages if we consider certain types of subject in English. Here it is quite common to find points of time or periods of time filling the subject slot of a sentence, as in 'The next second confirmed my suspicion', or 'A day or two should see the end of our troubles', or 'Christmas morning found her bustling in the kitchen'. (It is mainly the verbs *to find* and *to see* that appear in this construction). The corresponding pattern is barely possible in Danish, which normally con-

---

[1] See my article 'The Growth of Cataphoric Personal and Possessive Pronouns in English', in *Current Topics in English Historical Linguistics* (Odense University Studies in English. Vol. 4; Odense University Press 1983), p. 229

veys temporal notions in the form of adverbials (which is of course also possible in English). So this is another area where it must be brought home to the foreign learner that there is one acceptable possibility in his native language as against two in English.

Idioms constitute an area of great unpredictability from the point of view of the foreign student: some idioms are transparent, others are opaque, or they actually tend to lead the student astray. Most Danes, until they have been warned, assume that the expression 'they live like fighting cocks' refers to a state of animosity between the people referred to. The idiom 'to hang one's head' has its formal counterpart in Danish; it does not, however, suggest shame or guilt, as in English, but depression. Sometimes there is a formal difference between the two languages: English has 'the goose that lays the golden eggs', while in Danish it is the *hen* that does it. English has idioms with no exact Danish equivalents, and some Danish idioms can only be rendered by pale English paraphrases. Given all these incongruities it is no wonder that the foreigner grows bewildered and is reluctant to accept another important fact: that there *are* many instances of formal and semantic identity between the two languages as far as idioms are concerned: 'to take the bull by the horns', 'to say it with flowers', and 'to go up in smoke' are cases in point, and so is 'the apple of discord', although in this connexion it must be added that English also has available 'the bone of contention'. The so-called irreversible binomials—cliché-like co-ordinate pairs—are equally troublesome; many of them occur in parallel form in the two languages, for instance 'death and destruction', 'oaths and imprecations', 'bow and arrow(s)', and 'supply and demand', but in many others the ordering of the members is the opposite. Thus, corresponding to 'in and out', 'back and forth', 'double or quits', 'weights and measures', and 'a love-hate relationship' there are Danish binomials, but the order is inverted.

Formal similarity between English and Danish lexical items can be something between a hindrance and a help. It is of course a help in those many cases where formal and semantic similarity go hand in hand, but students may be led astray if there is only partial similarity. Take English *morning*, which is equivalent to Danish *morgen*, but which—unlike the Danish word—also denotes the period until one p.m. or so (incidentally, the exact period covered by *morning* seems to vary somewhat with individual speakers: I recently entered a London restaurant at one o'clock and was greeted with a 'good afternoon' by one waiter; the next customer immediately after me was greeted 'good morning' by another waiter). English *family*, in its central use, corresponds to Danish *familie*; but Danes have to be expressly reminded that the English word has a wider field of application: it can mean 'children' as in 'he has a wife and family' or 'she is one of a family of three'. Some of the English prepositions are identical or similar in form to their Danish equivalents, and they may correspond partially from a semantic point of view; this is true of *for*: in 'I work for him' the preposition corresponds precisely to Danish *for*. However, in an example like 'he was held for questioning' idiomatic Danish would not use *for*. This usage is nevertheless beginning to appear in Danish but must be labelled an Anglicism (of which more below).

There is a special group of these semantic will-o'-the-wisps, *les faux amis*. Typically, they are Romance loanwords that are found both in English and in Danish. Many of these loanwords mean the same in the two languages (this is true of adjectives like *puerile* and *senile*), so here there is no problem. But some do not, and they are insidious. English *eventuality* (as in 'in that eventuality') has its exact Danish formal and semantic equivalent, but *eventually* cannot be equated semantically with the corresponding Danish adverb (which means 'possibly'). There is a similar semantic mismatch between English words like *frivolous, genial, trivial*; *fabric, fundament, gymnasium* and the formally corresponding Danish words. A subgroup is made up of what may be termed pseudo-English words in Danish: their form is English, but they do not mean in English what they mean in Danish. Examples of these are Danish *butterfly* ('bow-tie'), *choker* ('choke' in a car), *sixpence* ('cloth cap'), *speaker* ('announcer'), *speeder* ('accelerator'), and *struggler* ('social climber'). The meanings of such words of course have to be unlearned.

The sheer size of the English vocabulary as against the more modest proportions of Danish poses certain problems for Danish students. Here again the situation is that while English has a richly developed system of stylistic and semantic contrasts, the corresponding Danish system is not nearly so fully developed. I should like to comment on two areas: the double-scale system of plain English *vs.* Latinate terms, and the many terms that are associated with the sexes.

Ever since the wholesale adoption of loanwords into English in the Renaissance it has been possible to refer to the same concept in two ways that generally contrast stylistically. We can either call a spade a spade, or we can call it 'an earth-inverting horticultural implement'. A dog is defined by the *OED* as 'a quadruped of the genus Canis...', by the *Oxford Advanced Learner's Dictionary of Current English* as '... a friend of man'. Quite apart from the suitability of one or the other type of expression in formally different contexts, and apart from considerations of variation, the contrast can be exploited—and has been—in literature not least for humorous purposes, as when Dickens has Mr. Micawber peter out in bathos: 'It is not an avocation of a remunerative description—in other words it does *not* pay'. One important factor that determines the choice of expression is the prestige value that often attaches to the Latinate term. Recent years have witnessed the spread of occupational terms of prestige like *funeral director* for *undertaker* and *rodent operative* for *rat-catcher*; *reconditioned* somehow sounds better than *second-hand* or *used*. Substandard speakers are fully aware of this prestige value, as appears from the following quotation from one of Katherine Mansfield's short stories:

'it was dropsy that carried him off at the larst. Many's the time they drawn one and a half pints from 'im at the 'ospital. . . It seemed like a judgmint.'—Alice burned to know exactly what it was that was drawn from him. She ventured, 'I suppose it was water.'—But Mrs Stubbs fixed Alice with her eyes and replied meaningly, 'It was *liquid*, my dear.'

(*The Garden Party*, Penguin 1955, p. 44).

The number of these 'hard words' in English is overwhelming compared with the vocabularies of most other languages, and this is an area that demands careful study if the foreigner is to acquire a sense of its stylistic potentialities.

A more circumscribed semantico-stylistic area—but still one that is quite well developed in English—consists of two sets of terms that are more or less closely associated with the sexes. It may perhaps be summed up in the phrase: 'He pops the question, and she names the day', which reflects the traditional sex roles. (I am concentrating here on items that are not self-explanatory to the foreigner, as are *bitch* and *stag*—or should be). A number of sexual roles and qualities are reflected linguistically. If somebody is small and neat, we have a choice between *petite* and *dapper*, depending on whether it is a woman or a man who is to be referred to. For some reason the terms normally reserved for the description of women appear to be more numerous than the terms relating to men. A member of the female sex may be *a young person*, or she may be *no spring chicken*, or she may be a *battleaxe*. A young person may be either *coy* or *forward*, and some girls are *flighty* or *bubbling over* or *svelte* or *pretty* or actually *beautiful*. Irrespective of age, a woman may be *buxom* or *catty* or *kittenish* or *dowdy* or in some cases *mannish*.

As for the men, there are *lounge lizards* and *lone wolves*, and they may be *chivalrous* or *womanish* or *effeminate* or *lecherous* or *horny* or—if they are old enough—*hale* (and perhaps *hearty* as well). The tricky thing is that in some cases at least the transfer of a term from one sex to the other is possible, albeit with certain consequences. *A nagging wife* is in the nature of a cliché; but if one occasionally comes across *a nagging husband*, such a person tends to take on female characteristics. If a member of the male sex is referred to as *beautiful*, this does not normally imply unqualified praise.

In Danish higher education we have among teachers of English a number of native speakers—Englishmen, Americans, and Australians. Some of them have been with us for many years, and if they have acquired a good command of Danish, this may sometimes affect their native language. It was once said that nobody acquires a foreign language without losing his own; this is perhaps putting it too strongly, but it is difficult to resist linguistic interference. One may see such native speakers of English form adjectives like *hair-fine* (on the analogy of Danish *hårfin* 'subtle', and possibly with *hairline* as a subsidiary agent) and use the expression '*on* the arena' (by analogy with Danish 'på arenaen'). The great writer Karen Blixen (alias Isak Dinesen)—of *Seven Gothic Tales* and *Out of Africa* fame—was nearly, but not quite, bilingual in her native Danish and in English, and she was a very fastidious artist. Nevertheless, when she wrote in English, her style was tinged by Danicisms, and correspondingly her Danish prose contains a number of Anglicisms. In *Out of Africa* she refers to a person's *arrestation*, meaning his arrest. The long form does occur in English, but very rarely, and it is labelled 'more or less a Gallicism' by the *OED*. It seems likely, though, that Karen Blixen was inspired by the Danish word *arrestation*. Another oddity is *an eluding reply*, where the form one would expect is *elusive*. This *-ing* adjective probably owes its existence to influence from an adjectival Danish present participle (*undvigende*), and Karen Blixen was obviously led astray by the circumstance that in many cases adjectival present participles have their exact counterparts in English (compare the parallelism between for instance *entertaining* and *underholdende*). Anglicisms in Karen Blixen's Danish are as numerous as Danicisms in her English.[2] — It is interesting to note that when *Seven Gothic Tales* was published in the United States in 1934, the critic Mark Van Doren, commenting on the language, spoke of 'a few slips from idiom which are so attractive as to seem premeditated',[3] and another critic, Janet Lewis, has this to say of Karen Blixen's English: 'I can detect practically nothing of the foreigner in her use of English.'[4] Such statements are a bit surprising to the language teacher, who is in a position to identify most of these 'slips' as Danicisms.

---

[2] See my 'Studier i Karen Blixens engelske og danske sprogform', *Blixeniana 1982*, Copenhagen 1982, pp. 263—308.

[3] See Aage Kabell. *Karen Blixen debuterer*, Munich 1968, pp. 92f.

[4] See *Isak Dinesen, Storyteller*, edited by Aage Jørgensen, Aarhus 1972, p. 57.

If even as fastidious a writer as Karen Blixen is unable to avoid Anglicisms—for she clearly does not want to use them—it is small wonder that English influence on Danish should make itself heavily felt in TV programmes and in newspapers. Journalists who are exposed to English-language sources often have to work against a deadline and do not always have time to consider whether a given English term might not be rendered by a genuine Danish word or phrase. It is easier to adopt a foreignism bodily or to supply a loan-ranslation, and this accounts for many of the Anglicisms that crop up in Danish newspapers—not only patent Anglicisms like *high-brow*, *job*, and *stress*; there is also the insidious process that may be termed semantic borrowing, whereby an existing Danish word receives a new sense from the corresponding, sometimes formally similar, English word. I mentioned earlier the anglicized use of the Danish preposition *for*, and I may add here that English words like *longhaired*, *umbrella*, and *bottleneck* now appear in their figurative senses ('highbrow', 'co-ordinating agency', and 'anything obstructing an even flow of production') in the corresponding Danish words. English influence on Danish is also manifest, though to a lesser extent, in syntax, style, and idiom.[5] Thus students of English find themselves in a climate that favours Anglicisms, and it may be difficult enough for them to resist this influence; but obviously it should be their endeavour to keep the two languages apart.

Up till now I have dealt with contemporary English. If, finally, we consider the study of earlier English language and literature, we shall see that this presents special problems, and as far as I can see, these problems are roughly identical with the problems confronting native speakers of English. Let me adduce the testimony of an Englishman. C. S. Lewis states: 'Indeed I am ashamed to remember for how many years, as a boy and a young man, I read nineteenth-century fiction without noticing how often its language differed from ours. I believe it was work on far earlier English that first opened my eyes: for there a man is not so easily deceived into thinking he understands what he does not.'[6] There we have the problem in a nutshell: many linguistic items from earlier literature are obviously different from—or nonexistent in—modern English. In Iago's 'shrewd doubt' *shrewd* means 'serious', and when Salerio in *The Merchant of Venice* says 'Slubber not business for my sake', we are compelled to look up *slubber* (= 'treat carelessly'). Such deviations from contemporary English call attention to themselves and force the reader to turn to the dictionary.

[5] See my 'English Influence on Contemporary Danish', in *The English Element in European Languages*, Vol. 2, edited by Rudolf Filipović, Zagreb 1982, pp. 71—153.

[6] *Studies in Words*, Cambridge University Press 1967, pp. 311f.

The real danger, however, is language that is formally identical with modern English, and which *might* make a kind of sense if one simply imposed the semantics of modern English on it. But this would lead to misinterpretation. Thus Dr Johnson's dictum on *Lycidas*, that it is 'easy, vulgar, and therefore disgusting', is apt to mislead unsuspecting contemporary readers, since both *vulgar* and *disgusting* had less negative overtones then than today ('commonplace, unlearned' and 'distasteful', respectively). C. S. Lewis comments on the expression *I dare say*, which today means something like 'probably' or 'I shouldn't wonder if' ('I dare say you are right'). But in earlier English it was much stronger, being synonymous with contemporary English 'I venture to say', and this sense is sometimes found as late as Jane Austen. As Lewis puts it: 'In *Northanger Abbey* the egregious Thorpe says of General Tilney, "A very fine fellow; as rich as a Jew. I should like to dine with him. I dare say he gives famous dinners." (Ch 12). Thorpe would not wish to dine with a man merely on the ground that, for all he knew to the contrary, the dinners might possibly be good. *I dare say* here means "I bet" or "I'll be bound."'[7] It is the same with the verb *to develop* in Dickens. Here it can have its contemporary meaning; but Dickens also retains the older sense of 'disclosing, revealing' as in this example from *Pickwick Papers*: 'Nathaniel Pipkin determined that, come what might, he would develop the state of his feelings.' (Ch 17). Even texts from the twentieth century can occasionally cause problems. In *The Language of English Literature* Raymond Chapman calls attention to the following passage from Evelyn Waugh's *Decline and Fall* (1928):

'Can you read and write, D.4.12?' asked the newcomer.
  'Yes,' said Paul.
  'Public or secondary education?'
'Public,' said Paul. His school had been rather sensitive on this subject.
  'What was your standard when you left school?'
  'Well, I don't quite know. I don't think we had standards.'
  The Schoolmaster marked him down as 'Memory defective' on a form and went out. (Part III, Ch 1).

Chapman comments as follows: 'The confusion between the speakers arises because the schoolmaster uses the idea of *public school* to mean a free school in the state system as opposed to paying 'secondary schools', while Paul takes it in the special sense of the most expensive and prestigious type of secondary school. The state schools at that time were divided into *standards*, the secondary into *forms*. The point is lost today when the state system includes both primary and secondary schools, and itself has forms instead of standards.'[8]

---

[7] *Studies in Words*, p. 309.
[8] *The Language of English Literature*, London 1982, p. 110.

In this discussion of the problems confronting advanced Danish students of English I have emphasized the importance of realizing that the student's native language may impede his acquisition of the target language, and that an explicit contrastive approach may help to overcome this difficulty. This of course does not imply any underrating of the value of the immanent approach, the description of the foreign language as an autonomous structure. But eclecticism is a sound procedure. If—as I believe—we cannot disregard the factor of interference, the contrastive approach and the immanent approach should go hand in hand.

ON ANGLICISMS IN DANISH

0.0. INTRODUCTION

0.1. *Previous research*. Despite the fact that the influence exerted on the Danish language by British and American English has been considerable throughout the 20th century, and particularly since 1945, this influence is a somewhat neglected field of study. Books describing the Danish language have dealt more or less cursorily with Anglicisms (Bang 1962, Skautrup 1944–1968), and a number of articles have been published on the subject (Dahl 1942 and 1956, Larsen 1982, Sørensen 1971, 1975, 1978, 1981 and 1982). The only monograph is Sørensen 1973. The year 1955 saw the foundation of the official advisory body *Dansk Sprognævn* (*The Danish Language Committee*), whose task it is to follow developments in the Danish language and advise the public about usage. Over the years *Dansk Sprognævn* has published a series of reports on Danish, containing alphabetical lists of new words and phrases, many of which are Anglicisms (*Nordiske Sprogproblemer* 1955–1967, *Ny Ord i Dansk* 1968–1971). The latest *Sprognævn* publication is Petersen 1984, a bulky dictionary of neologisms in Danish, mainly based on the extensive material collected by the Committee. However, in these alphabetical presentations the Anglicisms appear among other neologisms, and they have only to a limited extent been subjected to systematic analysis. There is a need for further detailed studies of a largely unexploited material.

0.2. *Historical retrospect*. Anglo-Danish cultural relations span a period of over a thousand years, and as always when cultural relations are involved, this is reflected linguistically. During the early part of this period, which begins with the Viking raids and settlements, it was largely Danish that contributed to the English language.[1] The most striking examples of this influence are the Scandinavian-inspired forms *they, them*, and *their* and the numerous English place-names ending in *-by, -thorpe*, and *-thwaite*. There are, however, occasional instances of English loans in Danish from the early period; thus Danish *blæk* 'ink' comes from Old

---

1 Cf. Björkman 1900 and 1902.

212 (31)

English *blæc*,[2] and the title of the Danish duke and saint Knud *Lavard* (who flourished in the 12th century) is adopted from Middle English *lavard* (< Old English *hlāfweard*).

During the Renaissance and post-Renaissance period there was not much cultural contact between the two nations, and the knowledge of English in Denmark was limited. In this connection it may be noted that Shakespeare's works were often translated not direct from English, but via German. Søren Kierkegaard quotes Shakespeare in German translation,[3] and as late as the 6th edition of Ludvig Meyer's *Fremmedordbog* (1884) we find the German version of a Shakespearian quotation, *gut gebrüllt, Löwe,* side by side with the English version. However, from the mid-18th century there was a growing interest in English, manifested in a number of loanwords; thus *klub* and *kutter* were adopted in the latter half of the 18th century, and the 19th century saw the adoption of several terms from nautical parlance, for instance *brækkage* (< *breakage*), *sjækkel* (< *shackle*), *skonnert* (< *schooner*), *slæk* (< *slack,* of a rope), and *stirrids* (< *steerage*). Another semantic field in which Anglicisms flourish in this period is the terminology describing the Red Indians. James Fenimore Cooper's novels were very popular and appeared early in translation; thus *The Last of the Mohicans* (1826) was rendered into Danish in 1827 and introduced words like *Moccasiner, Squaw, Tomahawk, Totem, Wigwam* and *Ildvand* (< *firewater*), the last being a loan translation.

When borrowing goes on over an extended period, it sometimes happens that terms in the donor language grow archaic or obsolete while the loanwords live on vigorously in the adopting language. This is true of Danish *muffedise* 'wristlet', borrowed from English *muffetee* (cf. *OED,* 2.), and of Danish *porter* 'dark brown bitter beer' (a shortened form of *porter's ale*), which has now largely been ousted by *stout.* In other cases English loanwords that have been in Danish for a shorter or longer time tend to fall into disuse; this applies to the two adjectives *prud* 'fair' (< late Old English *prūd*), which is now poetic or archaic, and to *najs* 'scrumptious' (< *nice*), which is hardly alive today except as a vulgarism. Again, some words with obsolescent senses may have these revived through inspiration from the donor language; cases in point are *social* 'marked by pleasant companionship' (as in *a social club*), a sense that was current in the Danish adjective in the 19th century, but which had become rare in the 20th century until English influence made itself felt; and *spektakel,* which today means 'noise, uproar', but which used to have a sense corresponding to *spectacle* when it means 'a public display appealing to the eye by its mass, proportions, colour, or other dramatic qualities'; this obsolete sense has now been restored to the Danish noun through inspiration from English.[4]

2 Cf. *OED, s.v.* 'black', sb., 2. a: 'Black writing fluid, ink .
3 Skautrup III, 1953, 138.
4 I am indebted to Professor Poul Lindegård Hjorth for drawing my attention to the semantic vicissitude of *spektakel.*

Before Otto Jespersen's pioneering achievement had made itself felt, Danes knew little about the pronunciation of English, and it is characteristic of the early loanwords that their pronunciation shows imperfect adaptation to English and that their spelling is often made to conform to Danish orthographic conventions. Thus *fjæs* [fjɛʳs] is from English *face*, *hive* ['hiːvə] from *heave*, and *kiks* [kegs] 'biscuit' from *cakes*. Some English words in *-age* were mistakenly interpreted as being of French origin and are therefore stressed on the last syllable: *brækkage* [brɛˈkaːsjə] from *breakage*, *kottage* [kʌˈtaːsjə] from *cottage*.

In the following pages I shall concentrate on Anglicisms adopted in the 20th century and particularly since 1945.

1.0. ORTHOGRAPHY

1.1. In general, English loanwords retain their spelling in Danish; compare words like *bazooka, computer, juice* (Swedish uses the form *djus*), *quiz, sweater*, and *yacht*. It is, however, characteristic of some words adopted in the 19th century or earlier that they have been given a Danish orthographic appearance; *kiks* 'biscuit' (< *cakes*), *kutter* (< *cutter*), *strejke* noun and verb (< *strike*), *tjans* (< *chance*), and *tørn* 'tough job' (< *turn*) are examples of this.

1.2. A few graphic symbols tend to be replaced by others, thus *c* > *k* before back vowel or consonant: *boykot, kricket* (but *city*); *ph* > *f*: *foto*; *x* > *ks*: *bokse* 'to box'; in some words English double consonants become single, which results in spellings like *buldog* and *mandril*. But there is vacillation: the spelling *cricket* also occurs, the definite singular form of *pub* is spelt either *pubben, puben*, or *pubˀen*, and words like *foxtrot* and *sex* are only spelt thus.

1.3. Compound words alternate between being spelt solid (this is the Danish convention) or in two words; thus we find examples like *beatmusical* and *happyending* contrasting with spellings like *Tweed jakker* 'Tweed jackets' and *leasing tilbud* 'leasing offer'.

2.0. Phonology

2.1. The fate that English phonemes undergo when they appear in loanwords in Danish is determined by a number of factors: (1) similarities and differences between the two sound systems; (2) psycholinguistic and sociolinguistic factors; (3) the educational backgrounds of speakers; and (4) the degree of integration of the loans. In theory these can be set up as independent factors, but they often interact.

2.2. (1) Some phonemes are identical or nearly so in the two languages, e.g. /h, n, m, ŋ, s; iː, aʊ/. In others there is partial similarity between the sets; thus English /b,

(33)

d, g/ are formed in practically the same places as the corresponding Danish phonemes, but the English sounds are normally voiced, the Danish sounds always unvoiced, and besides there is neutralization between Danish /b, d, g,/ and /p, t, k/ in final position. When Danish /b, d, g/ are substituted for the English series, the result is slightly un-English. Some English phonemes have no equivalents in Danish, for instance /θ/, /z/, and /ʌ/; in these cases most Danes will substitute a sound that they feel is rather close to the English sound, so that one hears pronunciations like ['bisnes] *(business)*, ['srilr] or ['trilr][5] *(thriller)*, and ['kari] *(curry)*.

2.3. (2) When a speaker has occasion to use a direct English loanword in Danish, it ideally requires code-switching from one sound system to the other. This is difficult, and loanwords are therefore often approximated to the Danish sound system. There may be another psychological factor at work here: a speaker who employs too perfect an English pronunciation may be thought by others to be trying to show off, and hence such a speaker will tend to stick to pronunciations favoured by most Danes.

2.4. (3) Today most Danes have at least some knowledge of English, but speakers whose knowledge is limited tend to use pronunciations based on the orthographic conventions of Danish, hence pronunciations like ['juːry] for *jury* and [ˌpalmoˈliːvə] for *Palmolive*. There is also a tendency for the vowels of weakly stressed syllables to retain their full quality; thus *sixpence* is ['sigspɛns], *slogan* ['sloːgan]. Some speakers note that the English digraph *ea* often corresponds to /iː/ and wrongly transfer it to a word like *steak*: [sdiːg].

2.5. (4) If English loanwords are felt to be (almost) fully integrated in Danish, they tend to be treated like normal Danish words; for example, some of them are pronounced with the Danish glottal stop: *gear* [giˀr], *mart* [marˀd], *plaid* [plɛˀd], *smart* [smarˀd], *spurt* [sburˀd], etc. Further, compounds of the type *comeback* are invariably stressed on the last element: *comeˈback*, *feedˈback*, *knockˈout*, *lockˈout*, etc.[6] This pronunciation is probably influenced by the stress distribution found in Danish verb-particle combinations.

2.6. It will have appeared from the preceding sections that there is a great deal of vacillation in the pronunciation of English loanwords in Danish, and that the structure of the English sound system is often disregarded. On the one hand, the same English phoneme may be equated with a number of Danish phonemes. Thus English /ʌ/ is given five different values in Danish: (1) One may hear an approximation to the English sound in words like *pub* and *struggler*. (2) /ʌ/ becomes /ɔ/ in words like *bluff*, *humbug*, and *slum*. (3) It is /œ/ in one or two words like *bluff* and *trust*, this being characteristic of the pronunciation of the older generation. (4)

---

5 It should be noted that Danish /r/ is uvular.
6 As in German; cf. Carstensen 1973.

There is a spelling pronunciation /u/ in words like *kutter* and *puck*. (5) In at least one word, *karry* (< *curry*), the vowel is /a/. On the other hand, different English phonemes may merge in the same Danish sound. Thus /ʌ, ɐ,əʊ,ə/ all become /ʌ/ as in *cup* [kʌb], *hot* [hʌd], *pony* [pʌni], and *computer* [kʌmˈpjuːdr]. But in spite of vacillation and imperfect imitation of the English sound system Danish speakers employ pronunciations that are on the whole intelligible, if not fully acceptable, to native speakers of English.

3.0. MORPHOLOGY

3.1. Nouns

3.1.1. Geder. Modern English lacks formal gender distinctions, unlike Danish, in which nouns either belong to the common gender—this is true of *c.* 75% of them—or are neuter. When English nouns are adopted into Danish, they must of necessity be treated as either one or the other. This gender assignment is governed by a number of factors.

For one thing, morphological features may be relevant. For instance most Danish nouns in *-al* are common gender nouns, and this may account for loans like *musical*, *professional*, and *terminal* being treated as common gender nouns. Danish nouns derived from infinitives (e.g. *et knus* 'a hug', < *at knuse* 'to hug') are usually neuter. Analogously, we have *et check* 'control' corresponding to *at checke*; other neuter loanwords are *flop*, *gear*, *hit*, *smash*, *stress*, and *tip*.

In some cases the influence of Danish translation equivalents is operative: there is a tendency for English nouns to take the same gender as the words that customarily translate them. It is *en suitcase* because its translation *kuffert* is a common gender noun, but normally *et case* (= 'case-study') because the latter word is translated by the neuter *tilfælde*. It is *en joke* owing to its translation *en vittighed*, etc.

In other cases the gender of a superordinate noun determines the gender of the hyponyms ranged under it. For example the hyponyms of *en hund* 'a dog' are all common gender nouns in Danish, and so are loanwords like *buldog, collie, foxterrier*, and *sheepdog*.

There is, however, some vacillation in gender assignment, and sometimes the same form belongs to different genders, depending on what it means. Thus *en lift* means 'a carry-cot', while *et lift* means '(the offer of) a ride in a car'.

3.1.2. The singular of some English loanwords ends in an *-s* that has erroneously been taken by Danish speakers to form part of the stem, but which is actually the English plural morpheme. Examples are *et drops* 'a boiled sweet', *en kiks* 'a biscuit', *en rollmops* 'a pickled herring fillet', and *et slips* 'a tie'. In one or two cases the forms with and without *-s* are considered equally acceptable: *en clip(s)* 'a paper clip', *et* *tip(s)*. In spoken substandard Danish incorrect forms in *-s* abound: *en drinks, en fans, en hotdogs, en sweaters, en tons,* and *et tricks* can all be heard.

3.1.3. The commonest Danish plural morpheme is *-(e)r*, less common ones being *-e*, zero, and mutation. In English loanwords these Danish morphemes compete with the English *-s* morpheme as illustrated in the following diagram:

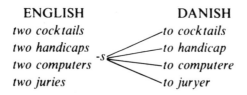

ENGLISH   DANISH
two cocktails   *to cocktails*
two handicaps   *to handicap*
two computers   *to computere*
two juries   *to juryer*

The choice of morpheme depends on the degree of integration of the word involved, so that words that are felt to have become fully naturalized tend to be inflected with Danish morphemes; but there is much vacillation. Thus one finds *babies* or *babyer; curlers* or *curlere; films* or *film; interviews, interviewer,* or *interview;* etc. Mutation plurals are only found with *man — men: he-men, gentlemen.*

3.1.4. There are three types of definite plural forms. (1) If there is vacillation between the plural morphemes *-s* and *-er*, the definite form ends in *-erne: festivals, festivaler; festivalerne.* (2) Some words that add *-s* in the indefinite plural drop the *-s* and form a definite plural in *-ene: checks — checkene, shows — showene.* (3) In other words that add *-s* in the indefinite plural the *-s* is retained when *-ene* is added: *gags — gagsene, jeans — jeansene.*

3.2. Adjectives

3.2.1. Danish adjectives add endings for definiteness (*-e*), neuter (*-t*), and plural (*-e*); thus we have *en gammel mand* 'an old man', but *den gamle mand* 'the old man'; *et gammelt hus* 'an old house'; *de gamle huse* 'the old houses'. Most English adjectives that are adopted unaltered do not add these endings: *den danske dark horse* 'the Danish dark horse'; *et "tricky" spørgsmål* 'a tricky question'; *de var liberale og yderst fair* 'they were liberal and extremely fair'. There is, however, a certain tendency to treat such adjectives in the same way as Danish adjectives: *hotte melodier* 'hot tunes' is an example of the Danish plural ending being transferred to a loanword (note also the doubling of the consonant).

3.2.2. Past participles in an adjectival function often retain the ending *-ed: en useeded engelsk spiller* 'an unseeded English player', although sometimes the Danish ending *-et* occurs: *hvis tæppet er tuftet* 'if the carpet is tufted'. If an ending is required, the rules of Danish are normally adhered to: *den blendede whisky* 'the blended whisky'; *merkantilmindede folk* 'commercially minded people'.

3.2.3. *Comparison*. English adjectives adopted into Danish are normally compared analytically: *mere/mest cool* 'cooler/coolest'; *mere/mest sophisticated* 'more/most sophisticated'. An adjective like *hot* is, however, easily made to fit into the Danish system of synthetic comparison: *hot — hottere — hottest*.

3.3. Adverbs

The Danish adverbial ending *-t* (as in *godt organiseret* 'well organized') is not added to English loanwords: *en fair spillet kamp* 'a fairly played match'.

3.4. Verbs

3.4.1. The Danish infinitival ending *-e* is practically always added to adopted verbs: *at booke, bowle, croone, entertaine, lynche*, etc. A single consonant is doubled after a short stressed vowel: *at droppe, handicappe, kidnappe*, etc.

The present active adds *-r* as in Danish verbs: *han crooner* 'he is crooning'.

The Danish passive in *-s* (*der spises* 'people are eating', literally 'there is-eaten') may be transferred to verbs of English origin: *tingene skal times rigtigt* 'things must be properly timed', literally 'things shall be-timed properly'; *firmaer, som blacklistes* 'firms that are blacklisted'.

3.4.2. All verbs borrowed from English are conjugated regularly (the weak conjugation), also those that are irregular in English: *han postede brevet* 'he posted the letter'; *han fightede godt igennem hele kampen* 'he fought well throughout the match'.

3.4.3. When phrasal verbs like *to knock out* and *to lock out* are adopted into Danish, they are treated as units, orthographically as well as morphologically; for instance the infinitive is *at lockoute* with the ending added to the particle, and corresponding to an example like *The workers have been locked out* Danish has *Arbejderne er blevet lockoutet*.

4.0. SYNTAX

General remarks. English and Danish are cognate languages that have many syntactic patterns in common.[7] It is therefore not always a simple matter to prove syntactic influence. In a number of cases one can, however, point to constructions that conform to English syntax while deviating more or less from normal Danish

7 Cf. Sørensen 1984.

usage, and considering the cultural relationship between the English-speaking nations and Denmark it is reasonable to interpret such cases as evidence of English influence. This is sometimes a matter of degree: a Danish minority construction may have been reinforced through English influence.

4.1. The nominal phrase

4.1.1. *Premodification and postmodification.* In contemporary English premodification is widespread, and this has influenced Danish, which today favours constructions like *et væg-til-væg tæppe* 'a wall-to-wall carpet' and *en vent-og-se-holdning* 'a wait-and-see attitude' (there is no consistent use of hyphens in Danish). In a single instance postmodification, too, has made its influence felt; this is the use of *ever* qualifying a superlative, as in *the greatest scandal ever*, which has produced the new Danish construction *den største skandale nogen sinde.*

4.1.2. *Occupation, name, age.* In a Danish nominal group, terms indicating occupation and name will normally occur in that order. But some journalists favour the opposite, English-inspired order: *Erling Dinesen, arbejdsminister* 'E. D., Minister of Labour'. The occasional postposition of a person's age is also inspired by English: *forfatteren Clifford Irving, 41* 'author C. I., 41'.

4.1.3. *Time as subject.* In English one frequently finds indications of time functioning in the subject slot: *The next morning found her bustling in the kitchen. — The near future will see many changes.* This is barely possible in Danish. Parallels do, however, occur, and where this is the case, they may well have been modelled on English: *De senere år har set enkelte forsøg...* "Recent years have seen a few attempts...". *De sidste 14 dage af 1975 fastslog, at...* "The last fortnight of 1975 established that..."

4.1.4. *The articles.* As is well known, the English combination of adjective and proper name without a preceding definite article is commonly associated with emotional overtones: *lovely 18-year-old Ann, chicly dressed Laura.* The corresponding Danish phrase normally requires the article, but in recent years the English construction has been imitated in Danish, especially by journalists who wish to get on intimate terms with their readers: *katteelskende Minnie Caldwell* "cat-loving M.C.", *30-årige Nicholas Alveras* "30-year-old N.A.". It should be added that Swedish may also have contributed towards influencing Danish in this respect.[8]

When a noun is in apposition to a name in English, it often appears without the article. The same construction is becoming current in Danish, especially in journalese: *Folkets Dagblad, officielt organ for kommunistpartiet* "The People's

---

8 Cf. Hjorth 1969.

Daily, official organ of the Communist Party"; *Thomas Alva Edison, amerikansk opfinder* "T.A.E., American inventor".

4.1.5. *The use of the plural.* The distributive plural is not nearly so common in Danish as in English; we normally find *side 3 og 4* "page (sg.) 3 and 4", but there is a tendency to use the plural: *siderne 3 og 4* "pages 3 and 4", which may have been reinforced by English (and possibly also by Swedish).

A number of Danish nouns do not normally appear in the plural; when they do, it may be due to English influence. This applies to *energier* 'energies', *indsigter* 'insights', *politikker* 'policies', and *tjenester* 'services': *MacMillan takkede Heath for hans tjenester* "M. thanked H. for his services".

4.2. Pronouns

4.2.1. *Cataphora.* In English it is by no means rare to find a personal pronoun appearing before the noun with which it is coreferential: *When he came home, John had a beer.* In Danish this is not nearly so common. Where it occurs, one may sometimes suspect English influence. For instance it is a favourite with Karen Blixen (Isak Dinesen), who was bilingual in English and Danish. In the following example *hun* 'she' precedes the name *Lucan: Langsomt, idet hun samlede al sin Kraft, saa Lucan op paa hende* "Slowly, gathering all her strength, L. looked up at her".

4.2.2. *You — du.* The well-known employment of *you* as a kind of generic pronoun (*you never know*) has had a curious influence on contemporary Danish. The Danish indefinite pronoun *man* 'one' is not infrequently replaced by the second person singular pronoun *du*, especially in the speech of young people. In part this may be due to a rough translation equivalence being set up between *you* and *du*, in part the phonetic similarity between the two pronouns may play a rôle. One may find *man* and *du* alternating in the same passage: *Man er fantastisk afhængig af heldet. Der kan ske det, at du har en lang research på et spor, der ender blindt* "One is fantastically dependent on luck. You may happen to conduct protracted research along a trail that leads nowhere".

4.3. Verbal syntax

4.3.1. *Verb plus particle.* A verb plus its particle forming a semantic unit is a common type in Danish. English has the same type: *back up* = 'support', and recent years have seen numerous such combinations invading Danish in the form of translation loans from English. Several of these analytic expressions, like *koge ned* 'boil down' for synthetic *sammentrænge* 'condense', are characterized by stylistic vividness since they are often metaphorical.

Here, first, are some examples of intransitive combinations: *bakke ud* < *back out, checke ud* < *check out, droppe ud* < *drop out, komme op* < *come up* (of a topic of debate). Next some examples of transitive combinations: *bakke op* < *back up, bringe op* < *bring up* (a topic for discussion), *følge op* < *follow up, rulle tilbage* < *roll back* (i.e. 'reduce prices'), *tone ned* < *tone down*.

A related English type consists of the elements verb (+ adverb) + preposition. This is also copied in Danish, which has *komme op imod* < *come up against, lede op til* < *lead up to, løbe ind i* < *run into* (e.g. difficulties), and *være oppe imod* < *be up against*.

4.3.2. *New transitive function.* A number of Danish verbs that used to be solely intransitive have in recent years had their grammatical potential expanded to transitive functions, at least partly under English influence. Examples are: *eksplodere en bombe* 'explode a bomb', *flyve BEA* 'fly BEA', *gro blomster* 'grow flowers'. A few Danish prepositional verbs sometimes drop their prepositions because the corresponding English verbs are transitive: *at influere verdens supermagter* "to influence the superpowers of the world" (normally *influere på*); *at plædere arabiske synspunkter* "to plead Arab points of view" (normally *plædere for*).

4.3.3. *'The book sells well'.* This example illustrates the notional passive with active form, a type that has been transferred into Danish in a number of cases; thus we have an exact parallel to the above example in *bogen sælger godt*. Other examples are: *Hun fotograferer godt* "She photographs well", i.e. is photogenic, and *stadig flere bøger lukker dårligt op* "ever more books open poorly", i.e. are difficult to open. The last example is distinctly awkward.

4.3.4. *The passive.* When an active English sentence is converted into the passive, it does not matter, as far as acceptability is concerned, whether the direct or the indirect object becomes the subject of the passive version; we have both (1) *A compensation was awarded him* and (2) *He was awarded a compensation*. In principle there are the same possibilities in contemporary Danish, although to most Danes of the older generation the equivalent of (2) is often doubtfully acceptable. It has, however, spread in recent years under English influence. Examples are: *Jeg blev fortalt, at ...* "I was told that ..."; Danes belonging to the older generation prefer *Det blev fortalt mig* "It was told me"; *Clark blev forevist billeder* "C. was shown pictures"; *Bogen blev ikke ydet retfærdighed* "The book was not done justice".

4.3.5. *Nominal style.* A mannerism that occurs especially in British and American journalese is the nominal, i.e. verbless, construction seen in: *The maximum penalty for insurrection: death by firing squad*. This has caught on in Danish: *Penge tjener Chung i et supermarked. Lønnen: 17 kr. i timen* "C. earns money in a supermarket. The pay: 17 kr. per hour". *En trøst: Vinhøsten tegner virkeligt godt.* "A consolation: The wine harvest is really promising". The verbless construction is also found in the frequently used expression *ingen tvivl om det* < *no doubt about that*.

5.0. LEXIS

Problems concerning the delimitation of the inventory. While the ascertainment of syntactic influence presupposes a comparison between the structures of the two languages and is thus only obvious to the specialist, lexical influence might at the first blush be imagined to be conspicuous. This is indeed the case as far as most direct loans (5.1) are concerned, for even if some of them have been phonologically and morphologically adapted to Danish, they are recognizable as foreign elements. But if we consider lexis in its entirety, we should note the importance of what the scholar to whom this volume is dedicated calls "das innere Lehngut": [9] to the man in the street, loan translations (5.3), translated idioms (5.4), and semantic loans (5.5) are rarely immediately recognizable as being Anglicisms.

On the other hand the non-specialist will include among English loanwords the so-called *pseudo-Anglicisms*. These are words whose elements are indeed English, while the combinations of the elements are unknown in Britain and the USA. Thus Danish uses *cottoncoat* in the sense of '(proofed) raincoat', *covercoat* for 'covert coat', *stationcar* for 'station waggon' or 'estate car', *babylift* for 'carry-cot', *smoking* for 'dinner-jacket', and *dressman* for 'male mannequin'. The last two have entered Danish via German, while other such forms may have been coined by Danish businessmen. Another group of words, *les faux amis,* is characterized by being employed in senses that differ from the senses of the corresponding words in English. This applies, for instance, to *butterfly,* used for 'bow-tie', to *sixpence* for 'cloth cap', to *speaker* for 'announcer', and to *struggler* for 'social climber'. Thus not everything that appears in English garb is necessarily English in the full sense of the word.

Occasionally it may be difficult to specify the precise degree of indebtedness to English. Let me exemplify. About 1850 the verb *to mix* was adopted as *mikse.* Danish has another verb, *bikse,* a jocular word meaning 'mix together', dating from *c.* 1900, which may have been formed on the basis of *mikse* (or it may have arisen as a blend of *blande* 'mix' and *mikse*). In its turn the form *bikse* produced two nouns: *biks* 'rubbish' and *biksemad* 'a dish of hashed meat'. There is another recent noun *biks* meaning 'a small shop' (a somewhat derogatory term), and this may owe its existence to the joint influence of the three words *biks* 'rubbish', *biksemad,* and the English loanword *boks* (< *box*). The tentative formulations used here are due to the fact that there is simply not enough evidence available concerning the histories of these words; but it is reasonable to assume that some English influence was at work here.

5.1. *Direct loans.* Strictly speaking, these are loans that have entered Danish without any formal alterations; examples are *beat, dry, freak, copyright, deadline,*

---

9 Carstensen 1984, 48.

and *widescreen*. It is practical, however, to include here also loans that have undergone more or less adaptation: *advokere* (< *advocate* vb.), *coatning* (< *coating*), *elektorat* (< *electorate*), *implementere* (< *implement* vb.), and *pesticid* (< *pesticide*). It is characteristic of some of these loans that they do not retain the entire semantic spectrum that they have in English, but only part of it; thus *design* is only used in the sense of 'artistic pattern(ing)', and *pencil* in Danish always means 'propelling pencil'.

A number of English affixes have found their way into Danish. Among the prefixes may be mentioned *anti-* (as in *antihelt* 'anti-hero'), *ex-* (as in *ekskonge* 'ex-king'), and *super-* (as in *supermagt* 'superpower'). Among the suffixes, *-ation* is in competition with the Danish suffix *-ering*, so that one finds either *eskalation* or *eskalering*, and English *-ing* is either retained or it becomes *-ning*, which produces vacillation between forms like *kidnapping* and *kidnapning*.

5.2. *Formal adaptations*. In a number of cases we may note the formal influence exerted by English words on their Danish equivalents. Thus the standard Danish term for the holder of a title (in sports) is *titelindehaver*, but *titelholder* and *holder* alone are beginning to be used on the analogy of English (*title*)*holder*. Similarly, what was until recently termed *mineudlægger* (literally 'mine-out-layer') is now usually *minelægger* owing to English *minelayer*. *Sidevirkning* and *sideeffekt* have begun to compete with the normal term *bivirkning*, the two new arrivals being supported by English *side-effect*. What in English is *baby seal* is normally *sælunge* ('seal-young', 'the young of a seal') in Danish; but in the spring of 1978 *babysæl* was the term frequently used in newspapers to refer to the victims of Alaskan hunters. In most of these examples we have to do with compounds whose elements correspond semantically to each other in the two languages while they differ somewhat formally; an adaptation then takes place in the Danish term so as to make it conform more closely to its English equivalent.

5.3. *Loan-translations* are compound words in which each of the elements renders an English word. Examples are: *arbejdsfrokost* (< *working lunch(eon)*), *blodbank* (< *blood bank*), *frynsegoder* (< *fringe benefits*), *græsrødder* (< *grass roots*), *troværdighedskløft* (< *credibility gap*), and *tænketank* (< *think tank*).

In some of these compounds one element may be productive. This applies to the first component of *gruppedynamik* (< *group dynamics*), *gruppepraksis* (< *group practice*), and *gruppesex* (< *group sex*). In the following compounds it is the last element that is productive: *generationskløft* (< *generation gap*), *indkomstkløft* (< *incomes gap*), and *teknologikløft* (< *technological gap*).

5.4. *Idioms*. Numerous English idioms are translated into Danish. Some of them will probably turn out to be ephemeral, but others have been in fairly frequent use for some time. The reason why they tend to attract especially journalists is probably that they are felt to be racy metaphors while the Danish locutions that they are ousting are rather pale and abstract by comparison. Examples are: *som en tyr i en porcellænsforretning* < *like a bull in a china shop* (the Danish idiom this replaces is *som en hund i et spil kegler* 'like a dog in a game of ninepins'); *få enderne til at mødes* < *make ends meet* (replacing *få pengene til at slå til* 'make one's money last'); *kalde en spade for en spade* < *call a spade a spade* (replacing *kalde en ting ved dens rette navn* 'call a thing by its right name'); *holde en lav profil* < *keep a low profile* (replacing e.g. *holde sig i baggrunden* 'keep in the background').

5.5. *Semantic loans.* Semantic borrowing is the process whereby an existing Danish lexical item receives a new sense from the corresponding, sometimes formally similar, English word. Thus the Danish adjective *langhåret* has received from English *longhaired* the figurative sense of 'intellectual, highbrow' (for instance of classical music). Danish *åbning* 'aperture' corresponds to English *opening*, which has extended the semantic sphere of the Danish word, so that it may now also be used in the sense of 'chance, opportunity, job'. Similarly, the Danish word for 'umbrella', *paraply,* has borrowed from its English equivalent the recent sense of 'co-ordinating agency', often in the compound *paraplyorganisation* 'umbrella organization'. Danish *tilstedeværelse* corresponds to English *presence*; the English word has recently acquired the sense of '(the influence of) armed forces' (often when premodified by *military*),[10] and the Danish word may now be used in the same way. The Danish translation equivalents of 'buying' and 'selling' *købe* and *sælge* can now, owing to English influence, be used about ideological matters, e.g. *at sælge en politik* 'to sell a policy'. Until recently the adjective *komfortabel* could not be employed to refer to a satisfactory election result; but now Danish has *et komfortabelt flertal* on the analogy of *a comfortable majority* (the traditional Danish adjective here is *pæn* 'nice'). In all these cases Danish words have had their spheres of application extended under English influence.

The same is true of some Danish prepositions. In a number of cases there is orthographic identity or similarity between English and Danish prepositions: *for* and *over* are orthographically identical in the two languages, *of* is close to Danish *af,* *after* to *efter,* and this may be part of the reason why Danish prepositional usage is influenced by English. For example, *after 40 minutes* has its contemporary Danish counterpart in *efter 40 minutter* (although the normally preferred formulation is *efter 40 minutters forløb* 'after the lapse of 40 minutes'). English *for* may indicate destination, as in *100 men left Brussels for Kinshasa,* and its Danish cousin may be observed in the same function: *100 mand forlod Bruxelles for Kinshasa,* where Danish would, however, normally prefer a different formulation (. . .*forlod B. med K. som mål* " . . .left B. with K. as their destination"). English *over* often means 'on account of' as in *a conflict over a problem.* A corresponding Danish formulation may be met with in an example like *Labour var splittet over Fællesmarkeds-*

10 Cf. *OED-Supplement,* III, 1982, *s.v.* 'presence', 1.e.

spørgsmålet "Labour was divided over the Common Market issue", although the prepositional phrase used in such a case would normally be *på grund af* 'owing to'.

5.6. *Back-formation and conversion.* The process of deriving a verb like *tape-record* from the compound noun *tape-recorder* is common in English. A similar process is possible in Danish, and in a number of cases it has probably been given a fillip by English. Thus we have *at båndoptage* corresponding to English *to taperecord* (the Danish noun is *båndoptager*), *at dagdrømme* corresponding to English *to daydream*, *at globetrotte* corresponding to English *to globetrot*, and *at hjernevaske* corresponding to English *to brainwash*.

The process of making a word belonging to one word-class (e.g. nouns) do duty as a member of another word-class (e.g. verbs) without any formal change is known as conversion; thus English has *a black-list* and the derived verb *to black-list*, and these forms have inspired Danish *en sortliste* and *at sortliste* (alternating with *en blacklist* and *at blackliste*). Similar examples are *en kontakt* 'a contact' and *at kontakte* 'to contact' *post* 'mail' and *at poste* 'to post (a letter)'. It will be noted that such Danish nouns and verbs are not always quite identical in form since all infinitives end in *-e*.

5.7. *Acronyms.* This type of word has been enormously on the increase in recent decades, especially among British and American journalists, and Danish has acquired its fair share of these abbreviations. Many of them are adopted unchanged, for instance, *EFTA, GATT, LP, NATO, PR, SALT,* and *WHO; hi-fi, laser,* and *radar.* When these are used in Danish, they do not require any explanatory comments, unlike lesser known acronyms like *VIP* and *WASP.* Many Danish journalists are tempted to introduce any foreign acronyms they come across.

Sometimes the initials are changed so as to conform to Danish. Thus *EDP* becomes *EDB* (*el*ektronisk *datab*ehandling), and *GNP* is replaced by *BNP* (*b*rutto*n*ational*p*roduktet).

5.8. *Hybrids.* Compounds consisting of an English and a Danish element are frequent and testify to the fact that many English loans lend themselves to integration with Danish without any difficulty. Most of these hybrids are written as one word.

In the commonest type the English component comes first: *booking-kontor* 'booking office', *gospelsang* 'gospel singing', *popkunst* 'pop art', *scrapbog* 'scrapbook', *slipstrøm* 'slipstream'; but there are also hybrids in which the Danish term comes first: *matroslook* 'sailor look', *målaverage* 'goal average', *præmiequiz* 'prize quiz'.

In a few cases an English loanword combines with a bound Danish morpheme; this is seen in *partnerskab* 'partnership' and *partnerske* 'female partner'.

5.9. *Competition between direct loans and translations.* Very often there is competition between direct loans and their translations. In some cases direct loans will after a time be crowded out by their translations; this applies to *hearing* 'radio or TV programme in which experts are heard', which is now practically always *høring*, and to *pressure group*, which has been ousted by *pressionsgruppe*. But it would be possible to draw up a long list comprising direct loans that are in free variation with their translations. Here are some examples: *design* 'artistic pattern(ing)' and *formgivning*; *in* 'in fashion' and *inde*; *out* 'out of fashion' and *ude*; *konsumerisme* (< *consumerism* 'doctrine advocating continual increase in consumption goods') and *forbrugerisme*; *singer/song-writer* and *sanger/sangskriver*; *thinktank* and *tænketank*.

5.10. *Where do the loans occur?* There is no doubt that Anglicisms occur with the greatest frequency in the media. Thus journalists, who often draw on English-language sources, are chiefly responsible for the English infiltration of the Danish language. Although practically all aspects of modern life have their share of Anglicisms, it may be useful to list the main semantic areas where English influence is particularly prominent; a few examples from each area will be given below.

Politics and economics: *skyggekabinet* (< *shadow cabinet*), *duer* (< *doves*), *høge* (< *hawks*), *Finlandisering* (< *Finlandization*), *vækstrate* (< *growth rate*), *lokomotivlande* (< *locomotives*).

Modern warfare: *kanonbådsdiplomati* (< *gunboat diplomacy*), *terrorbalancen* (< *the balance of terror*), *afskrækkelsesvåben* (< *deterrents*), *nedfald* (< *fallout*), *overkill*.

Science and technology: *rumalderen* (< *the Space Age*), *knowhow*, *overlydshastighed* (< *supersonic speed*), *computer*, *input*, *hardware*.

Commerce: *boss*, *diversificering* (< *diversification*), *gyldent håndtryk* (< *golden handshake*), *joint venture*, *image*, *marketing*, *PR*.

Clothes: *maxi*, *mini*, *unisex*, *sailor-look*, *blazer*, *housecoat*, *whipcord*.

Food and drink: *dressing*, *hotdog*, *sandwich*: *at grille* (< *to grill*), *at simre* (< *to simmer*); *drink*, *gin*, *sherry*, *cocktail*.

Social conditions: *befolkningseksplosionen* (< *the population explosion*), *kernefamilie* (< *nuclear family*), *statussymbol* (< *status symbol*), *drop-out*, *samfundstaber* (< *social loser*), *hårde stoffer* (< *hard drugs*), *syrehoved* (< *acid head*).

Sports and games: *boksning* (< *boxing*), *fodbold* (< *football*), *mål* (< *goal*), *frispark* (< *free kick*), *fair play*, *seedning* (< *seeding*).

The film industry: *studie* (< *studio*), *talentspejder* (< *talent scout*), *stand-in*, *stuntman*, *script-girl*, *trailer*.

Radio, TV, and music: *dampradioen* (< *the steam radio*), *sæbeopera* (< *soap opera*), *ankermand* (< *anchor-man*), *dåselatter* (< *canned laughter*), *muzak*, *punk rock*, *disc-jockey*.

Literature: *den hårdkogte roman* (< *the hard-boiled novel*), *thriller*, *bestseller*, *plot*, *nærlæsning* (< *close reading*), *paperback*.

Most Anglicisms tend to occur first in more or less technical parlance, but in time many of them become popularized.

5.11. *Statistics*. It appears from Petersen 1984, which deals with neologisms in Danish in the period 1955–1975, that approximately 25% of them are of foreign origin, the vast majority of that percentage stemming from English. On the basis of the lists at the end of the book it is possible to form an idea of the ratio between the different categories of loans. If we stick to Petersens's classification, the following picture presents itself:

Direct loans

nouns	(e.g. *pesticid*)	301
verbs	(e.g. *briefe*)	31
adjectives	(e.g. *faktuel*)	20
adverbs	(e.g. *offshore*)	6
phrases	(e.g. *do-it-yourself*)	4
first components	(e.g. *drive-in*)	5
hybrids	(e.g. *backinggruppe*)	40
		407

Loan translations

nouns	(e.g. *armvridning* 'arm-twisting')	285
verbs	(e.g. *dryptørre* 'drip-dry')	29
adjectives	(e.g. *ikkevoldelig* 'non-violent')	24
phrases	(e.g. *ingen kommentar* 'no comment')	26
first components	(e.g. *fuldtids-* 'fulltime')	5
		369

Semantic loans

nouns	(e.g. *hovedjæger* 'headhunter')	127
verbs	(e.g. *gro* transitive 'grow')	39
adjectives	(e.g. *høj* 'euphoric from drugs')	21
adverbs	(e.g. *efterfølgende* 'subsequently')	4
pronouns	(*du* 'you, one')	1
phrases	(e.g. *lav profil* 'low profile')	12
first components	(e.g. *græsrods-* 'grassroots')	5
		209

There is a further list, not included here, which contains words whose indebtedness to English is uncertain.

(46)

I have subjected my own material to a similar analysis (excluding the items contained in Petersen's lists) and present my figures below:

Direct loans

nouns	1589
verbs	187
adjectives	131
adverbs	8
phrases	49
first components	87
hybrids	98
	2149

Loan translations

nouns	210
verbs	45
adjectives	53
phrases	188
first components	14
	510

Semantic loans

nouns	103
verbs	78
adjectives	34
adverbs	2
phrases	6
first components	3
	226

These figures invite a number of comments.

In the first place it is interesting to note the distribution of the loans on word-classes. Clearly it is the nouns that dominate, verbs and adjectives being modestly represented and the remaining word-classes very modestly indeed.[11] To the above list of direct loans I might, however, have added a dozen interjections, and at least one of them, *O.K.*, occurs very frequently in spoken Danish. This raises the problem of how frequently the loanwords are used. It makes a difference whether we operate

11 This tallies with Einar Haugen's findings 1953, II, 406.

with *tokens* or with *types*. There are numerous tokens of *O.K.* in Danish while some of the nouns and verbs in my material occur rarely. Unfortunately it is impossible to be more specific than this since as far as I know there are as yet no analyses available that might shed light on the type—token ratio.

Another point that calls for comment is the fact that the Petersen lists reveal a preponderance of translation loans and semantic loans over direct loans, while the reverse is true of my own material; here, in fact, direct loans are almost three times as numerous as the other two categories taken together. There may be two reasons for this. In the first place Petersen's lists only include loans that are fairly commonly used, while I have, as it were, scraped the barrel, including in my material rarely used words and words that I have only noted once, some of them being terms from commercial and technical parlance that hardly lend themselves to popularization. There may, however, be a further reason for this discrepancy between the two sets. It might be the case that in recent decades—those covered by Petersen's dictionary—there has been a tendency to rely on "das innere Lehngut" to a greater extent than on direct loans, so that, to take an example, *hovedjæger* would be preferred to *headhunter*. At the moment it is, however, impossible to say anything definite on this score; for one thing we need extended analyses of word frequencies since in many cases direct loans and semantic loans occur side by side.

If we add together the loanwords from the two sets (and I have here left out of account a number of pseudo-Anglicisms), we reach a grand total of close to 4,000 items. Is this a sufficiently large number to entitle us to speak of Danish being infiltrated by English? Answering that question would presuppose a calculation of tokens. One might, however, gain a rough impression of the extent to which Danish is indebted to English if it were possible to compare Danish with other languages. The only relevant figures I know of are those given in the preface to the recently published *Dictionnaire des Anglicismes* (1980). Here the editors inform us that their dictionary lists more than 2,700 Anglicisms, a good many of which are, however, obsolete, while some 1,500 are current today. In recent years there have been frequent complaints that French is developing into *franglais*; if there is any substance to that complaint, Danish would seem to be rather heavily Anglicized, and it should be borne in mind that lexis apart, Anglicisms are making themselves felt in Danish syntax as well.

We need more information about the impact of English on its neighbours. As far as German is concerned, much has already been provided by our Paderborn colleague. We all look forward with great anticipation to the completion of the *Anglizismen-Wörterbuch* to which he is devoting so much work; meanwhile I take this opportunity of wishing him every success with his venture in years to come.

BIBLIOGRAPHY

Bang, Jørgen, *Om at Bruge Fremmedord*. Copenhagen 1962.

Björkman, Erik, *Scandinavian Loan-Words in Middle English*. Vol. I: Halle 1900, vol. II: Halle 1902.

Carstensen, Broder, "Die Betonung substantivischer Wortverbände vom Typ *the make-up* im Englischen und Deutschen", *Wiener Beiträge zur englischen Philologie* 75 (1973), 36–49.

Carstensen, Broder, "Wieder: Die Engländerei in der deutschen Sprache", *Die deutsçhe Sprache der Gegenwart*. Göttingen 1984, 43–57.

Dahl, Torsten, "English influence as reflected in the Danish language", *Studia Neophilologica* 14 (1942), 386–392.

Dahl, Torsten, "Engelske spor i moderne dansk", *Festskrift til Peter Skautrup*. Aarhus 1956, 251–256.

Dictionnaire des Anglicismes. Les Mots Anglais et Américains en Français. Paris 1980.

Dollerup, Cay, *Omkring Sproglig Transmission*. Anglica et Americana 3, University of Copenhagen 1978.

Haugen, Einar, *The Norwegian Language in America*. Philadelphia 1953.

Hjorth, Poul Lindegård, "Omsværmede Clive Roots", *Nyt fra Sprognævnet* 3 (1969), 1–3.

Larsen, Fritz, "Changing Danish", *Pre-Publications of the English Institute of Odense University*, November 1982, 132–146.

Meyer, Ludvig, *Fremmedordbog*. Copenhagen ⁶1884.

Nordiske Sprogproblemer 1955. Copenhagen 1956.

Nordiske Sprogproblemer 1956. Copenhagen 1957.

Nordiske Sprogproblemer 1957 og 1958. Copenhagen 1959.

Nordiske Sprogproblemer 1959 og 1960. Copenhagen 1961.

Nordiske Sprogproblemer 1961 og 1962. Copenhagen 1963.

Nordiske Sprogproblemer 1963–1965. Copenhagen 1966.

Nordiske Sprogproblemer 1966 og 1967. Copenhagen 1968.

Ny Ord i Dansk 1968–69. Copenhagen 1972.

Ny Ord i Dansk 1970–71. Copenhagen 1978.

OED = Oxford English Dictionary. A corrected re-issue of *A New English Dictionary on Historical Principles*. Oxford 1933.

OED-Supplement = A Supplement to the Oxford English Dictionary. Vol. III: O–Scz. Oxford 1982.

Petersen, Pia Riber, *Ny Ord i Dansk 1955–75*. Dansk Sprognævns Skrifter 11. Copenhagen 1984.

Skautrup, Peter, *Det Danske Sprogs Historie I–IV*. Copenhagen 1944–1968.

Sørensen, Knud, "Knock-out og come-back. Om trykket i en engelsk låneordstype", *Nyt fra Sprognævnet* 7 (1971), 1–2.

Sørensen, Knud, *Engelske Lån i Dansk*. Dansk Sprognævns Skrifter 8. Copenhagen 1973.

Sørensen, Knud, "Om anglicismer i moderne dansk", *Nordiske Studier. Festskrift til Chr. Westergård-Nielsen*. Copenhagen 1975, 221–231.

Sørensen, Knud, "Om engelske betydningslån i moderne dansk", *Danske Studier* 1978, 134–140.

Sørensen, Knud, "Fra *Seven Gothic Tales* til *Syv fantastiske Fortællinger*", *Danske Studier* 1981, 45–72.

Sørensen, Knud, "English influence on contemporary Danish", in R. Filipović (ed.), *The English Element in European Languages*, vol. 2. Zagreb 1982, 71–153.

Sørensen, Knud, "Cognate, but sui generis: Difficulties confronting advanced Danish students of English", *Moderna Språk* 78 (1984), 1–11.

BIBLIOGRAPHY

'On the Pronunciation of Recent French Loan-Words'. *English Studies* 37 (1956), 162-168.

* 'Substantive with two Epithets'. *English Studies* 37 (1956), 261-264.

'Latin Influence on English Syntax. A Survey with a Bibliography.' *Acta Congressus Madvigiani* V (1957), 131-155.

Engelske Oversættelsesøvelser (with Børge Maaløe and Paul Bay). Copenhagen 1957. Fourth edition 1976.

* 'Subjective Narration in *Bleak House*'. *English Studies* 40 (1959), 431-439.

Thomas Lodge's Translation of Seneca's "De Beneficiis" Compared with Arthur Golding's Version. A Textual Analysis with Special Reference to Latinisms. Thesis Copenhagen 1960.

* 'Thomas Lodge's *Seneca*'. *Archiv für das Studium der neueren Sprachen und Literaturen* 199 (1962), 1-12.

* 'English and Romance: Some Aspects of Style'. *Zandvoort Number of English Studies* 1964, 21-25.

* 'Nicholas Haward's Translation of Seneca'. *Huntington Library Quarterly* 29 (1966), 203-214.

'Understanding English: Difficulties Confronting Danes'. *Moderna Språk* 60 (1966), 388-393.

Engelsk Grammatik (with Poul Steller). Copenhagen 1966. Third edition 1988.

'Lingvistik og sprogundervisning'. *Meddelelser fra Engelsklærerforeningen* No. 41 (1967), 1-11.

* 'Johnsonese in *Northanger Abbey*'. *English Studies* 50 (1969), 390-397.

'Lingvistik og engelskundervisning' (with Poul Steller). *Engelskundervisning analyseret i ni artikler*. Copenhagen 1969, 45-72.

'Engelskundervisningen i Danmark historisk betragtet'. *Engelskundervisning analyseret i ni artikler*. Copenhagen 1969, 127-137.

* 'Language and Society in L.P. Hartley's *Facial Justice*'. *Orbis Litterarum* 1971, 68-78.

'On the Stressing of *be, been,* and *as*'. *English Studies* 52 (1971), 305-309.

'The Teaching of English in Denmark: A Historical Survey'. *Paedagogica Historica* XI, 1 (1971), 90-101.

'*Knock-out* og *come-back*. Om trykket i en engelsk låneordstype'. *Nyt fra Sprognævnet* No. 7 (1971), 1-2.

Review of F. Brengelman, *The English Language. English Studies* 52 (1971), 483.

'A Reply to Dr Schubiger's Note'. *English Studies* 53 (1972), 350.

Review of K.C. Phillipps, *Jane Austen's English, English Studies* 53 (1972), 365-367.

Review of Rodney D. Huddleston, *The Sentence in Written English. A Syntactic Study Based on an Analysis of Scientific Texts. English Studies* 54 (1973), 88-92.

* 'Latin *Oratio Obliqua* and English Free Indirect Speech'. *Classica et Mediaevalia Francisco Blatt Septuagenario Dedicata*, 1973, 595-607.

Review of William Caxton, *The Book of the Knight of the Tower*, ed. Offord. *English Studies* 54 (1973), 276-278.

Engelske lån i dansk. Dansk Sprognævns skrifter, vol. 8, 1973.

Review of Norman Page, *The Language of Jane Austen. English Studies* 54 (1973), 595-596.

Review of James Muir, *A Modern Approach to English Grammar,* and of Sven Jacobson, *Studies in English Transformational Grammar, English Studies* 54 (1973), 618-619.

Aspects of Modern English Prose Style, Copenhagen 1975.

'Om anglicismer i moderne dansk'. *Nordiske Studier. Festskrift til Chr. Westergård-Nielsen,*1975, 221-231.

* 'A Note on *at all'. English Studies* 56 (1975), 498-503.

Review of Randolph Quirk, *The Linguist and the English Language. English Studies* 57 (1976), 270-271.

Review of P.A. Erades, *Points of Modern English Syntax. English Studies* 57 (1976), 383-384.

Review of Xavier Dekeyser, *Number and Case Relations in 19th Century British English. English Studies* 57 (1976), 566-572.

Review of Emma Vorlat, *The Development of English Grammatical Theory 1586-1737. English Studies* 58 (1977), 79-81.

* 'Asseverative IF and its Congeners'. *English Studies* 59 (1978), 248-254.

'Om engelske betydningslån i moderne dansk'. *Danske Studier* 1978, 134-140.

Numerus i moderne engelsk (with Arne Juul). Copenhagen 1978.

'A Discredited Generalization Comes True'. *The Dolphin* No. 1 (1979), 97-101.

'Is End-Stressing on the Increase?' *English Studies* 60 (1979), 54-55.

* 'Preposition + X + Complement'. *English Studies* 60 (1979), 42-48.

Review of M. Cohen, *Sensible Words. English Studies* 60 (1979), 87-89.

'Bloody: et bandeords grammatik'. *SPRINT* 1979, No. 2, 29-31.

* 'Co-ordinate Prepositions with a Single Complement'. *Essays Presented to Knud Schibsbye. Publications of the Department of English, University of Copenhagen,* Vol. 8, 1979, 207-228.

* 'From Postmodification to Premodification'. *Acta Universitatis Stockholmiensis* LII (1980), 77-84.

* 'Some Observations on Pronominalization'. *English Studies* 62 (1981), 146-155.

'Fra *Seven Gothic Tales* til *Syv fantastiske Fortællinger'. Danske Studier* 1981, 45-72.

232

* 'Determinative *that of* vs. Zero'. The New University of Ulster: *Occasional Papers in Linguistics and Language Teaching,* Vol. 8, 1981, 137-146.

Review of Mats Rydén, *An Introduction to the Historical Study of English Syntax. English Studies* 62 (1981), 488.

Review of Jan Svartvik & Randolph Quirk, *A Corpus of English Conversation. English Studies* 63 (1982), 85-86.

Review of Hans Hertel & Sven Møller Kristensen ed., *The Activist Critic. English Studies* 63 (1982), 86-87.

Review of Roger Lass, *On Explaining Language Change. English Studies* 63 (1982), 87-88.

'English Influence on Contemporary Danish', in *The English Element in European Languages,* ed. R. Filipović, Vol. 2, 71-153, Zagreb 1982.

'Studier i Karen Blixens engelske og danske sprogform I-II'. *Blixeniana* 1982, 263- 308.

Review of Stig Johansson, *Plural Attributive Nouns in Present-Day English. English Studies* 63 (1982), 468.

Review of Magnus Ljung, *Reflections on the English Progressive. English Studies* 63 (1982), 469-470.

* 'The Growth of Cataphoric Personal and Possessive Pronouns in English', in *Current Topics in English Historical Linguistics,* Odense University Press 1983, 225-238.

* Review of Vol. III of *A Supplement to the Oxford English Dictionary,* ed. R. W. Burchfield. *English Studies* 65 (1984), 86-90.

* 'Cognate, but sui generis: Difficulties Confronting Advanced Danish Students of English'. *Moderna Språk* 78 (1984), 1-11.

'Charles Dickens: Linguistic Innovator'. *English Studies* 65 (1984), 237-247.

Review of Ralph W.V. Elliott, *Thomas Hardy's English. English Studies* 66 (1985), 375-377.

Review of W.F. Bolton, *The Language of 1984. Orwell's English and Ours. English Studies* 66 (1985), 377-379.

Charles Dickens: Linguistic Innovator. Acta Jutlandica LXI, Aarhus University Press 1985.

* 'The Distributive Plural and its Limits'. *English Studies* 66 (1985), 338-350.

Review of Andreas Haarder, *Sangen om Bjovulf. Danske Studier* 1985, 155-158.

Review of H. Yonekura, *The Language of the Wycliffite Bible. English Studies* 67 (1986), 78-80.

'On Countable and Uncountable Nouns', *The Dolphin* No. 13, 1986, 17-28.

* 'Phrasal Verb into Noun'. *Neuphilologische Mitteilungen* 87/2 (1986), 272-283.

* 'On Anglicisms in Danish', in *English in Contact with other Languages.* Studies in honour of Broder Carstensen on the occasion of his 60th birthday. Budapest 1986, 31-49.

'Engelsk indflydelse på moderne dansk syntaks', in *1. Møde om Udforskningen af Dansk Sprog,* ed. K. Ringgaard, 1987, 135-144.

Review of *The Pickwick Papers,* ed. James Kinsley. *English Studies* 68 (1987), 292-293.

Review of Vol. IV of *A Supplement to the Oxford English Dictionary,* ed. R. W. Burchfield. *English Studies* 68 (1987), 293-296.

Titles marked with an asterisk (*) are reprinted in this volume with the permission of the original publishers.

TABULA GRATULATORIA

Danmarks Lærerhøjskole
Afdeling for Engelsk
København

Dansk Sprognævn
København

Handelshøjskolens Bibliotek
Århus

Det Lærde Selskab i Aarhus
Århus

Roskilde Universitetsbibliotek
Roskilde

Statsbiblioteket
Århus

Det Universitetshistoriske Udvalg
Aarhus Universitet
Århus

Aalborg Universitetsbibliotek
Aalborg

Jens Axelsen
Holte

Paul Bay
Vejby

Ulla Bjerregaard
Allerød

Andreas Heide Doelsmand
Odder

Lene Byriel
Århus

Ulf og Vera Böiken
Hørsholm

Graham D. Caie
København

Jørn Carlsen
Århus

Paul Christophersen
Cambridge

Jens Bjerre Danielsen
Århus

Niels Davidsen-Nielsen
København

Xavier Dekeyser
Antwerpen

John M. Dienhart
Odense

Ole Fenger
Århus

Knud Gram-Andersen
Virum

Lara Hallgrimsdottir
København

Donald Hannah
Århus

Erik A. Hansen
Århus

Niels Bugge Hansen
København

Hans Hauge
Århus

Erik Hvid
Holbæk

Andreas Haarder
Odense

Anders Iversen
Århus

Bent Jacobsen
Århus

Arnt Lykke Jakobsen
Frederiksberg

Ruth Jensen
Århus

Arne Juul
Frederiksberg

Allan Karker
Mundelstrup

Torben Kisbye
Århus

Mogens Kragh
Virum

Shirley Larsen
Århus

Svend Erik Mathiassen
Århus

Hans Frede Nielsen
Odense

Jørgen Erik Nielsen
Glostrup

Bent Nordhjem
København

Holger Nørgaard
København

E. Ransgård Olesen
Hvidovre

Flemming Olsen
Lyngby

Kjeld Pedersen
Ulfborg

Kurt Møller Pedersen
Lemvig

Pia Riber Petersen
København

Viggo Hjørnager Pedersen
Ballerup

Birger Petterson
Skjern

Gerda Poulsen
Århus

Marianne Powell
Århus

Bent Preisler
Århus

Althea Ryan
Århus

Lars Ole Sauerberg
Odense

Jørgen Schmitt Jensen
Århus

Helge Schwarz
Frederiksberg

Jørgen Slettebo
Sønderborg

N.J. Skydsgaard
København

Povl Skårup
Århus

Sven Sorgenfrey
Frederiksberg

Tyge Stavnstrup
Rødovre

Bent og Jytte Sunesen
Charlottenlund

Frode Søby
Århus

Anna Trosborg
Hinnerup

Gudmund Tybjerg
Tønder

Torben Vestergaard
Aalborg

Karl-Heinz Westarp
Hårup